THE TRAGEDY OF

NIJINSKY

BY ANATOLE BOURMAN

IN COLLABORATION WITH

D. LYMAN

GREENWOOD PRESS, PUBLISHERS
WESTPORT, CONNECTICUT

Originally published in 1936
by McGraw-Hill, New York

First Greenwood Reprinting 1970

SBN 8371-2965-6

PRINTED IN UNITED STATES OF AMERICA

TO
VASLAW — MY FRIEND
HIS MOTHER, HIS FAMILY
AND HIS ART
this book is most humbly dedicated

PREFACE

A ROSE petal carried on a breath of wind through an open window in a graceful parabola of crimson and green—that was Vaslaw Nijinsky in *Le Spectre de la Rose,* a single aspect of the human being who transcended human limitations and danced into the heart of poesy. No one can explain the mystic quality that was an integral part of his art, or describe in words precisely the source of his inspiration. A description of the methods he employed to achieve his effects and a shadowy screen of words depicting a fraction of his splendor are all that anyone can hope to attain.

Physically, Nijinsky was all but a demigod. Every muscle in his vigorous young body was so perfectly developed that the doctors in St. Petersburg often brought him before them in order to study the action of the living tissues rippling beneath his satiny skin.

"There is not a single undeveloped muscle visible in his body. All are developed far above the average," they announced.

His sinews and tendons were neither stiff nor protruding, nor were his muscular masses clumsy in outline. Yet, even the tiny intracostal masses were delicately visible when he tensed himself, while the mobility of his facial muscles permitted an uncanny adoption of unfamiliar racial characteristics. When Nijinsky played the Negro in *Scheherazade,* he was more, far more, than a dancer. He was the embodiment of a race. His face, normally Mongolian in cast, became negroid. His whole body was transformed until Nijinsky the Pole disappeared, and a Negro, lusty and sensual, lived out his life behind the footlights. In the closing moments of the ballet, when

Nijinsky fled from a vengeful soldiery, it was a primitive fleeing the nameless terror of dying who ran across the stage, pursued by incomprehensible Destiny, and fell backwards, landing on his skull, spinning an instant before he dropped, a victim both of his fear and of the fated sword cut.

When he danced that role, Nijinsky made every witness of the tragedy feel it. That was one of his mighty gifts. His power literally transported his audiences into the era and story that he played, until factual reality receded, losing itself in the greater reality of his art.

Nijinsky's pantomime mastery in the role of Harlequin in *Karnival* was unsurpassed. He imbued the character with worldliness, retaining glamour and romanticism alike, and yet his Harlequin personified all that masquerade implied. As the Prince in *Giselle,* he excelled afresh. *Petrouchka* proved, past doubt, even in the early years of his career in Russia, that the amazing young Pole could depict the charm of a puppet without forcing his audience into a recollection of his birth as a mere mortal. He was simply Petrouchka, grotesque and amusing, brought to life.

Greek influence predominated in *Paphnis and Chloë* and in *Narcisse.* Presented in Paris in 1912, both reflected the molded classicism of ancient terpsichorean spectacles in Nijinsky's interpretation utilizing familiar themes from mythology. *The Blue God,* composed by Fokine the same year, was inspired by India and portrayed both its color and its mysticism in a tropical setting. In that ballet, Nijinsky became the sensuous devotee of a strange faith to captivate his public afresh.

Never has any other dancer been able to seize upon one's imagination and sweep one into forgetfulness of the mechanics of dancing as Vaslaw Nijinsky. This was unquestionably due to the marvelous physical development I have already described as well as to a freedom of motion imparted by a technique perfect to watch. Like all great creative artists, Nijinsky was never satisfied, never contented with his own supremacy. He spent at least two hours a day in grilling practice, concentrating always on most difficult steps, striving perpetually for soft arm and body motion, asking me again and again to repeat his accompaniment in order that he might more closely approximate his own ideal in matchless execution.

He was the only dancer to achieve the entrechat-dix, a step that called for terrific elevation for its completion according to the technical standards of ballet and one which, alone, must have placed him among the immortals. His elevation provided Fokine with endless opportunities to astonish the world with ingenious routines in which Nijinsky seemed to float across the stage.

Without exaggeration, he leaped between fifteen and twenty feet with each grand jeté, provided the stage was large enough to permit it, and, once launched in his flight, appeared to stop for a fraction of a second as he reached his maximum elevation before his forward course was pursued. That trick never failed to bring a gasp of surprise from his audience. It was attained with equal ease in his arabesques and proved a source of curiosity to every dancing master and dancer who watched it.

I questioned him regarding the technique of its attainment.

"The secret lies in my back, Anatole," he replied, "for as I leap, my back muscles are timed and coordinated with my abdominal muscles, and somehow, I can stay in mid-air for nearly a second—long enough, at least, to miss a few beats of music if I'm not careful to count my rhythms exactly."

His back and abdominal muscles were cultivated assiduously by Nijinsky, who used a simple exercise during the years I knew him. He used to lie on his back, prone on the floor, his toes caught under a low bar or a heavy piece of furniture, and then with infinite patience he very, very slowly raised himself to a sitting posture and lowered himself with the same slow motion. This he repeated at least twenty times daily, permitting no jerkiness to mar the utter harmony, or distort the rhythmic steadiness, of his movements. This exercise is one which I have never seen described as an important factor in Nijinsky's development.

He never sat down to rest during his practice but worked ceaselessly, even at the height of his acclaim, until perspiration ran off his face and body in streams and spotted the floor. His arch and instep he always massaged before and after practice. Later in his career, a man trained in massage was employed to keep his entire body fit, to give him a thorough massage after every performance. Consequently, despite twelve years of almost super-human physical effort, during which time Nijinsky continued his practice unremittingly, thus increasing his muscular development, he was never in the slightest degree muscle-bound. That was an achievement for the Russian system of training, which, properly given, permits the development of un-believable strength without impairing the freedom of muscle play or giving rise to a condition frequently met with in improper training. Nijinsky considered bar work essential as a foundation for any dancer.

Nijinksy, during his classical period, never landed heavily. There was no jar, no thump discernible to ruin the lightness permeating his interpretations. He was never the athlete leaping and bounding, owing to the perfection of his plié and ballon. With his splendid thigh muscles to impel him upwards, he was one of two living dancers to succeed in completing three turns in mid-air. These tours-enl'air were equaled only by Stanislaw Idzikovsky, whom Nijinsky, with commendable and unconscious modesty, proclaimed "the greatest living dancer" when he saw Idzikovsky on the stage.

Pirouettes were executed with nonchalance by Nijinsky, whom I have seen complete twelve turns perfectly. Six or seven revolutions were nothing at all to him, and never did he mar them by tipping off balance for an instant. However, Fokine considered pirouettes "the machinery of dancing" without any particular beauty, without particular significance except that of a spectacular trick to catch the eye of an audience. Neither Fokine nor Nijinsky believed in depending upon unbeautiful motions to attain public approval, and so neither made much of the pirouettes, which were, again, impossible for any other dancer I have ever seen, or heard of. In them Nijinsky turned with the speed of a top, until his face was a blur and he literally seemed to be a spinning top. But the public rarely saw him in that triumph of skill.

The softness that has frequently been interpreted as effeminate by critics was due more to incomparably finished and controlled coordination than to any innate effeminacy in his execution of the dance.

It was when we forsook classicism, his forte for the greater part of his career, that he created a sensation. With his first venture into choreography,

Nijinsky modified the classical laws of the old ballet and the beautifully modeled body grace that was Fokine's tremendous contribution to the dance, progressing into angular figures and heavy leaps with his *Le Sacre du printemps* in 1913. He used his amazing technique then as a foundation for the absolute modernism he embraced wholeheartedly in his primitive exposition of the Stone Age. The piece was primordial, clumsy, all but brutish. It nearly wrecked the health and nervous systems of the entire company and, I believe, was responsible for aggravating his own mental and nervous condition. At that time, the first indication of an overwrought mind and body betrayed itself in an uncertain temper which sometimes verged on frenzy when we failed to execute the intricate figures he conceived to fit a diabolically difficult tempo abounding with counts and counterrhythms. Even he forgot the routine he himself had conceived and stormed furiously at the company.

During the final months of his career, a further penetration into the abstract haunted his disordered mind with absurd "creations" based upon geometrical planes, cubes, triangles, and spheres impossible to execute in a three-dimensional world. The new modernism, he thought, must bring into physical manifestation a fourth dimension that, alas, seeems to have swallowed his mind and his art into its mystic, impenetrable realms.

What quality thrills the strings of Kreisler's violin when he draws his bow across them and opens the well-streams of emotion and dream? What magic is evoked when Paderewski's hands linger and dart and linger again above a keyboard and send the very spirit of inspiration surging through his hearers? What mystery and power brooded over Vaslaw Nijinsky and made him supreme among the mighty priests of Terpsichore?

Genius . . . it is the only answer.

ANATOLE BOURMAN

October 6, 1932
Springfield, Massachusetts

CONTENTS

Contents

ILLUSTRATIONS

FOREWORD

It is my conviction that, in a book of this sort, the reader should have the privilege of examining the authority, motives, and attitudes of the authors, and so better weigh the significance of their work as a whole, for upon authors devolves the special duty of interpreting a human life whenever they venture into the field of biography.

As the life of that Titan of the dance, Vaslaw Nijinsky, was unfolded to me, it revealed itself as a moving drama, primarily appealing in its warm, human qualities, dependent for its setting upon voluminous material on the personalities touching it and on the ballet. There was, naturally, a temptation to transform a simple, unaffected representation of the man, Nijinsky, into a polished literary exposition of towering genius, almost legendary in its power, even though the legend has had less than two decades to grow and its hero is still alive. That temptation I have resolutely denied in order to recapture the atmosphere of familiarity and sincerity Anatole Bourman created around the figure of his best friend.

Because my collaborator, I am persuaded, frequently exerted a definite influence on the character of Nijinsky, I have deliberately retained much of his personality in order that, through his eyes, I might pull into sharp focus not only a man, but a whole background, a whole tradition, and thus provide a balanced account of Nijinsky's pilgrimage through the experiences of a life to great, too bountiful, or too complex to endure in sanity—however the reader chooses to interpret it.

Aside from the mechanics of writing, there was little labor and much joy involved in creating this book, for my collaborator's memories were vivid, flowing naturally, intense with feeling. To reveal his close friend, he revealed himself unconsciously as we worked. His motive was primarily unselfish, for he remembered what Sergei Diaghilev once said to him, "I have given the world Nijinsky's art, but only you can give it his life!" He remembered, too, the repeated requests of dancers and dance lovers who knew of his long association with Vaslaw Nijinsky and implored knowledge of Nijinsky, not only as an incomparable dancer, but as a fellow mortal.

They asked, "What was his early life? His heredity? How was he molded by his environment? How was he equipped to face the common task of living and adjusting himself to the world about him?" To answer those questions, Anatole Bourman gave his most treasured memories, now overcome with regret for some childish prank, now nearly bursting with enthusiasm over Nijinsky's triumphs, now rebelling against the ironies of destiny, and, again, forcing me to wait ten long minutes while he plunged into sorrow which had to be put from him before he could go on reliving a past that furnished me with a veritable magic looking-glass through which I could enter into the life of a man and an artist whom I never knew, but who now seems a familiar entity—Vaslaw Nijinsky.

Choreographers, ballerinas, and followers of the modern dance seeking fresh light on the man who had few friends in a multitude of admirers realized that only one well acquainted with Nijinsky's childhood, youth, and maturity could present a full-length portrait of him, logically tracing his growth into genius, disclosing something of the psychology behind his tragedy. The evidence proves that Anatole Bourman is such a man.

I could discover no evidence that any other living person knew Vaslaw Nijinsky as did Anatole Bourman, for apparently no other contemporary survives to relate at first hand the entire scope of his school background, its ignorant cruelties, its prejudices, elegance, and humor—elements which must have created deep and indelible impressions on the subtle mind-stuff of the sensitive boy, Nijinsky. No other friend now alive had the privilege of watching Nijinsky develop and change while sharing nearly twenty out of the twenty-nine years he lived before madness dropped the final curtain on his public career. So I have come to believe that no one but Anatole Bourman is equipped to draw those extensive influences into a logical sequence, throwing new light on the humanity of Nijinsky, which paralleled the course his genius ran.

Realizing circumstances are merely the crucible in which human frailty is tested, I have been content to set forth the manner of that testing in this case, leaving the reader to draw his own conclusions so far as possible. Yet I believe I have so directed the beam of light my collaborator has thrown upon Nijinsky's early years that the discerning reader will be able either to trace the thread of subconscious maladjustment and its causes, or to travel the more superficial route of kindly revelation.

Four classmates of Vaslaw Nijinsky and Anatole Bourman might have provided this same revelation had they escaped the evil destiny apparently overshadowing their class at the Imperial Russian Ballet School in St. Petersburg, sparing only my collaborator. Those four boys were all dead before any reached the age of twenty-nine. George Rozai died of influenza in his early twenties; Gregori Babitch was killed by a jealous husband when he was twenty-three; Iliodor Lukianov poisoned himself at the age of twenty-one; and Michail Fedorov was killed "by mistake" during the last Russian Revolution.

This knowledge has contributed to my desire to produce an accurate word portrait of a Nijinsky whom so pitifully few really knew. To attain this end I have permitted myself to be swept on with unsimulated feeling into the depths of emotion, hurt, hope, sorrow, and disillusionment where Nijinsky lived while he entranced a world with his art. Behind the glitter of blinding success, his personality, as I see it, struggled for integration—and lost. If I have failed in setting forth a heartfelt delineation of that drama, I have failed greatly.

If my collaborator's estimate of Nijinsky's life gives rise to controversy, I can only remind critics that Nijinsky's mother and sister are able to verify the major events in his school life, though even they cannot verify the wealth of intimate anecdote set forth in this biography, for they could not share personally those years Nijinsky and Anatole Bourman spent together as students resident in the Imperial Ballet School under rigid discipline, at the mercy of schoolmates, and subject to other important influences immediately after graduation when both lacked the wisdom born of sophistication.

The first person, used by Mr. Bourman in his original Russian manuscript, has been retained, as it seemed to me best adapted to portraying the beauty, emotion, and truth of his narrative, which he translated verbally to me so that it might be interpreted, related, and assembled into this book. We hope it may fulfill the widespread demand for a detailed biography of Vaslaw Nijinsky in relation to his environment and the personalities touching the circle of his life, each contributing something towards the growth and understanding of a giant genius, who, beneath his greatness, remained mortal, prey to mortal aspirations—and alas!—to mortal ills.

D. LYMAN

February 6, 1933
Longmeadow, Massachusetts

POSTSCRIPT

As we go to press, we are reminded that Mme. Eleanora Nijinsky, mother of Vaslaw Nijinsky, is now dead. His sister, however, remains a prominent personality in the ballet world, and should be able to verify the major events in Nijinsky's school career.

D. LYMAN

January, 1936

PART I

SCHOOLDAYS

I

ENTRANCE AT THE IMPERIAL
RUSSIAN BALLET SCHOOL

It was mid-August, 1900, when, in common with hundreds of other youngsters, I entered the massive building of the Imperial Russian Ballet School. About me were scores of nine- and ten-year-olds: all aspiring to enter the world's greatest school of the dance; all prepared to pass before the most critical judges ever appointed to discover dormant artistry capable of perpetuating a national tradition. There were boys and girls like myself from old Russian families, some boasting a noble line; and there were boys and girls whose clothing told its own story of want and poverty. For once, neither heredity nor fame could count against worth in Old Russia. Throughout the Empire it was common knowledge that none could pass the judges who was not mentally and physically fit, nor could anyone devoid of grace and the promise of talent hope to emerge among the few chosen to dance into the heart of St. Petersburg, at the expense of the royal court. Of all the children who sought fortune through the ballet the year that I entered, only fifteen girls and fifteen boys could be selected to train under the most expert ballet masters in the world!

Surrounded by scores upon scores of others assembled in the huge hall, I watched the governors of the ballet systematically ranging us in lines of one hundred to pass before the greatest dancers and doctors in Russia. Clumsiness in gait, flaws in deportment, any crudeness that lurked beneath our best behavior would be discovered unerringly and acknowledged with dismissal. While thoughts of my own trial passed through my head, my eyes fixed on a boy just ahead of me in line. If I felt uncertainty, what must he feel? A more unprepossessing lad was hardly to be hunted out than that slim, fearful creature standing as though he would jump at his own shadow. It seemed as though the spirit had been beaten out of him, so timid he was, with only the faintest trace of a smile to brighten the lurking tragedy of his appearance.

Slowly the queue of one hundred, which included myself and the strange boy, wound towards the judges until it reached them. There it halted while the distinguished group, with one accord, bent forwards, exclaiming with subdued excitement over the boy before them: "His body, it is perfect!" "He is the most symmetrical human I have ever seen!" And then, "What is your name, boy?"

In a quavering voice, the lad answered in Russian, "Vaslaw Nijinsky!" A Pole, I thought, with one of the worst Polish accents I had ever heard! That alone would bar him, for every student accepted by the Imperial Russian Ballet School was required to speak perfect Russian, and to be alert mentally. The boy, Nijinsky, had spoken with hesitation, distraught at the unexpected reaction he had evoked. He seemed almost stupid, I thought, knowing he could not be one day older than eleven or one day younger than nine to apply at the school. Even if he managed to slip by the doctors with the body they admired, there were still mental examinations to pass. He personified to me the spirit of rivalry surging through us all.

Time after time we filed in the elimination inspections and time after time, the boy Nijinsky and I were ordered to stand with the successful candidates. At last, only a score remained of these sons of artists, nobles, peasants, factory workers, and landed gentry, who had gathered with such high hopes —and among them were still Vaslaw Nijinsky and I. The mental tests were before us!

It was evident from the first that this Nijinsky was a slow thinker, but even that made no difference to the examiners who continued to enthuse over his measurements and his reactions to the eye and ear tests. His senses and his coordination were apparently phenomenal. I was passed and stood distastefully watching his final tests. Against all my nine-year-old judgment and prejudice, he was taken in the midst of admiring medical men, psychologists, and ballet masters. Vaslaw Nijinsky and I would be classmates.

Rapidly I gave the family data required. My great-great-grandfather was brought to Russia from Holland by Peter the Great; my great-grandfather built the Brest-Litovsk Fortress mentioned in the first treaty the Soviet government signed with Germany; my father, however, did not follow the military tradition of the family from which I, too, was departing; my cousin was chief of the Imperial Engineer-Officers' Academy and an adjutant in Grand Duke Peter Nicolaievtch's service; another cousin was Colonel Vladimir Bourman of His Majesty's Ulansky Cavalry. All that might be said of Anatole Bourman, but what, I wondered, was the background of Vaslaw Nijinsky.

I soon found out. He was born in Kiev; his father was the Thomas Nijinsky who, against all precedent, had been invited to dance on the stage of the Imperial Russian Theater, though he had never attended the Imperial Ballet School. His reply had been an outright refusal to give up "the Road"! His mother, Eleanora Nicolaievna Nijinskaya, was a dancer who had astounded all Russia by retiring at the height of her career to care for her three children, Stanislaw, Bronislava (called Bronia), and Vaslaw.

Once our respective family histories were recorded, we were notified to report as day scholars at the Imperial Ballet School for two years. At the end of that period six, of the fifteen chosen, would be kept to live at the school at the expense of the royal court. Seven years of study must pass before any of us might read our names as members of the Imperial Corps de Ballet.

II

THE SOUL ALONE

Fᴿᴼᴹ the moment the most prominent ballet master in Russia stepped onto the ballet floor before the fifteen of us, we quaked. Nicolai Goustavovitch Legat was a name known wherever dancers gathered. No wonder we were too awed in his presence to do more than attempt the rudimentary positions he showed us. But Nijinsky!—Without hesitation, the Pole took every position like an inspired artist and executed each step as though it had long been familiar. We crowded around him demanding the name of his teacher.

"My father and mother always danced, but they left me at home while they traveled. I have never seen them dance," he explained.

That first triumph was enough to focus jealousy against him, since reports of his excellence brought older students flocking to our class to watch the "first-year genius" at work. His improvement, in comparison with ours, was a succession of little triumphs. None in our class could compete with him from the start, and so we unanimously hated him and devoted ourselves to making his life one long round of ridicule. Born to conquer and to suffer, Nijinsky found his talent responsible for his first unhappiness and it was his talent that indirectly caused the final tragedy of his life to overtake him.

Every one of us rejoiced when it was discovered that Vaslaw Nijinsky might be a king on the ballet floor, but in academic pursuits he was a nonentity! It is necessary to have known something of Old Russia to understand the prejudice leveled at Nijinsky because of his Polish antecedents. He was made to feel inferior at every turn; he was ignored in our games, and utterly despised. Privileges which I automatically accepted as a Russian were ab-

solutely denied him; he was someone to be ordered about, to be sneered at
and scorned. Whether or not he deserved criticism, Nijinsky found it. We
shouted with laughter at the picture he made, standing alone, watching us
at play, resignation drawn in the set of his head and the slump of his body,
for he knew no invitation to join us would come. Again, he would stand with
his nose in a book, repeating his next lesson incessantly in an attempt to
achieve something more than a failing mark.

In the classroom, Nijinsky was still isolated. Our desks seated two, but no
one would sit with a Pole. When we were dismissed and rushed out into
Theater Street, shouting and laughing, Nijinsky followed us hungering for
whatever consideration we flung at him. He was never punished for noisi-
ness, or for breaking rules. He was never anything more than an onlooker
—even at lunchtime, when we went into the dining room and gathered
together in a knot to share the good things packed away in our knapsacks.

No memory of Vaslaw with any delicacies brightens my recollection of
him. The rest of us might have cutlets or cakes and sweets tucked into our
lunch boxes at our mothers' orders, but never Vaslaw! A little sandwich of
scraped cheese, often without butter, was all that he could afford. There was
never a leaf of lettuce, or a scrap of meat. For that, we dubbed him "Polish
Cheese"! Some of the senior students heard us at our baiting and tried to
make his life more endurable by sharing their food with him. Again, he
failed to betray a trace of false pride but, instead, accepted their gifts, expressing his appreciation with far more breeding than we displayed.

With censure on every hand, Nijinsky cultivated the tenacity of a bull-
dog in his struggle to make his grades, assuming the handicap of a dull brain
with the same philosophic attitude that marked his realization that, to us, he
was an outlander. For two years he maintained that same dogged persever-
ance without a sign of his innate sensitiveness, always apparently grateful for
the merest suggestion of kindness, registering no complaint, even against the
obvious preferences of the school staff for those of us who were from wealthy
families.

From the first weeks of our training, we were sent onto the Imperial stage
as extras, a part of the mob that surged in the background. We were un-

necessary as dancers, but were learning to be natural before audiences in order that poise and stage presence might become practically subconscious qualities. Those of us appointed for that privilege received fifty kopecks for transportation to and from every performance, and at the end of the month we had often accumulated as much as ten rubles.[1] That was a tremendous sum for a ten-year-old, and a boon to those in the class who were poor. But Nijinsky was again haunted by an ill star; for he was rarely chosen to appear on the stage, and the few rubles which unquestionably would have spelled welcome relief for his mother were denied.

Madame Nijinsky was constantly threatened with poverty because of Vaslaw's father. He was a gypsy at heart, appearing and disappearing without warning. One day he might happen home laden with gifts for his family, recounting his Bohemian experiences, and flinging money about like a lord. Then, as suddenly as he had arrived, he departed for more dancing and more experiences, leaving a pitiable sum to be stretched over a period of months. There was no telling when Thomas Nijinsky would be back!

Meanwhile, Vaslaw's expenses went on. His ballet slippers alone were a tremendous item on his mother's budget. Other boys might use the same slippers for a month, but Vaslaw worked so strenuously that his must be new every week. Broken or soiled footwear was not tolerated, for it ruined the effectiveness of an ensemble, and the two rubles a week necessary for Vaslaw's dancing shoes proved a frightful drain on the slender resources of the Nijinsky household. In addition, there was Stanislaw, who had fallen from the second story of a building in Kiev and injured his head. He was mentally unbalanced and needed special care, lest he go off into mad frenzies at the hospital where he had been for years.

As the close of our training period approached, Madame Nijinsky and Vaslaw waited with eagerness unconcealed. If he was accepted as a boarder at the school, his mother would be relieved of all expense in connection with his food, clothing, and education. There would be money for Stanislaw's care, and for food!

It was a great holiday for Madame Nijinsky when she sat in the large

[1] A ruble was worth about fifty cents.

dance room of the Girls' School and heard Vaslaw's name read as one who had been accepted as a permanent pupil in His Majesty's Imperial Russian Ballet School. It was a source of grave concern when the principal added, before the hundreds assembled, "Nijinsky is accepted—but conditionally. His record in academic studies is poor, and it must improve if he is to remain here!"

With the five others who were chosen to remain—Iliodor Lukianov, George Rozai, Gregori Babitch, Michail Fedorov, and myself—Nijinsky was measured for his uniform, in order that we might return after a three months' summer vacation to find a full wardrobe awaiting us.

There would be ballet uniforms, and dress uniforms, six changes of linen, and two overcoats, one for summer and one for winter wear. A rich array— and more than Vaslaw had ever called his own!

III

SCHOOL RESIDENTS

T HERE was the pride of accomplishment in our carriage when the six of us reported for classes in September. We were no longer "conditional scholars" when we strode through the huge school doors opening into the center of the building. That structure covered the equivalent of three city blocks and housed all of the executive offices controlling the Imperial Russian Theaters: the Wardrobe, Stage-set, Make-up, and Administration departments on its first floor; the Girls' Ballet School occupying the whole second floor, the Imperial Dramatic School and the Boys' Ballet School allotted the third floor.

All the dignity eleven years could muster radiated from us as we passed through the famous portal guarded by the three old soldiers whose names are known to ballerinas throughout the world: Alexis, Gurian, and Jacob. This time, they who had watched so many great ones grow from adolescence to maturity and fame stood silently holding the door open for potentially the greatest of all male dancers to pass. They saw Vaslaw Nijinsky with the same attitude of indifference that they had shown for Karsavina, Kshessinskaya, Pavlowa, and a host of others. He was ordinary to look at, that Vaslaw, with his brown hair clipped close in short straight bristles above his low forehead; his brown eyes peering submissively under heavy slanting brows that accentuated the Tataric cast of his features; his thin sensitive lips rarely curved in a half-smile.

With shouts of delight we donned our uniforms for the first time, standing stiff and erect, like small soldiers, and promenading before the great mirrors like peacocks. Our dress uniforms particularly entranced us. They were of fine blue cheviot, each finished with a military collar of rich velvet, bearing on its points the engraved silver lyre surrounded by palm leaves and surmounted by the royal crown which was the insignia of our school. Our caps, made on the model of the officers', bore the Imperial crest with the school symbol and lent an air of jauntiness to our whole appearance, while silver buttons decorated our double-breasted coats, adding further to our glory. In the winter, astrakhan collars were provided for our overcoats, which were lined with scarlet silk.

Five of us never donned those clothes without bursts of pride; throwing our chests out, deigning a public appearance only when we were so well brushed we fairly screamed propriety. The sixth member of our class, Nijinsky, slouched around without regard for whatever impression he might create, taking the rebukes of the governors without a murmur when they reproached him for his unkempt appearance. He straightened his cap, or buttoned his coat offhandedly, but he never conducted himself as though he enjoyed any distinction as a member of the Imperial Ballet School. It was only when he dressed in his ballet uniform for practice that he walked as though life were worth living; and only when he stood upon the ballet floor that he was galvanized into an extravagant zeal that pulsed in every fiber. Ballet seemed to be his life, his whole existence. There were fire in his eyes and confidence in the set of his head when Legat indicated a particularly difficult step. From the time he was a beginner, when he leaped, he had a trick of staying suspended in mid-air, motionless, as though the atmosphere itself supported him in his flight. All this served as fuel for the jealousy that was beginning to eat deeply into the heart of George Rozai, a lad who harried Nijinsky ruthlessly when he realized that, were it not for Vaslaw, he would be the foremost dancer in our class! Our daily routine presented ample opportunity to exhibit our petty meannesses, for our day began promptly at seven-thirty, when the servants appeared and pulled back the heavy green draperies that shuttered our dormitory windows. At the same moment a deep-throated brass hand bell shattered any thought of extra sleep. The more ambitious among us dashed out of bed and began the work of arousing the heavy sleepers with vigorous thumps, and Nijinsky was one who received more than his share of stirring!

Hot water was unknown to us. We scurried along the cold corridors into the lavatory to wash together, dipping icy water from an enormous copper reservoir in the center of the floor. Haste was essential if we were to be properly washed and dressed and in the dining room before grace was said by one of the students. We set about eating white bread and tea under the eagle eye of the governor seated at the head table. Overeating was frowned upon, for our first class was ballet, which directly followed a morning constitutional around the block, and our wind must be good. The ballet masters utilized every ounce of our strength to build artists, before our brains were clouded with dates and the worries of French grammar, which we heartily despised.

After noon luncheon, part of the students were sent to pursue academic study, which formed an important part of our curriculum, and the rest went to the Marinsky Theater for rehearsals, until five in the afternoon, when our dinner was served. We had more than enough soup, meat, vegetables, and sweets to satisfy our needs, and usually returned our plates to the kitchen well filled, even after we had made gourmands of ourselves. Every move of ours was watched by a monitor who was responsible for teaching us table deportment in preparation for the days when, as ballet artists, we might associate with the crowned heads of Europe with unstudied ease and assurance. Clumsiness or ill-bred remarks brought a sharp rebuke from the monitor, who meted out punishments with the power of a minor god until we revolted at his decisions and appealed to the governor for a final settlement.

Classes in the higher arts followed the five o'clock meal, with certain of us assigned study in pantomime, or in the violin, piano, or other instruments. Others occupied boxes at the opera or attended rehearsals. Supper followed at nine, when huge portions of meat were served to provide us with muscle and energy, according to the belief of the school staff that meat built strength. At nine-thirty we youngest students were expected to be in bed and ready for sleep, while the older boys were permitted to stay up until eleven at night; then they were dismissed and sought their beds, so exhausted that they fell into an immediate and heavy sleep.

Both Nijinsky and I eventually learned what a rigid program like that of the school could do towards making sleep something to be craved at the end of a sixteen-hour day. How we used to laugh when we were traveling together and saw fond parents expecting their children to be finished artists at the end of ten ballet lessons! Before we could attain the right to a place in the Corps de Ballet, we were required to spend seven years under the strictest discipline and training in the world, and many a student who went through that course never danced a solo!

IV

LESSONS WITH
OBOUCHOV AND LEGAT

$\mathbb{M}$ASTERING the art of dancing was stern business in a stern climate for us of the old school conducted under the direction of Nicolai Legat, who waited for us outside the huge salle de ballet, with every window flung wide to admit the freezing winds that blew down from the north on a St. Petersburg that swathed itself in furs and, even then, shivered. Exactly one minute before class began, Legat ordered the windows closed. We took our places on the floor and his strong fingers began the pizzicato that was our sole accompaniment. In ten minutes our blood tingled! We had to work to keep warm! —and we worked until the heat from our bodies created an aura of steam around us while our breath made us look as though we held white plumes between our teeth. I have often remembered how cold it was, and thought of Legat, unable to exercise as we did, patiently teaching us, now shouting excited orders at us, now counting sharply to emphasize the tempo that he set by plucking the strings of his violin.

Always happy and smiling, he made his lessons a joy, and loved us both as a friend and as a teacher. His pencil and sketching block were never far from him, for he was by way of being a genius at caricature, and utilized his talent to produce a volume of cartoons, some not without irony, but all of them reflecting Legat's merry dealings with his students. His book, which proved a sensation, had no effect on him, however, for he continued his policy of voicing criticism or praise only when it was thoroughly earned, and played no favorites in any of his classes.

We were under his direction only two years before we were transferred to Michail Konstantinovitch Obouchov, to whom belongs the full credit for developing Nijinsky from an inchoate genius into a supreme master of the ballet as an art.

Obouchov it was who spent hour after hour drilling Nijinsky until his technical skill was as marvelous as the leaps which defied the laws of gravitation. An exceptionally strict teacher, Obouchov was also extremely outspoken, remaining a firm disbeliever in praise during the years we spent with him. I never heard him grow enthusiastic. "Pretty good!" was the acme of approval from his lips. His marking betrayed the same tendency. Twelve was the maximum mark to be acquired, but Obouchov never gave more than an eight or a nine, except to Vaslaw, who was once honored by an eleven, though even he failed to achieve a twelve. "Why should I mark any of you with a twelve?" the master would fume. "Perhaps there is some school in the world better than this, and some dancer who may deserve the highest mark. Here none are perfect!" Nevertheless, he recognized Nijinsky's genius with the highest grade that he ever gave and he perceived Nijinsky's needs with far more penetration than his mark indicated.

More and more Obouchov became aware of the jealousy that hounded Vaslaw from every quarter. He unobtrusively observed the cruelties we inflicted upon his star student until he became incensed against the five of us. One day he exploded with wrath which was vented characteristically.

"Wolves!" he screamed at us. "You are nothing more than a pack of wolves harrying a helpless lamb! How can you be jealous of a gift God has bestowed? How can you fly in the face of a Providence that made Nijinsky a genius? Polish, is he? What difference does it make if a man is born Polish, or Jewish, or French? He is your brother just the same. He has a right to live!" Then, his anger spent, Obouchov pleaded with us: "He must live in this school, this Nijinsky! Make him happy! He can bring honor to your school and to you because you knew him!"

That harangue was the first of many, for I can see, now, that we were breaking Nijinsky's spirit with our insults. We loved Obouchov; we respected him so completely that we changed. Vaslaw was permitted to play with us, to receive invitations, to share our jokes, and then our master smiled and let the warmth of his approval encourage us in his classes. Still, it is difficult to change the heart of a wolf; and even while Obouchov visioned the future of Nijinsky's inborn supremacy and expanded with Vaslaw's changing status, Rozai hid fresh tricks in his mind and schemed to bring about Vaslaw's downfall.

We had completed more than two years' training, and at last we were deemed capable of dancing on the stage. Such music as Tchaikovsky's *Nutcracker Suite*, Puni's *Hunchbacked Horse*, and Drigo's lightly rhythmic *Compositions* were featured in the ballet then, and permitted the whole school, forty boys and forty girls, to take part. It was the ballet *Pahita* that was chosen for our debut, and the chance to dance a spirited mazurka offered Vaslaw his first real thrill. The rest of us rejoiced in the gorgeous blue, gold, and white costumes that we would wear, with high boots and jingling spurs, and the foregone conclusion that we would make a bis [1] with the ballet because it was the Tsar's favorite.

If we were excited, Vaslaw was elated! He lived in a world of his own, executing the mazurka as none other. His very soul responded to that dance, and I know he thought: "This is a Polish dance, and beautiful. I am Polish and I have suffered because I am Polish—but this dance is mine!" Step by step the sixteen of us who were to appear in it were trained at rehearsals, held downstairs in the Girls' Hall, where Alexander Victorovitch Shiryaev always directed us.

The prospect of rehearsing with the girls put us into a state of nervous tension, relieved by the scrubbings and brushings we inflicted upon ourselves and each other. Shiryaev was noted not only as a splendid ballet master, but as a brilliant artist—one who was willing to explain at length until the intricacies of ballet were unraveled for us and we understood the meaning of dance composition and formation. He it was who provided the foundations

[1] Stop the show.

for towering successes by graduates of the Imperial Russian Ballet School which have been hailed by the world as triumphs.

A rehearsal with him was a tremendous red-letter day for us, until a cloud descended to obscure our elation.

Varvara Ivanovna Lihosherstova, directress of the Girls' School, was the inevitable cloud. She always discovered something wrong! Her discipline was as unbending as court etiquette. If one boy spoke too often to his partner, if another laughed, Varvara Ivanovna would dart a piercing glance in his direction, and desserts were lost for a week or visiting privileges were gone in the twinkling of an eye, for she protected her girls with the jealousy of a hen with one chick. She prohibited flirting or joking between boys and girls, and no excuse for transgressions was acceptable, punishment was certain, and there could be no quarter expected. All this never touched Nijinsky, for he was too timid off the ballet floor to infringe on the slightest regulation.

Final rehearsals customarily took place in the vast repetizionnoe zalo,[2] where the "real" artists and stars of the Imperial Theater rehearsed with us daily from twelve until four, an air of seriousness prevailing while the mighty Marius Petipa ruled supreme. Although he had spent sixty years in Russia, he had never learned to speak the language properly—it was in a purely original admixture of French and Russian that he snapped his directions at us. Whenever we were under his strict baton, we puffed up with pride in our own importance.

The whole Ballet School could be accommodated for the more important spectacles. Eighty boys and girls united with the company of two hundred and fifty and worked with the silence and precision of mature students, a phenomenon I have yet to witness in any other country. The zalo was two stories high, and was walled with a mirror at one end, which created the illusion of a room twice its actual size. Not a whisper or a giggle broke the stillness when we were not at work; and whenever Petipa spoke, his voice was clearly heard in the farthermost corner.

Richard Drigo himself played for us with a first and second violinist, while we danced without sparing a thought for his greatness. Years later, Anna

[2] Rehearsal Hall.

Pavlowa reminded me of the way Drigo was treated during those rehearsals. "Do you know, Bourman," she said, "I used to scream at Drigo, 'It is too fast! Do it again, Drigo! Again, I say! Slower!' And then after roaming all over the world I have worked with musicians who didn't know how to sit at the piano, and I have been afraid to ask them to repeat a phrase! I beg these people with my prettiest smile, 'Please, please repeat it!' And how I treated the splendid Drigo!"

We prayed for long rehearsals to escape the dull routine of our classes, until our teachers, well realizing what we were up to, would put an end to our hopes by lining us up and directing a barrage of questions at us. It was an ordeal that usually found our minds perfectly blank when it came to names and chronology and declinations. Inevitably a long list of failures resulted.

While rehearsals caused us to lose class after class, they were never proffered as legitimate excuses for failure in mathematics, history, languages, or any other course. Since spring examinations betrayed any laziness or stupidity, we worked and studied ceaselessly, sandwiching in our own diversions whenever occasion offered.

Weekly rehearsals at the Marinsky Theater were scheduled for Fridays, and on that day we were piled into the enormous coaches that the natives of St. Petersburg nicknamed "Kovcheg Noya"—Noah's Arks—and in those we rolled in state to and from the theater to rehearse with the orchestra. Immediately upon our arrival, we changed into practice suits and took our places in boxes to await our numbers.

It was not enough for us to watch accomplished artists in rehearsal. With Russian thoroughness, it was considered wise to ground us in the fundamentals of music. Drigo directed the orchestra of one hundred and twenty pieces which provided a classical fare fit for the most discriminating connoisseur. And why not? In that organization were not only Leopold Auer, who taught Heifetz, Zimbalist, and Mischa Elman, but Krueger, Wolf-Israel, Zabel, the master harpist, Verjbilovitch, the world-famous cellist, Walter Kune, and other equally renowned musicians, as well as dozens of men who held full professorships in the Imperial Russian Conservatory of Music. A professorship in Russia was no empty title as it is in some countries where nothing but an instrument is required, for every professor in the conservatory was given his title only after he had proven his superiority over hundreds of gifted musicians determined on winning a post in the organization.

Again, this opportunity to watch the foremost musicians at work with the world's premier artists was judged necessary, even though we understood that until we had earned the right to success, our stage appearances would be unimportant, for the simple reason that we would be given no opportunity to exhibit our own capabilities.

The commonly accepted fact that everyone who attended the Imperial Ballet School must have talent was sufficient for us! We were content to take the insignificant roles designated, and to dance as extras. Even then, Nijinsky's work was unusual, but who dreamed that the slim figure leaping in unison with scores of other slim boys would one day startle the whole world with his genius? Obouchov was only the more severe with him because he realized Vaslaw's potentialities, and we only tolerated him because the master wished it!

V

RECONCILIATION

As we grew in stature, we improved in understanding, until to Lukianov, Babitch, Fedorov, and myself, Nijinsky was no longer an enemy. Rozai still maintained an armed neutrality, which sometimes flamed into active hate, but for the most part we contented ourselves with occasional slurs against Vaslaw's nationality. Quick to sense our change of front, Nijinsky began to open his heart to us, and in common with the rest of us declared his love for his favorites in the Big Ballet and among the girls at school.

Like us, he imagined himself in the throes of an immortal passion every other week, and scratched the name or initials of his beloved on mirrors, on walls, in the lavatories, in books, and on scraps of paper, whenever the notion possessed him. In our rehearsal hall there stood a piano dating back to the days of Napoleon, which, if it has not been destroyed during the Revolution, would be welcomed by any museum, for on it are scratched the names of the greatest dancers born to fame.

There, on the ancient redwood, anyone may discover the adorers of Karsavina, Pavlowa, Kshessinskaya and Trefilova. Nijinsky's name and mine are there, along with those of the great, the near-great, and the never-great, who traced the record of their amours in the fond belief that those school-loves and school-dreams were eternal. I remember once watching Vaslaw painstakingly trace the name of his first beloved, Tonia Tschumakova, who later became the wife of Legat. To keep up the tradition established for us, we each boasted four loves: one in the Big Ballet; one in training in the Girls' School; one outside the school, and one in the Dramatic School.

The dramatic students were not difficult to know, for their school was conducted on our floor. Each was at least a high-school graduate, and all were picked for both talent and personal beauty. They ranged in age from eighteen to thirty, and universally admired Nijinsky, although they were fond of every "ballet boy" and brought repeated reproofs on themselves by peering at us through a crack in the door when we were at class. Ivanova-Setchenova, the daughter of a Russian general, was singled out by Vaslaw for his special attention. Timmé, now one of the few great Russian dramatists still in her country, was my favorite.

We waited eagerly until their class was done with its lessons in plastic and ballroom dancing, before we invaded the hall and claimed our favorites as partners, always under the gimlet eyes of our governor. Ivanova and Timmé awaited our coming as the ancient Hebrews watched for manna, for ballet boys were far more graceful than dramatic students—and how we reveled in our supremacy! Vaslaw was even more sought after as a fencing partner, for his lightninglike speed and adroitness made him a marvel with the foils.

Despite these more refined diversions, we contrived opportunities to slake the Tatar in us which reveled in bloodshed and cruelty that is hardly credible to an Occidental mind. The one mistake that the school made was to fail in providing organized and supervised sports, an oversight indirectly responsible for the several tragedies that marred Nijinsky's earlier years at school.

In those days we had a game similar to baseball in its intent, but infinitely rougher, called lapta. A ball, about the size of a baseball, but made of solid India rubber, was thrown at a runner, the object being to strike him while he was between goals. The ball, termed the "Arab," was so heavy that it left deep bruises whenever a hit was scored, and Nijinsky, with his sure aim, was the most brilliant shot among us. A hit delivered by him unfailingly resulted in black and blue marks that were sore and angry for days, and again it was his excellence that precipitated Rozai's jealousy.

"Vaslaw! You think you are good," Rozai sneered, "but I will set you a task that will beat you. I'll bet every chocolate that my parents bring me for the next four weeks that you can't hit me with the Arab at thirty paces!"

We gasped. Thirty paces was well over sixty feet, and who could throw any Arab that far! We rallied around Nijinsky, insisting that Rozai was crazy, that he was bent upon urging Vaslaw into certain failure.

Rozai broke in. "You can't do it, Nijinsky! If you fail, I'll take your desserts for two months!"

"All right. Pace the distance!" retorted Nijinsky. "There, now, turn your back!"

"Turn my back on a Pole? Never! You can't hit me!" and Rozai thrust out his stomach and grimaced. Back went Nijinsky's arm, almost too speedily for our eyes to follow, and the ball rocketed straight as an arrow to catch Rozai squarely in the mouth. He swayed for an instant, his hands covering his face, and then, with a groan, he fell, blood gushing from his mouth and nose.

Poor Vaslaw! He was as pale as a ghost when he saw blood forming a pool around Rozai's head. Suddenly he seemed to realize what had occurred and dashed to Rozai, lifting his head tenderly, and whispering: "Poor boy! Rozai, forgive me! It was an accident! You made me so angry! Speak to me, Rozai!"

I can see Rozai yet, groggy, livid with anger and jealousy, his lips and nose a pulpy mass, his mouth further disfigured by the loss of four teeth! We lifted him and carried him to the infirmary, where he was washed and doctored. After a fortnight, his looks were enough restored to justify his return to classes. I sensed the passion that was simmering in Rozai, but still, not caring especially for Nijinsky's friendship, I let it pass as a groundless notion.

Nijinsky, meanwhile, had become our hero. He had thrown the Arab thirty paces, and better yet, he was excelling at a secret sport that thrilled us with its audacity. He was a boxer par excellence! Every night, when we didn't go to the theater, we held our pugilistic exhibitions in the lavatory. There we gathered after picking two boys, evenly matched, to fight until they dropped, or until our own blood lust was satisfied. None dared refuse the order, for refusal brought the mob of us into furious action. In consequence, the lesser of two evils was to fight at our command! Our boxing was patterned after that instituted by Peter the Great two hundred years ago, when he ordered strong men brought before him and reveled in their fistic encounters, declaring all blows fair, without exception. The same rule governed our battles. Unless he fought like a tiger, the boy who begged mercy and shouted "I give up!" was lost. If he fought like a demon possessed and struck hard and fast, he was excused—until the next night.

Nijinsky was matched with Lukianov, the only boy strong enough to stand up to him, for Vaslaw's muscles were like tempered steel. If any of us had contested with either Vaslaw or Lukianov, we would have risked more than beauty—we would have risked our lives!

Fighting was fun, but not lusty enough to satisfy us! We invented another pastime that Nijinsky loved! It was never indulged in without the full consent of the pair who took part, each of whom usually challenged and accepted, with spirited assurances of victory. Although the whole class were devotees, Nijinsky never fought with any but an older boy, Bekeffi. Like the rest of us, when his chance came, Vaslaw stripped to the waist with Bekeffi, and each took his heavy leather belt, lashing at the other unmercifully— and woe be to the boy who managed to get in line with the belts that fell with increasing weight and violence on bare skin until long, bloody welts crisscrossed their bodies from shoulders to knees.

That game went on night after night until the spring medical examinations disclosed the entire class with skin that rivaled that of a zebra! Then it was prohibited on pain of immediate expulsion.

Babitch's ingenuity was equal to the task of providing other entertainment, however, and when we returned from our summer holidays, it was to discover a new standard for judging vacations! We might be brown and sunburned, but if we presented too refined an aspect, Babitch declared that we had had a poor time of it! The staff unconsciously abetted him by remarking, "What? All dressed up? You must have had a bad summer!"

"To prove that you had a good time, take a buttonhook, and stand another boy before you, and then both of you tear the clothes off the other with the hook!" proposed the bright Babitch. It was a grand idea, but as usual Vaslaw turned it into a tragedy!

Vaslaw and Babitch stood face to face, each angling for seams, pockets, and sleeves with his buttonhook. The rest of us were likewise engaged when a sharp cry from Nijinsky spoiled our sport. He had aimed for Babitch's collar, and caught him by the corner of the mouth instead! When we turned, it was to face Babitch, the handsomest boy in the class, with his cheek ripped open for two inches and bleeding like a fountain!

Nijinsky's malign destiny followed him as long as I knew him. His superior strength brought trial after trial upon him, and though we might not take Nijinsky into our hearts, we had our own unbreakable code of honor. As soon as he was able to talk, Babitch was put through a third degree by the staff, intent upon expelling the boy responsible for the scar Babitch carried until the day he was killed by a jealous husband years later, but true to our code, Babitch swore that he had forgotten who half-killed him! We all suffered from equally short memories and there the matter ended.

VI

LESSONS IN PANTOMIME
WITH GUERDT

Nıjınsky learned his clever miming as did the rest of us, with Pavel Andreyevitch Guerdt, the pride of the Imperial Ballet, who with only one other dancer, Maria Petipa, achieved the glory of being billed as "soloist to His Majesty." Neither Anna Pavlowa nor Vaslaw Nijinsky gained that honor! Yet, my memories of "d'Immortel" as we called him, are of a man to whom art meant more than any honor the Tsar could bestow. Guerdt, at sixty, looked not a day over forty with his plentiful blond hair and his fresh complexion, every inch of his five-feet-eight lending the illusion of height in his soldierly carriage. On the stage he always portrayed a young lover with consummate skill, turning time backwards with the ease of an Olympian god. In his pantomime, he was incomparable. It was this giant of his art who was chosen to impart all that he could to us.

With infinite patience, he explained each role, and then he stood off to survey his little mimes before he said in his marvelously expressive voice, "Play it now as you *feel* it!"

Our efforts were watched as intently as though each of us were a genius as great as our master until he picked out those who had satisfied his standard of veracity. Then he would say to the chosen few: "I like your expression. I like your method, and I approve the light that shone in your eyes, but it is not enough! See! I will show you how *I* would do it!"

And then the great Guerdt would teach us. Love, suffering, jealousy, hypocrisy, joy unbounded—the whole gamut of human emotions he played with the ease of a master who understood the human heart.

If we were nobles this week, next week we were surely beggars. Before our eyes, Guerdt performed the miracle of transforming fifteen- and sixteen-year-old girls into ancient hags, twisted and warped in mind and body. It was fascinating to watch him take a beautiful and eager young girl like Karsavina and train her to play a crippled old creature nearing ninety. We were spellbound in the illusion that it was no longer Karsavina, but a human wreck that dragged itself laboriously through life, as she struggled across Guerdt's pantomime hall.

Those who begged, implored as did the lowest and most miserable beggars in Old Russia, writhing in mute supplications at the feet of a student who cast the obnoxious creatures from him in horror. These were destined to be the artists of the next generation, and Guerdt was training artists, not amateurs! Whole lessons were given on a single word like "Yes," "No," "Go," "Come." One word, but in it every shade and nuance possible was depicted. A dozen intonations were expected of the least among us, but if we could manage twenty-five interpretations, Guerdt showed us fifty more!

He adored Nijinsky's efforts from the moment he began teaching us. I have sat in Guerdt's class and watched Vaslaw playing with such power and conviction in his gestures that the goose flesh crept eerily over my whole body, and fear itself invaded me. Nijinsky starred, and Guerdt watched him, entranced, until he played love scenes with unsimulated ardor and the girl who served as his partner crimsoned with embarrassment.

The ever-watchful Guerdt would let the scene go on, apparently gripped by the emotion surging through his pupil, until Nijinsky bent forward to kiss his partner. Instantly, the master's voice rang out, "Stop!"

The two would separate abruptly, the girl grateful and Nijinsky abashed that he had not been permitted a kiss. Guerdt well knew Vaslaw's violence, and at the same time he understood his sensitiveness. He would relieve the situation with a chuckle, commenting, "It was enough, Vaslaw! I know how a kiss is done!" and the class continued.

VII

VISITING DAYS AND
SPRING EXAMINATIONS

For some little time life went smoothly enough. We met our families and friends every Thursday in the First Ballet Hall and learned the fragments of news that were of importance to us. Vaslaw's sister, Bronia, had been admitted to the Girls' Ballet School, and he seldom met Madame Nijinsky in our hall, but, instead, went downstairs to visit with his mother and sister.

There was an unwritten law among us that every "Mamma's Boy" in the school must share whatever fruits and candies his doting parent brought on that red-letter Thursday, for the rest of us never enjoyed the indulgences that fell to the lot of a "Mamma's Boy." Those mothers never missed a Thursday. They arrived in rustling satins with at least two pounds of rich chocolates, many kisses, and a wealth of concern for their darlings. We singled out one Potanin for our special attention, and I delivered our ultimatum.

"Potanin, you are eating too much candy and getting fat and clumsy," I pronounced. "Too much candy will ruin you! From this time forth, you are to keep one-seventh for yourself, and divide the rest with us!"

Nijinsky listened intently, and voluntarily shared the small gifts his mother brought. Not so Potanin! He brought a handful of chocolate liqueurs to us, with many apologies, explaining that his mother had brought him only a few candies. I stared at him indignantly, for every one of his pockets bulged!

"Boy! Here is something *very* wrong! We must see that he takes us more seriously!" I gave the signal, and in an instant six of us were rolling the wretched Potanin on the floor, punching him, pommeling him, jumping on him, until his uniform showed big, wet, sticky patches oozing around every pocket! We thrust our hands into the mess and smeared it over Potanin's face and hair with a thoroughness that left nothing to be desired—except a hard scrubbing! Never again did any boy dare to cheat. Sharing sweets became a community affair, and even the school punishment, devised by the staff to maintain discipline, was not too great a price to pay for the treasures that fell into our open hands from that day onward! What was the loss of desserts for a paltry fortnight compared with a supply of candy that remained constant all the years of our training?

Both Nijinsky and I felt the supervision of our parents incompatible with our growing dignity, and so we devoted ourselves to explanations of our growing maturity. Our mothers were told, tactfully, that a weekly visit was unnecessary. Where once we had begged them to come, we made excuses in order that we might entertain the girls from "outside" who were capturing our interest.

Even though he showed a perfectly healthy concern over girls, Nijinsky's first love remained the ballet, and his greatest single drawback was his apparently permanent Polish accent. In vain the staff sent him regularly to the Alexandrinsky Theater to hear Madame Savina, whose fame as an actress far exceeded Pavlowa's fame as a dancer, and to listen to interpretations by Vera Komisarjevsky, Mitchurina, Pototskaya, Davydov, and Varlamov. Despite a passion for drama, and an appreciation for it that was rooted in his very being, Nijinsky's accent stayed with him.

Nothing seemed to touch it! Nothing! Russian pronunciation cost him long hours of discouraging practice, and engaged his attention along with academic subjects when spring examinations presented their annual threat of failure or dismissal. Nervousness and a feeling of insecurity invaded the whole school, for our programs were so heavy that it was almost impossible to pass everything in the long curriculum. If expulsion wasn't the penalty for failure, an extra year at school was; in any case, it was wisest to pass!

As spring drew on, our jokes and loves receded while we went around with long faces, a book perpetually under our noses. Nights no longer were given over to sleep; instead, they found us creeping through the shadowy corridors into deserted schoolrooms to cram, or rising at five in the morning to discover just why Napoleon invaded Russia, and just who his generals might have been! Well knowing that no excuses were acceptable when it came to getting through with a passing mark, we devised tricks, legal and illegal, to manage successful exams.

Shpargalki—cribbing—was a common thing. Answers to a whole series of questions, maps and data of every conceivable variety were laboriously traced on fingernails, the palms of our hands, or our cuffs. Whenever any one of us put a hand to his head with an air of concentration, one of the jury of twelve teachers ranged before us would command, "Come forward!" The guilty one always responded, and stood quaking until he was ordered, "Show your hands!" Unclenched fists would reveal, for all to see, minute tracings completely answering the questions before us!

That scheme was too old to be effective, and so Nijinsky, to whom examinations were more of a nightmare than to any other lad in the whole school, invented a plan that brought honor to every one of us for three consecutive years! It was customary for the jury to prepare card questionnaires bearing simply a number on their backs. These were put on a long table and we filed past, each of us drawing a card and presenting it to the examiners, who registered its number. When Nijinsky learned that the cards were prepared twenty-four hours ahead of the fatal day and left in the offices of Principal Vladimir Parfirievitch Pisniachevsky, he conceived the brilliant notion of marking every card with a symbol which would enable us to make our choice.

At first his idea met with a landslide of objections, but he persisted with characteristic stubbornness until he had persuaded us of its feasibility. Consequently, we stole the keys to Pisniachevsky's office from one of the servants, and tiptoed into the sacred apartment in the wee small hours, to mark every last card destined for our class with a symbol disclosing plainly whether the questions covered chapters one through five, chapters six through ten, chapters eleven through fifteen, or chapters sixteen through twenty! Each of us had one series of chapters in each subject thoroughly prepared, an infinitely easier task than to memorize names and dates in a whole book!

The innovation was marvelous, working precisely as Nijinsky promised, for three years, when for some unknown reason, the staff hit upon the plan of preparing questions only five minutes before the final examinations and we emerged with our just quota of failures. Until that tragedy engulfed us, we had passed every examination with flying colors to the envy of the whole school, for when—when, in all history, had a class shown such intellectual mastery as ours? Surely we were destined to be a great and wondrous group!

Regardless of the destiny that has left only Nijinsky and myself alive, and none but him renowned, to Vaslaw goes the credit for three years of excellent marks which broke the school record for classes past, and set one for future generations to struggle for while they wondered at our surpassing intelligence!

VIII

SECRET RENDEZVOUS AT NIGHT—THE WATERMELON

One of my most amusing memories is of a series of night rendezvous fraught with romance and danger for the five or six boys and as many girls who rivaled Romeo and Juliet in risking life and limb under the rigorous code of the school. Like all budding adolescents, Nijinsky, Lukianov, and I had conceived undying love for a maid of our choice for whose glance the whole world might be lost with a graceful gesture! In our cases, it was a student in the Girls' Ballet School with whom we each stole pitifully few words to whisper that, in the darkest hour before dawn, we would seek her presence.

Days and nights of feverish uncertainty followed until we could determine when the heaviest sleeper among the guards was due to serve as night watchman for our dormitory. When that was assured we drew up a plan of campaign that was perfect.

We plotted like demons for the promise of a kiss! Lukianov, because of his superior strength, was to stand at the guard's head, a three-pound dumbbell poised and ready to fall if the guard moved, I was to stand behind the guard's bed with a huge wet towel (I don't know why it was wet!) to be thrown over his head in order to prevent his recognition of any of us, and Nijinsky, noted for the stealth of his movements and the delicacy of his touch, was to slide his hand under the pillow, remove the keys hidden there, and unlock the doors noiselessly!

31

Over and over, we cautioned Lukianov, "If the watchman wakes up, don't kill him—just make him dizzy!" How we imagined that any fourteen-year-old could gauge his strength to that extent I can't imagine! One blow from a dumbbell wielded by Lukianov was bound to kill! Our first rendezvous passed without accident.

We went through the program without mishap, although the tenseness of those fifteen or twenty minutes that passed while Nijinsky's slender fingers inched their way under the pillow can well be imagined. The trip through the long, cold corridors and down the broad stairway to meet our beloveds is as vivid as though it had happened yesterday—so, too, is the breathless wait while Vaslaw tinkered with the keys and fitted them to the heavy locks!

And the girls! How comical they were, crowded like little white ghosts in one corner of the great empty ballet hall! They wore long white starched petticoats over their nightgowns, with odd short jackets and nightcaps that were enough to kill romance in the hearts of any but the Don Juans we fancied ourselves! Tonia Tschumakova, who is today dancing her way into the hearts of Russians, was Nijinsky's love at the time, while Helena Smirnova, now in South America, was my adored. Each of us took our Juliet off in a corner and whispered magic words, stopping only long enough to plight undying troth with a stolen kiss! After ten minutes of that inspiring occupation, we trooped soundlessly back to the guard, locking the doors behind us, and standing half-petrified with fear in the darkness while Vaslaw replaced the keys!

The other boys heard of our escapade and treated us with the deference due any willing to fly in the face of man and the devil! We planned another rendezvous—in which the guard, Vassily Repeyko, was closer to death than we ever were. All went well until Nijinsky began to slide his hand under the pillow to replace the precious keys, when, to our utter horror, Repeyko groaned and moved his arms! Our nerves were stretched to the breaking point, and beside me I could hear Lukianov's breath coming in short, sudden gasps while his body tensed. The arm holding the dumbbell tightened! Somehow I managed to convey the idea of withholding the blow. Lukianov's sharp breaths alternated with Repeyko's dreamy grunts. Eternity passed before the guard turned suddenly and began a symphonic snore! Lukianov's taut muscles relaxed, and Vaslaw's work of inching the keys into their cache went on to the rhythmic snorts of Repeyko. It was over, and so were our moments of daring all for love.

I sometimes wonder if the memory of those ridiculous excursions amused Tschumakova and Smirnova when Nijinsky's fame grew until he was an international figure! Funny enough they are to look back upon and remember now, but then— Ah! Then we lived the romance and glamour we portrayed on the stage as unequivocally as any who ever plighted troth on pain of death!

Vaslaw was no longer an enemy. He had proved himself a real boy in spite of his genius; he fought with us, he plotted with us, and he played with us. He had even helped us to discipline a cat that scratched one of the boys who was prowling up the "black stairs" [1] where scores of mangy, hungry felines congregated to steal garbage! The cat had scratched a member of the Imperial Ballet School—and death was the penalty our jury of six decreed while the animal was locked in the music room. No one felt like playing executioner until one of us hit on the splendid idea of throwing pussy from the third-floor window into the court. Away went pussy, describing a parabola through the air, and landing on all fours! She looked up at us disdainfully, and trotted back up the "black stairs"!

That was too much! We hunted her up and tossed her out again, with no better luck. The fun went on, until one of the boys tried the experiment of somersaulting pussy! That seemed to disturb her sense of balance, and before our eyes she was crushed on the cobbles of the court. We suffered agonies of reproach when we discovered that the cat who was killed was not the one who had dared to scratch a student in His Majesty's service. She was the innocent victim of a new sport!

After the annual horror of spring examinations passed, our thoughts yielded to the splendor of spring. Bird songs and soft breezes stirred the spirit of adventure in us, and we recalled the glory of apples, pears, grapes, and

[1] Back stairs were jocularly referred to as "black stairs" in Russia.

melons that would be stacked in the Stchukin Dvor, Russia's largest fruit market, when the blossoms scenting the winds would yield up their fruit.

It was then that we planned a series of raids on teams that came from the north and south and east and west in the fall with loads of luscious fruit at prices so low that even beggars could buy! It was more fun to steal than it was to purchase, and during our years at the school Vaslaw and I filled our pockets many a time from the stock of a simple peasant!

Since watermelons were one thing we couldn't steal, we collected a kopeck or so from each of the six of us, and in the event one of us was minus the kopeck, we accepted service in lieu of cash! Nijinsky was almost always penniless, and to him usually fell the business of buying the melon and lugging it from the Stchukin Dvor to the school. On the occasion in question, he had sweated and strained to deliver a forty-pound globe of a melon to us. Forgetful of him, we fell to quarreling over its division. I had given two kopecks; Lukianov had given more, Babitch less, and so on. With our pencils we marked off our respective shares, forgetful of Vaslaw, who stood puffing and wiping his sweating hands and head, apparently not deeply concerned over our battle until he discovered that his share was infinitesimal. Then his wild fury lashed out for the first time.

"Crazy fools!" he shrieked at us. "Do you think I am insane! Am I your servant to sweat and strain with the weight of that melon for a beggar's share? Ingrates, I'll show you!"

With the speed of a lightning stroke, Nijinsky's arms shot out and heaved the melon straight through the window onto Theater Street. For a second we stood speechless—Vaslaw as stunned as we—until the sound of shouting came up from the street. We rushed to peer out.

There was the stately carriage belonging to one of Russia's greatest Names with its top broken, surrounded by a crowd of people gesticulating, shouting, and pointing up at our window. It was enough! We ran like deer, and when two coachmen, a policeman, and several governors arrived in high dudgeon we were innocently occupied in another part of the building.

"Melon?" we queried. "What melon?"—and I suspect the school paid the carriage bill!

IX

ROZAI'S REVENGE

Despite our efforts to make Nijinsky one of us in the eventful life of the school, Rozai was obsessed with an opposite intention. If it was not a slur against Vaslaw's nationality that was flung at him, it was a disparagement of his talent, until it was evident to the most disinterested bystander that even if the rest of us tolerated our unwelcome genius, Rozai did not. He was the sort of boy who couldn't endure a secondary place in life and devoted himself deliberately to cultivating the jealousy that was, by that time, part of his character.

Schelkatchi, a game that decreed a sharp snap on the back of the skull, delivered by the wiry fingers of any lad who scored a triumph in the art of snapping pen points at his opponent, offered Rozai his first opportunity to vent his fury against Nijinsky. Vaslaw won whenever marksmanship meant victory, and so most of us received a resounding crack on the head from his muscular third finger. Rozai was no exception, although he was Vaslaw's closest rival. The law of averages inevitably gave him his chance to crack Vaslaw's skull one fine day when the sun poured through our school windows in a golden flood and the world seemed benevolent enough! Nijinsky bent his head before the triumphant Rozai in the accepted fashion while the rest of us rejoiced in the rare spectacle of a genius prone before an ordinary mortal. Rozai's lips twisted into an unpleasant, tight smile when he delivered his schelkatchi on Vaslaw's shaven head, while his whole face was transfigured by a diabolical grin as Vaslaw spun around and around, grabbing his head in his hands and shrieking with pain, in spite of the fact

35

that he had won a reputation for stoicism that was the envy of the class! In a flash, the three of us leaped at Rozai, chasing him through the school like hounds after a fox, certain that he had caught Vaslaw with a knife, and bent upon delivering our own brand of justice for the trick.

We caught him, and beat him until he could hardly stand up, when we found a heavy steel thimble on his finger. Even wolves may turn on a jackal! Still smarting under the disgrace of Nijinsky's hit with the Arab, Rozai's hate festered like a canker until our beating brought it to a head. He glared at Vaslaw with implacable fury when the poor lad smiled at him, perfectly willing to forget the pain of the huge lump that had been raised on his crown by the thimble, eager only to reestablish a semblance of friendliness. Rozai pretended response, his eyes flickering with anger, his fists clenched, his voice trembling with rage—and we let it pass as "temperament" until it was too late to do more than spend weeks of regret!

The next day found us in the First Ballet Hall as usual, practicing leaps for elevation after Obouchov's lesson. We had cleared the chairs usually pressed into service, and sought something higher when Rozai proposed springing over a heavy wrought-iron music stand that stood in a corner. It was an inspiration! The stand, weighing pounds, could be raised and lowered at will for our jumps as well as for the short, swift flights of Nijinsky. Rozai, as author of the idea, claimed the honor of adjusting the stand for each of us, bent on excelling one another and, some day, perhaps to equal Vaslaw. One by one we ran and, after each success, stood to discover our nearest rival, until Nijinsky's turn came. By common consent, we walked back to the far end of the hall. Why wait for fresh humiliation by his superiority? Only Rozai remained to set the stand at Nijinsky's limit. The devil must have possessed him when he raised it inches higher!

Vaslaw was midway up the hall, running with every ounce of strength in him when we faced Rozai and the stand to witness Nijinsky's defiance of the gravity that held us closer to earth than he ever stayed. His slippers, heavy with rosin, barely touched the floor until with a tremendous bound, he soared through the air like an eaglet. For an instant he hovered above the stand, and then, inevitably, he crashed, the stand toppling onto him with a dull thud. Before we could cover the space between, a senior had burst into the hall and lifted Vaslaw in his arms. Only then did we perceive that Nijinsky had pitched head foremost and injured himself painfully, for blood poured from his mouth and nose and ears, while his chest seemed misshapen. We did our best to help the senior to the hospital with his burden, and scurried back to the hall, one thought uppermost. Rozai!

The staff was there ahead of us! They had Rozai before them, defiantly professing innocence. It was the senior who settled the matter. He listened to Rozai only for a few moments, and then he spoke, "That boy fixed the stand. I was watching from the hall, and saw him raise it to a height that would have taxed me. Also," the student's eyes narrowed, "I saw him scatter something on the floor."

At once the staff moved towards the fallen stand. The floor was covered with soap shavings! Rozai was taken off for further examination, and we went to classes. After all, it was not too serious, and why worry over Nijinsky?

It was at luncheon that we learned the truth. Nijinsky was still unconscious, and had been removed to His Majesty's Hospital where the best doctors in St. Petersburg were at that moment working to save his life. His head was frightfully injured and his chest was crushed. It was most uncertain that he could live through the day. His mother had been called to his bedside. Obouchov wore an air of misery that reflected itself in all of us —except Rozai who, regardless of the threat of expulsion and disgrace that hung over him, went about with a little smile in his eyes. He had repaid Nijinsky for his mighty genius! He was happy, actually happy!

That afternoon, his father, a horse trainer in the service of Gertzog [1] Leychtembergsky, arrived, but the Gertzog had power, and it was enough to keep Rozai at school with only a minor punishment. The class revolted at the injustice and buzzed with threats against Rozai; but, after all, what could we do? There were only four of us, and each had a guilty conscience to contend with on his own account.

It was then that every spark of potential manhood in me asserted itself, and I swore an oath after the fashion of Old Russia, before I hurried off to

[1] Duke.

recount the whole story to my family. Father was indignant, and while my mother and sisters wept, he stormed at Rozai, at me, at every one of the boys who had tortured Vaslaw over his birth and his accent. Even if I hadn't sworn the oath that never can be broken, I knew then that never again in all this world should I listen to treachery or injustice against Vaslaw if he might only live and be willing to accept my friendship.

"We will go to him at the hospital Sunday!" my father announced, and on Sunday we went.

Five days had passed since the accident, but Vaslaw was still unconscious. As we entered the hospital, we saw his mother standing quiet by his bed, crying as though her heart would break over the slender body, swathed in bandages.

My father went to her and, speaking in Polish, he kissed her hand. A full-blooded Russian, he had been born in Poland and understood Poles as few Russians could.

Madame Nijinsky was baffled by our presence. She had known from the beginning that I was as much Vaslaw's enemy as any boy at school, but she smiled her thanks when Father promised that Mother and Nastia, my sister, would visit Vaslaw daily. He kept his word. Every day, my mother and sister made the pilgrimage to the hospital to stand for a little time with Madame Nijinsky, while for days Vaslaw hovered between life and death, now laboring for breath, and again hardly breathing at all, but fighting, fighting to live.

A week later I went to see him. He was alone, motionless, and pale, unable to speak, and staring blankly at the ceiling. He saw me. Slowly he reached his hand out, his eyes alone shining to tell me how grateful he was for friendship. I tried to hide my emotion by recounting news of what was going on at school, for we supposed he considered his misfortune an accident. As I spoke, he motioned weakly for the paper and pencil at his bedside and wrote, "I think Rozai may have had something to do with this, but it does not matter. He is forgiven."

His manliness affected me more than I cared to show. I vowed my oath of friendship to him, not for a year but for life. Again his eyes glowed and he traced, "I trust you. When I am well again, I shall be happier among the wolves."

Once my prejudices were swept away, it was simple to understand why artists, dramatic geniuses, the staff, and the great dancers of the Big Ballet kept Nijinsky's bed surrounded with flowers which perfumed the whole room with their fragrance. I could comprehend why Obouchov lived in an atmosphere of worry and abstraction until it was certain that Nijinsky would recover. The rest of us, to our amazement, discovered that the Pole had taken the joy of the dance with him. To be sure, Rozai did his best, and if we hadn't known Nijinsky's interpretation, Rozai's might have been our ideal. As it was, his efforts were no more than feeble imitations of Vaslaw's proficiency.

At the close of his third month in the hospital, word came that Nijinsky had been permitted to stand, but that owing to extreme weakness, he must learn to walk anew. The whole class visited him. Even Rozai basked in his slow smile when he told us he would be back at the end of the month. His splendid young body had triumphed, and within four weeks he returned, moving slowly from class to class, watching the ballet lessons patiently, since dancing was forbidden to him for months to come. He sat quiet, his eyes alight with joy when we did well. How we "wolves" danced for one of his infrequent smiles!

Nijinsky remained under the doctor's care until fall, when the reopening of school brought the old familiar Vaslaw back, to Obouchov's undying delight. The master fretted over him constantly, stopping classes to demand: "How do you feel, Vaslaw? Are you tired? It is better to go slowly!" Obouchov's primary concern was for the genius he had discerned with Vaslaw's first lesson, and he watched like a hawk for any signs of moodiness on the part of a Nijinsky who had nearly been killed by an unreasoning hate. Under Obouchov's wise direction, Vaslaw grew stronger daily until it was apparent that Rozai's brief supremacy was over, and the king of dancers was back to wear his crown and to claim a new place in our hearts.

My friendship with him grew hourly, but not everyone in the class had sworn the oath I had. Some reverted to the fierceness of the wolf in them, once more delighting in petty scheming against the Pole. I enjoyed every prestige of birth, and although I was the smallest boy in class, I ruled with an iron will, until I was as sincerely hated as Vaslaw had been—with the difference that I was also feared.

Even my championship couldn't stay the jeers that were designed to tear down Vaslaw's pride. One insult, although it was heartbreaking to Vaslaw, was the means of establishing a friendship lasting until within a few years of his final tragedy.

Although Nijinsky and his mother had become close friends of our family, visiting us weekly at our home, where they were welcomed whole-heartedly, months elapsed before Vaslaw mustered the courage to invite me to his home. In Russia, some apartments are erected with three buildings separated by a court. The first block faces the street and boasts a garden for a courtyard; the second is noticeably cheaper, and its court is flagged, but the third! It is the home of the poverty-stricken, and its court is malodorous with garbage dumped into a filthy container. Huge rats sit up and defy tenants and visitors alike. Mangy cats prowl, adding their own nauseous stench to the place where they wage war on their hereditary enemies. It was off such a court, on Sixteen Nicolaievsky Street, that Vaslaw lived, making light of the comedy of cats and rats that went on under his nose! He had wanted to be sure that I wouldn't laugh at him before he trusted me in his home! I made it my business to show him that his friendship was what counted, not his poverty, and in gratitude he reciprocated with friendship, rarely proffered to anyone during his life.

His good times and his troubles he shared. He sought my advice, and he fought for me if a soul dared to speak against me. He was no mad and unde-pendable friend. He was loyal and splendid until permanent forgetfulness claimed his mind and distorted his actions.

At school Vaslaw never mentioned his home to the boys, although he was guilty of no pretenses. Whenever the rest of us displayed expensive gifts or told of receiving simple remembrances, he smiled, remarking: "Of course you are happy with it! I should be, but those things are not for me! My mother cannot afford them!" I never saw him show a trace of envy, but I have often seen the light of resignation in his eyes.

Once he said, "Bourman, perhaps the boys think I am pretending. If they saw that I was really poor, they might understand and give me just a little peace!" The idea met with my immediate approval. "Of course, Vaslaw, they have not really known you—how could they understand you?"

The next day he gathered the class together and extended an invitation to them all to attend a supper party at his house, observing, "I have wanted to know you and to have you know me, but don't expect a palace. My home is very modest!"

To his delight, Rozai, Lukianov, Babitch, and Fedorov accepted at once, and he went off with me, explaining that I might help with his preparations and arrive at five Sunday, instead of at seven, when the rest would come.

Punctually at five I entered the court and pounded for admittance on Nijinsky's door. What a festive scene met my eyes! Mother Nijinsky had been up since early morning polishing and cleaning everything until it was more spotless than before, unbelievably enough. All the little treasures she had hidden away for holiday use were out in full sight, along with her best dishes and glassware for the table.

Vaslaw's face was radiant as the sun. He ran here and there, hunting for pencil and papers to make out the list of our purchases at Filipov's, the most wonderful Russian bakery in St. Petersburg. Off we went, Madame Nijinsky's last kopeck clinking with a few rubles in Vaslaw's pocket. At Filipov's we stood wide-eyed before all the good things ranged before us. Our list was forgotten while we chose bread as white as snow, this pastry for Rozai, that one for Babitch, a kind that we knew Fedorov adored, something for Mother Nijinsky and for me! I had to remind Vaslaw of himself! Then we hunted around for just the right sausages and meats, until every last kopeck was spent and we were laden with little bundles as we ran back home to complete the final preparations.

Before long, the most appetizing odors of sausages and gravy drifted into the dining room, and Madame Nijinsky came out of her kitchen to beam at Vaslaw rushing about the table, arranging and rearranging plates and glasses, standing off to appreciate the result. It was seven o'clock and he was still bustling around in anticipation. We sat down to wait. Seven-fifteen . . . seven-thirty . . . quarter to eight . . . eight o'clock. I understood then exactly what had happened.

How happy Vaslaw had been at seven! "Mother! mother! will the sausages be ready? . . . Should the knife be here or there? . . . The pastries for Babitch . . ." Minute by minute his enthusiasm had faded, until at last, at eight-thirty, he understood, too!

He stood motionless for the space of several minutes, staring straight ahead over the table, empty of guests, and then he sank down into the host's chair he had placed so carefully, sobbing until it seemed that he must reopen the newly healed scars in his chest. His mother tried to soothe him, stroking his head and murmuring consolation to him in Polish that became more and more broken with her own tears, until she wept with him.

I struggled to maintain my own composure, but the memory of Vaslaw's suffering, to be crowned by this humiliation, was overwhelming and when I watched Madame Nijinsky once more heartbroken over her son, it was too much—I began to cry!

I have no idea how long the three of us wept, but suddenly I thought of the good things waiting for us, and thumped Vaslaw on the back. "Come, Vaslaw! Why cry over some idiotic boys who have lost a good meal for their foolishness! The best cakes and sausages in St. Petersburg are waiting for us! Come on, Vaslaw! Why are you crying? Let's eat them and laugh!"

Then he raised his head and laughed a little and cried a little—and laughed again when the three of us sat down to eat.

It was over, except that our friendship was firmly cemented.

X

HOLIDAYS

In all my travels, there has never been a land that excelled Old Russia in its celebration of religious and national holidays. Christmas, Eastertide, the Birthday of the Tsar—these were gala occasions in the life of the Russia that is past. From the day I swore that Vaslaw was my friend, he and his family shared every state occasion with me and my family. How well do I remember Christmas, preceded by two weeks of merry shopping, every difficulty in life fading before the greater problem of seeking just the proper gift in St. Petersburg's great stores where mobs surged constantly, vibrant with their Christmas joys and Christmas hopes.

Vaslaw was with me when we went the rounds, losing me now and again to rush off to buy the gift he'd picked for me, while I hastened to take advantage of the chance to buy my gift for him! And then the Christmas tree that glittered in every home, alight with candles and aglow with tinsel! Laden with tiny bundles and surrounded with big packages, awaiting the ordained "divining" that took place each Christmas Eve, from the Tsar's palace to the meanest hut, when young and old gathered to discover what the future held!

Of many sorts were those "tricks" that we tried to pierce the veil between the "now" and "that to come." Some used a mirror, others poured wax upon cold water and told fortunes from the figures that it formed, using the stiffened wax to cast weird shadows on the wall. Sometimes it was a wedding ring we peered through to seek out a marriage partner, or it was tea leaves or coffee grounds that foretold coming events. Wherever I have roamed that custom has persisted, and overshadowing it, the remembrance of Madame Nijinsky, Bronia, and Vaslaw at my home where my brother and sister brought their friends. The three Nijinskys were always my guests, mingling with the girls from the gymnasium,[1] and the boys from military school, elegant in their splendid uniforms, cocksure and happy with their wealth and family prestige, until the moment for divination, when an air of half-laughter and half-mystery stole over us!

One of the first years that we were all together, Bronia invented a new game. "Boys and girls!" she shouted, her eyes gleaming, "as the clock strikes, write your hopes on a slip of paper, burn it in the flame of the Christmas candles, then swallow the ashes, and if all is done before the last tone of the clock is done reverberating, your wish will most surely come true!" A few moments and the whole gathering was busy scratching off those faraway dreams, and as the last note of the great chimes ceased, Vaslaw, his face a mass of gray ashes, grinned across the room at me. A few moments later he was leaning over my shoulder confidentially. "I wished that I might be a soloist at the Marinsky Theater, and earn one hundred rubles [2] a month— and change our apartment!" he whispered.

Our Christmas lasted two full weeks, and after the great day, the Nijinskys returned home bearing the presents my family had tendered, and as the holiday season went on and we received invitations from our rich friends, Bronia and Vaslaw always accompanied us to exclaim over the expensive gifts that were hiding away in their gay wrappings, for most of them cost between fifteen and twenty-five dollars at least, and so it was with joyousness in our hearts that we made the rounds, staggering home under the blessed weight of our Christmas treasures!

But if intimate family life was joyous, the gala performances at the theater were something to dream about, and to remember now that they are gone forever. Of St. Petersburg's three tremendous theaters, the Alexandrinsky for Russian comedy and drama, the Michailovsky for the greatest French presentations and artists, and the Marinsky—our theater where only ballet

[1] Equivalent of high school.
[2] Fifty dollars.

and opera might be seen, the Tsar loved the Marinsky best of all. Every Christmas, Easter, and birthday of the Emperor's was a red-letter day in our lives, for on those occasions the ruler traditionally chose the ballet, being careful always that it was one in which the whole company and school might participate. Weeks of anxiety preceded the great day, especially at Christmastide, for then the Tsar attended the special performance for the school children of the capital who represented the most aristocratic blood of the country.

I will do my best to convey something of the grandeur of those typical gatherings which brought the carriages of the royal household, resplendent in gold and scarlet, rolling up to the Marinsky a full hour before the performance started. In them rode the mighty ones of the Empire, clad richly, bearing themselves like subjects of a mighty king, waited upon by coachmen and footmen as stiff and straight as soldiers, uniformed in more scarlet and gold and wearing dashing tricorns to add further distinction to pageantry that might have been conceived in the pages of a fantasy.

It was impossible to meet the daughter of a soap or wheat king, for only princesses, countesses, princes, and those whose veins throbbed with noble blood received the hundreds of invitations that went out to the most exclusive boys' and girls' schools.

Every invitation passed through the hands of the school director, who was personally responsible for seeing that they reached only the cream of the students registered at his school.

So it came about that the bel étage, the balcony, the first row of loges were filled with the highest born young people of Old Russia, not one younger than nine, and not one older than twenty. To stand on the stage and sweep that splendor of youth with a glance was an experience! There the most famous names and houses of the most imperial of Russians were represented by faces that seemed masks of classic beauty and the embodiment of culture and refinement. That scene was dazzling with color, fitted like mosaic into the frame of gold and silver and burnished steel which betrayed the uniforms, the swords, the scabbards, and the helmets of His Majesty's Corps de Pages, arrayed in their black and gold glory, with snow-white trousers, high black boots, and crested steel helmets. The Pravovedy in their deep green and dully glowing gold, and the Lyceists in black heavily embroidered in scarlet, contrasted magnificently with the lads from the Nicolaievsky Cavalry School, gorgeous in black and red with shining golden buttons, striding in full of assurance, their long sabers swinging against their sides, and their spurs jingling softly against the counterpointing of conversation that filled the great Marinsky. Here and there sat a group of young women, conscious that they represented the finest names and the highest honor in all Russia, smiling with ill-concealed admiration at the young cavalrymen whose brilliant costumes were like the flourish of the very trumpets that sent them galloping in parade formation. Young men from the Nicolaievsky Cavalry Cossack School, in their long belted coats, and the three grades of cadets in crimson, blue, and white—they were a part of the pomp that was on review before the regal Tsar and Tsarina on the big holidays!

The orchestra seats were reserved for the directors and staffs of the distinguished schools, representing the aristocracy of mind that Russia claimed, approving the companies gathered in the boxes and loges where a governor or directress sat with students, awaiting the triumphant entry of the royal family.

That entrance was always made simply, without ceremonial, for the Tsar was at heart a simple man. A few seconds before the curtain was due to rise, Drigo entered, in such absolute silence that a pin dropped on the stage echoed through the most remote galleries, for no applause greeted the celebrated conductor. Why? It was simple to Young Russia—applause must be given to achievement, but how could youth appreciate the greatness of a man who apparently did no more than hold a little baton? And so it was in utter stillness that Drigo faced the royal box awaiting the arrival of Tsar Nicolai and his lovely Tsarina. At the moment the royal personages stood modestly enough in their places, the whole orchestra and audience rose and the Russian national anthem pealed forth until the very atmosphere tingled with vital inspiration while three thousand young voices caught the spirit of the gathering and swore their lives to the glory of the empire singing "Boje Tsaria

Hrani"—"God Save the Tsar"—in an ecstasy of patriotic exaltation. The man, Nicolai, inevitably stood bowed in silent tribute to the devotion of the youngsters until the last ringing notes of the great hymn died away, and the signal for the performance was given.

Be sure that Kshessinskaya, the Tsar's favorite, and the premier dancers of the day appeared, inevitably scoring an ovation that seemed more like a sudden, swift hurricane, for the applause stopped as though on signal and often left the artists in the ridiculous situation of completing a bow in death-like silence . . . because the directors stopped the enthusiasm of the audience in the royal presence!

We ballet boys and girls were always called into the royal box during intermission, and were the sole school so honored. Every person present would receive a box of chocolates, a Crimean apple, and a tangerine, but we knew that, by tradition, our boxes would be twice the size of any others! First the girls and then the boys entered the royal box, standing at attention and bowing to the Tsar, and kissing Tsarina Alexandra's hand.

Early in our careers, our class distinguished itself, for there were wild wagers made. One boy declared that he would force the Tsarina to present him with two boxes of chocolates, and the other, decrying the possibility of that, vowed that he would soil her glove! The first boy received his sweets, ran back stage and hid them, and returned to stand at the end of the line of boys, until he confronted the Tsar and Tsarina once more. In vain the Emperor reached to the director for another box. The impossible had happened! The tradition of Russia was about to be shattered—for it was unheard of that a ballet boy should be without his candy from the Tsar on Christmas Day. One of the Tsar's daughters came to the rescue, "Let me give my box to this boy!" The lad graciously refused, but the Tsarina insisted, and so it came about that Nijinsky to my intense relief was not expelled, but won his wager with Lukianov, and enjoyed his own box and that extra one with its one piece of candy missing—for the little princess had already sampled Nijinsky's extra gift!

Lukianov, the other daring one, had neglected to remove his lipstick, and so when he, as the Lobster in the ballet of *The Hunchbacked Horse,* kissed the Tsarina's glove, he left on it the trace of his blue lips. The Tsar had laughed, "How wonderful!" and the Tsarina had smiled, "But, of course! I shall keep those gloves as a souvenir!" and while the director perspired, and I have no doubt cursed us all, instructions were given to suspend any punishment for Lukianov's "absent-mindedness."

Many times I have heard tales of the Tsar's coldness and haughtiness, of his cruelty and lack of understanding. They have accused the Tsarina of possessing similar traits. To me those remarks are a source of amusement, for I knew them both. I have seen them scores of times, always pleasant, always gracious. They were, personally, among the most charming people that I have ever met. At the holiday season, we entered their box, with its immense candelabra, priceless paintings, and the Oriental rugs into which our slippers sank. Stepping into the royal presences as friends, we were sure enough of their pleasure and understanding for Lukianov and Nijinsky to play tricks without danger of anything more fearful than a smile!

Very often the Tsar would encourage a young dancer, or the Tsarevitch would play on the floor with his sword, or, with his sisters, he would lean over the rail and chat with the musicians in the orchestra pit, while the Tsar and Tsarina smiled happily, with never a rebuke because their children were not standing at attention like little wooden crown-bearers. We felt neither awe nor fear with Tsar Nicolai, but watched the directors and staffs with wonderment when they stood perspiring at stiff attention. Why should they fear the Tsar? He was a friendly man.

Great Lent and Holy Thursday were both important to Nijinsky, a Roman Catholic, and to me, an Eastern Orthodox Catholic. Here it may be well to note Vaslaw's freedom from religious prejudice, for despite his religion, he usually attended the great religious fetes at our Orthodox church at Eastertide, when the mightiest and holiest celebration in Old Russia was held. Zautrennia, we called it.

It began the Saturday preceding, and with Vaslaw, I stood in the vast nave of the church, with the world's most famous personalities about us, for many of them journeyed across Europe to stand at Midnight Mass for the blessing of Father Pigulevsky in the solemn beauty of his glorious service.

We took our places in congregations that included Karsavina, now Lady Bruce of England; Egorova, now Princess Trubetskoy; Guerdt; Nicolai and Sergei Legat; M. Dandre with his wife, Anna Pavlowa; Sascha Guitry, who was Alexander Guitry before the Russians hailed him as their beloved Sascha; Mademoiselle Balletta, the sweetheart of Grand Duke Alexis; Marie Louise Derval; Trefilova; Kshessinskaya; a hundred others of equal fame—they all stood, their eyes glistening with the lights from the candles on the high altar, and bowed their heads in reverence before the reborn Spirit of Christ on that most sacred of holidays under the old regime.

A little after eleven, the Krestny Hod—the Procession of the Cross—started from the main altar. Once I had the honor of carrying the immense golden crucifix, and preceded other ballet boys who held the precious banners depicting incidents in the lives of the Holy Family, and after the Crucifix and the banners came a group bearing enormous candles alight in honor of the Great Mass, and following them came Father Pigulevsky clad in richly embroidered vestments of old gold, a jeweled cross suspended on his breast. Following him was always the great chorus of picked voices to lead the people, singing as they joined in the ritual and followed the Cross.

If Chaliapin himself was there, he was not a soloist in that ceremonial; he was, like everyone else, a voice in the mighty chorus that swelled with greater power than any organist could coax from the most perfect organ, until the whole church rang with that holy, holy hymn, "Christos Voskrese" —"Christ is Risen"; and outside, the great, mellow-throated bells of Russia burst forth in rapturous ringing to spread the glad tidings of rebirth.

To the accompaniment of song and reverberating bells, the procession moved into the school, through all its halls and rooms, the whole congregation following and singing as it went. At the moment the Cross halted, Father Pigulevsky sent forth his voice in an exalted annunciation that pealed like a celestial trumpet, "Christos Voskrese"—"Christ is Risen"—and a thousand full-throated voices answered him, "Voistinno Voskrese"— "He is Really Risen!" Three times the words rolled out and three times they were answered in such voice that it seemed the very building shook with the fervor of their faith. Its grandeur was too great, too mighty for description. It enthralled each soul with beauty and impressed each with that sense that someone has called "the profound obeisance of the inward soul."

And when the great pronouncement was made, each turned to the one beside him, and in a spirit of complete brotherliness a kiss was given and a kiss returned. It made no difference that the one beside might be a stranger, for in Russia on that one day, a spirit of utter accord ruled—a greeting "Christ is Risen!"—an answer, profound with the faith of ages, "He is Really Risen!" and a kiss to seal the time-honored truth. It was the custom of the land, prevailing in church, in streetcars, in restaurants, and on the streets—all Russia rejoiced in the happy realization, "Christ was risen—a new day was beginning!"

We boys never missed an opportunity presented by the ancient custom. We kissed every girl we had longed to kiss—and tradition forbade her denial! It was a great time for us, fraught with joys more subtle than mere religious fervor could impart to any kiss! After all this we went home to enjoy Razgovliatsia, the great Easter feast. In the poorest hovel and in the richest palace there would be a table set, and on it paskha, made of sweet and sour cheese filled with pistachios, raisins, and candied fruits; kulich, a rich pastry made for each member of the family and each guest at table, and beside each place a gay Easter egg. This must always be! There was never any change in the ordained menu which also decreed that there must be a huge okorok, or cured ham, weighing sometimes fifty or sixty pounds. If the purchase of these dainties took every kopeck in the house, they must be found at Eastertide!

In the churches, aflame with torch illumination inside and out, in the streets where more torches flared and cast dancing shadows over streets made ruddy with their burning in the early dawn of spring, all St. Petersburg moved about eagerly shouting "Christos Voskrese" and rushing homeward for the happy feast at which all friends and relatives must be united. Nijinsky, his mother, and Bronia adored that holiday and always spent it with us, for we were like one big family in those days.

The feast was followed by a party when we sang and danced and shouted.

Nijinsky always arranged a special solo for the occasion. I can still see him dancing with all the fine abandon of youth in the largest room of our house, leaping into the pirouettes destined to make him famous—the pirouettes he invented to set the whole world marveling at his mastery of that most difficult of arts—the dance.

In honor of Madame Nijinsky, my father always arranged a special musicale, for she loved music with a strong and vital love. It seemed to give her something she craved, and since my father understood the hunger of her heart, it was the music of Poland—the folk songs, the mazurkas, the polonaises—that he played, after which he would speak of the beauties of Warsaw, which we called "The Second Paris"! That city was, for her, a treasure city, the repository of her sweetest memories. There she had lived her girlhood, and danced her way to fame, and there she had had her family. Therefore Father talked of Warsaw to make Madame Nijinsky's Easter one of supreme happiness for her.

So poignant were her memories that she sometimes wept, not for sorrow but for joy, and perhaps a little for a life that was all in the past. Father would comfort her, saying "But do not weep! One day you will go back and see old Warsaw, just as beautiful, and just as happy for you once again!"

Then Madame Nijinsky would draw Vaslaw and Bronia to her and kiss them gently. I recall one wish of hers that was voiced from her heart after she had watched her son dance and seen in his work the promise of his genius.

"Vatso!" she half-whispered in amazement at his skill. "I have one prayer —one hope! When you are famous and all the world knows you are a great dancer, go then to Warsaw and dance there your greatest dance—for me! For Warsaw holds my heart—my life!"

Yet, try as he might, he never kept that promise to his mother. There were too many obstacles placed in his way whenever Nijinsky attempted to fulfill his mother's wish. Perhaps it was because the Russians feared his great gifts would stir Polish pride to swift and triumphant patriotism. At any rate, that was one of Vaslaw's hidden sorrows—he never danced in Warsaw as his mother had asked on that solemn and happy Easter Day.

All night, and until the clock began to creep around towards noon, we danced and sang and were happy. Then the Nijinskys went back to their apartment, off the last mean court, carrying with them the very spirit of our fun, and we were quiet thinking of the holidays that had been gayer than ever since we had known the generous-hearted Nijinskys.

XI

LITTLE TROUBLES AND GREAT ONES

Oɴᴄᴇ a year, ballets were presented at our own school theater instead of at the Marinsky, and on those state occasions His Majesty was usually present to encourage us all in our aspiration towards a more perfect expression of the great inspirational art of Terpsichore. I shall never forget what a picture Vaslaw made the year that Lydia Kyasht and Karsavina graduated. His Majesty was unable to keep his promise to attend, but his uncle, Grand Duke Vladimir Alexandrovitch, was present in his place. His voice could have been heard for miles around when he remarked during a silence, "Oh, that Kyasht and Karsavina will one day be the jewels of our stage! They're fine! Wonderful!" Like all the Romanovs, he had a voice of thunder. He had obviously enjoyed the ballet, which had to do with the fantastic dream of a hunter who fell during his climb to a mountain peak, and dreamed of a frolic that was being played under the ice and snow upon which he rested.

In fine fettle the Grand Duke climbed the stairs to our dining room and decided to take supper with us. A jovial sort, it wasn't long before the strict discipline of the place palled and he rumbled out at the boys in general, "Eh, boys! Who is the best dancer in the school?"

The whole assembly responded, "Nijinsky!"

"Where is he, this Nijinsky? Come over here, boy!" commanded His Highness.

Vaslaw stood while the Grand Duke began his questions. It was his atrocious accent that gave him away. "O-ho! You're a Pole, my lad. I like Polish people and their art! That nation should be proud of you, for you are a great dancer!"

Nijinsky's slow wits were unequal to the task of replying without risking a faux pas. First a Pole, and then tactful, he had forgotten that for years all Russia had smiled tolerantly at the Tsar's passion for a Polish dancer, for he stood straight as a soldier when he inquired, "And His Majesty, the Tsar, does he like the Polish?"

Grand Duke Vladimir literally shattered the atmosphere with his laugh— "Like the Poles? He not only likes them, he adores them!" and while the school staff and the boys held their breath, the Grand Duke roared at his own joke, and then, "It will be good to see you in a responsible role, Nijinsky!" he remarked, and with a promise that he would see to it that the Tsar visited us, he was off.

Not many days later, the governors rushed into our class wild-eyed, disrupting a learned lecture on history to shout at us, "Fix yourselves! Fix your costume! Neat! His Majesty is coming!"

It was like a bombshell, for some of us had disheveled our hair in a desperate attempt to pound names and dates into our skulls. The Tsar was there before we were presentable, greeting us in the low, rich voice that was his.

"Health to Your Majesty!" we shouted, making a brave show of breaking into huzzas. Tsar Nicolai smiled his amusement. He was used to visiting classes of sixty or more at the military schools and try as we would, we six boys couldn't equal the noise of sixty, even for the Tsar! There was only one of us capable of giving a dependable answer, and that was Babitch who saved the rest of us from humiliating stupidity before the Tsar. Only a few moments remained before the bell rang. Suppertime and his Imperial Highness was dining with us, he had said!

Off we went to supper, Vaslaw tagging me. "Anatole," he whispered, "I have been deprived of desserts. I will have to stand and face the wall unless His Majesty requests desserts for me!" and Vaslaw's voice rose hopefully.

We sat down, quite at ease, until desserts were served. When Nijinsky and one other rose and stood facing the wall, surely enough, the Tsar noticed the phenomenon.

"What? Don't these boys like desserts?" he asked, unable to understand why two boys should leave anything so tempting as those desserts.

As one, the two answered, "We love desserts, Your Majesty, but we are being punished, and so we can have none"; they permitted the hope in their hearts to be reflected in their voices.

"For what?" The Tsar was still mystified, but the Grand Duke, who had accompanied him, burst into another of his thunderous laughs. "Do you have to ask? Look at their faces! For fighting!" And let it be recorded that there was understanding in the Tsar's face when he scanned the gorgeously shaded black and blue and green and yellow marks that surrounded Nijinsky's eyes and marred his high cheekbones.

"All right, boys, you had your fun, and now you must pay for it," said the Tsar, but the Grand Duke broke in, "That Polish boy there is the one they told me was the best dancer in the school—you remember?" The Tsar nodded, his face alight with a broad smile.

"Well, after one look at him today, you can see that he's not only a great dancer—he's a great fighter!" and the Grand Duke's laugh rumbled off into the distance as he and the Tsar departed, the Tsar reminding us that we ought to be good boys and study hard in order that one day we might be the greatest dancers on his stage. For the first time, we learned at first hand that the Emperor was averse to gaining personal popularity at the expense of discipline.

Meanwhile, word came that Drigo had composed music for the ballet, *Millions d'Arlequin,* or, as we called it, *Harlequinada.* The melody, especially the *Serenade,* was on everyone's lips, and the Tsarina, herself an accomplished musician, adored it, according to reports that reached us. Drigo gallantly dedicated the whole composition to her, and she expressed the wish that the first performance of the ballet be presented before her at the Winter Palace. To our delight, Nijinsky and I were among the ones chosen to appear in a royal command performance at the Imperial Hermitage

Theater. Who wouldn't be thrilled at the prospect?—for fabulous stories of the wealth housed in the Hermitage and its ornate theater had spread through the school.

Even the stories had failed to do justice to the grandeur that confronted us when our request to be conducted through the Hermitage museum was granted and we stood in manifest astonishment before the beauty that had been garnered from every source. We saw halls filled with beautiful cases in which rested the world's largest and most radiant gems—sapphires, diamonds, rubies, emeralds; awestruck, we gazed into the fiery hearts of them, pulsing and aglow with flashing spears of light, glancing off the mirrors of beauty hidden in their facets. There were the Tsar's crowns, studded with precious stones, and heavy with the weight of gold that held their treasure trove of jewels; there were swords marvelously inlaid and studded with gems!

In the art galleries, we stood in reverence, young as we were, before the masterpieces of Velásquez, Rembrandt, Michelangelo, Rubens, and the whole galaxy of immortal Russian and foreign painters. An impression that has remained with me all through the years is that of the enormous golden cage which held a full-sized peacock, his tail spread, and the whole constructed of platinum and gold, the natural colors of his feathers carried out in jewels. Lustrous emerald eyes were given him, while great stones blazed to form the eyes of each feather in his tail. Perhaps the bird sounds too artificial; nevertheless, so exquisite was the art that had formed him that we waited breathlessly for him to move before we discovered that it was a creature of metal and stones winking at us from its gilded environs! Such splendor cannot convey more than the veriest suggestion of the wealth collected there where all might see it.

If the world is amazed at the glorious objets d'art that the present Russian government is selling for tractors, the world has yet to see the real magnificence still in Russia, for I am sure that it has glimpsed only the least valuable pieces of art the country owns. Wherever I have traveled, I have always had the consciousness of greater treasures in Russia, and even in the Louvre I knew real art lovers must journey to the Hermitage to sate their appetites for beauty.

Two rehearsals were held in the Imperial Hermitage Theater, which seated an audience of only five hundred. Its stage was a little larger than that of the school theater, and was unable to accommodate the whole company. A special company was formed for the royal performance and rolled in pomp to rehearse. At the Winter Palace, adjoining the Hermitage Theater, we were met by Russia's most distinguished noblemen and escorted to our dressing rooms, huge apartments lighted by enormous candelabra slung on heavy wrought-iron chains. Were we hungry? Great tables laden with dainties, fruits, and punches awaited us, and we were invited to fill our pockets from them!

Finally the day of the gala performance dawned, and we spent nearly the whole day at the palace, where we were served luncheon and dinner in a room that seemed to dwarf us with its height. Butlers in scarlet coats, white breeches, white stockings, and buckled shoes bent their powdered wigs over us deferentially, while a dozen generals and adjutants surrounded us, ready to fulfill the slightest wishes of the ballet boys—kings for the moment despite our twelve or thirteen years and the white whiskers of the generals!

We ate until we were stuffed, unable to believe that the delicate porcelain bearing the double eagle and the royal crown, and the slender crystal glasses were made especially for the palace by a factory which did nothing else but make porcelain for the royal family! Knives, forks, and spoons of solid gold were placed before us for our use, all of them bearing the double eagle, the crown, and the interlaced initials of Nicolai II. We scorned the notion that the tableware was of real gold and determined to discover that for ourselves.

After dinner we enjoyed a short rest before the Tsar gave the signal to prepare for the most opulent performance I have ever witnessed. When I looked out into the audience, it was as though I gazed on a sparkling ocean of jewels. There was the Tsar's whole family in full dress; every Grand Duke and Princess of the royal line in the capital; the highest aristocracy, represented by Counts and Countesses whose forefathers had disputed for the Russian throne—and all wore crowns that blazed with an eerie radiance through the half-light. Foreign ambassadors and their wives could be discovered in the company which included many Oriental visitors—Maharajas,

Chinese, Oriental Princes, gorgeous in the costumes of their native lands. The soldierly young pages of His Majesty's Corps were stationed at attention here and there, to serve the company, contributing color and contrast to the assemblage. I have never seen anything in this world to excel the brilliancy and magnificence of that gathering, for during intermission, when thousands of lights were turned on, the scene dazzled one with its superb glitter coaxed from the hearts of jewels that gleamed with rich, deep hues on every side.

Prince Volkonsky congratulated us all on behalf of the Emperor and Empress and, our eyes still confused by the glory that had been showered on us, we returned to the school, excited, yet tired and ready for bed. Imagine our amazement when we were met at the school with orders to report as we were, overcoats, hats, and all, to the First Ballet Hall. There we stood just as we had come from the Winter Palace, until the doors were flung open and in walked a resplendent general in full-dress regalia!

"Boys," he said, "who among you took, by mistake, the gold knives and forks and spoons from the Winter Palace? Please give them back to me!"

It was a picture worthy of perpetuation that we made, pulling out from our pockets and tall Russian hats the tableware, the serviettes, salts and peppers, and all kinds of small keepsakes concealed there, while one among us wept and begged to keep those precious souvenirs. Nijinsky and I were in the same predicament while the staff stood horrified. We went through with the unhappy business of parting with the sole proof we had of our visit to the Winter Palace, until, in a few minutes, the situation was reversed. The General stood before us, his hands and pockets filled! "You will not be treated as thieves," he decided. "You are boys sworn to His Majesty's service, and you made a mistake! It is forgiven!" and as he pivoted to go, he added, "But don't do it again!"

To this day, I have been sure we were right, and that it was only the prigishness of a stodgy old officer that deprived us of our souvenirs, for what could a few knives or forks more or less matter to the Tsar? Furthermore, it was the custom for him to give remembrances to whatever ambassadors or honored guests he entertained at luncheon or dinner in the palace, and cer-

tainly we had given him more pleasure than a score of ambassadors! But anyway, I have no proof that Nijinsky and I dined together at the Winter Palace when we were thirteen!

XII

THROUGH THE REVOLUTION

W E LIVED a secluded life of our own at the school, unaware of the threat of revolution that was stirring through Russia in 1905. The nation was tense as a steel string, but when we stared out the windows of the school at mobs surging backwards and forwards, trying to distinguish some sense in the chaotic shouts that rose from the street, we never guessed it was a riot we watched. Our governors explained that it was merely factory workers and students who passed, shouting and screaming about something that courted madness and caused trouble to pile up both for themselves and for the nobility.

Meanwhile, in the big ballet, there were various meetings being conducted by the least attractive members of the company, who went about wearing serious faces and dirty linen, and consequently failed to make much of an impression when they gathered us together for a revolution of our own. In vain we sought reason for revolt—but what could we ask for, except pocket money? It was a foregone conclusion that one's parents furnished that. At last we hit upon something that we must have for our health and comfort—more cream in our milk! We approached the director with a special committee which presented our demands. He listened solemnly until all was expounded, and then burst into a roar of laughter. "You are right, my boys! You have everything but bird's milk, and I think the Tsar should, in all justice, provide bird's milk for the ballet boys! It will be attended to!" And we got milk that was too rich for us! Thus ended our "revolution," but in the outer world things were not so easily adjusted.

60

It began to be whispered that January 8, 1905,[1] would be a big day in St. Petersburg—that the Cossacks would ride and there would be high excitement! Nijinsky, Babitch, and I decided to be on hand for whatever there was to see, despite the fact that the day fell on a Sunday and the governors warned us to depart from church and go directly to our homes, without lingering in the streets.

I don't remember just how the three of us made our way to the Winter Palace; at any rate, we found ourselves there in the midst of a mob of thousands. On every side we were hemmed in by angry faces, waving fists, red flags. We stared at the light artillery that was leveled at the crowd, and at the Cossacks mounted on spirited horses standing motionless before many soldiers whose bayonets winked evilly in the pale winter sunlight streaming over the scene. Somebody shouted, and I saw a young officer try to make himself heard. Failing that, he raised his right arm and described a swift circle with a sword that flashed like golden flame. The mob, ignoring his request to break up, surged forward the moment the soldiery took aim with rifles belching steel and fire at us all.

Bedlam reigned. Hysterical women rushed frantically in all directions, leaving dark bodies motionless behind them on the crimsoned snow, trampling one another, shoving, striking, pushing, screaming. Another and another round of ammunition was spent on the fleeing people, stampeding more like animals than humans. Babitch, Nijinsky, and I held hands and ran like deer, ducking here and there, zigzagging for our lives through the turbulence.

Nevsky Prospekt was before us, filled with more swarms of humanity. A frenzy as riotous as that we had escaped faced us anew. The crowds were rampant, rushing through the middle of the thoroughfare. Not a streetcar or a carriage was in sight—nothing but people, white-hot and smarting for trouble! We plunged among them, bent on reaching the school. Many bore red flags, singing and shouting wild words which remained incomprehensible to us. One student caught sight of the Imperial crown on our caps and thrust a flag into our hands. Off we went, bearing it proudly aloft,

[1] Greek Orthodox calendar.

absolutely ignorant of the fact that there was anything unusual in wearing the symbol of Royalism on our caps and bearing the symbol of Communism in our hands. We were too young to understand what it was all about. All that we knew was that we had a flag to carry, and by turns we carried it, disputing for the honor!

Momentarily the mob increased until we reached the statue of Catherine the Great, from which we planned to turn down Theater Street. Suddenly, from nowhere, a troop of savage Cossacks appeared, armed with sabers that dripped red, and nagaykami, heavy leather whips with many strips, each loaded on the striking end with a lead pellet. I lost Nijinsky and Babitch— we scampered blindly in any direction. It was frightful. I slipped in blood that poured into the streets. Blood ran on the cobbles until it was a scarlet street that was under my racing feet. When I glanced at the buildings, there was blood on the walls, for the Cossacks sliced unmercifully with their swords, sometimes decapitating a man with a blow; thrashing anyone within striking distance with nagaykami, splitting a human body with a stroke to lay the quivering flesh open to the backbone. They lashed through a red haze, those fiercest of Russians—and innocent and guilty alike fell before their rabid onslaught.

Awful! Awful! My brain reeled when I watched old men and women die. They couldn't run as fast as I. The bodies of men, women, and children huddled in still heaps on the boulevards while I dodged down Theater Street. The door was ajar. A hand darted out and caught my collar. It was the doorman.

"You idiot!" he screeched at me, giving me a mighty shake. "You idiot!" It was impossible for a doorman to address an Imperial student like that, but nothing mattered. I leaned against the wall. A few moments later Nijinsky rushed in, pale and hatless, and more than a half hour passed in ghastly uncertainty before Babitch arrived.

Our teeth were still chattering with fear when we faced the principal and told him our whole story. He stared at us dumbly, unbelievingly. "How could you carry a red flag and wear the Imperial crown?" he muttered. Yet we were not punished,

Between the Cossacks and the police, the riot was so effectively quelled that we went to the Marinsky Theater to attend the benefit performance given on that date for Madame Olga Preobrajensky, who had sold every ticket in advance. The whole theater was empty and scores of artists and musicians were absent!

Only the next day did we ballet boys learn the full woe that followed in the wake of the Cossacks' ride. Babitch had had a beautiful sister, seventeen years old, the idol of every one of us—and she was missing! With tears in his eyes, her brother explained that his parents could never seek her in all of the police stations, hospitals, and morgues before the "great burial day," and begged us to help him hunt for her body. Vaslaw and I, with Rozai, Babitch, Fedorov, and Lukianov began our pilgrimage through the hundreds of bodies laid out on marble slabs, some of them horribly disfigured and dismembered, scanning every waxen face for the girl we had laughed with and loved, and sickening at the sight of mutilations that were unspeakably gruesome.

It was days before any of us smiled. Vaslaw was especially affected, for he had agonized over the child-bodies that confronted us, and over the old people—perhaps as innocent as we had been, but dead nevertheless. Babitch's sister was never heard of again. Perhaps she was one of those poor, mangled things—who had been happy before the Cossacks unleashed Terror in the name of peace.

We had met tragedy face to face in the midst of plenty. How could we play? Vaslaw's eyes were deep, black wells of agony that was scarcely fading when cholera struck the city.

"A plague! The cholera!" On every hand placards warned us not to eat uncooked fruits or to drink unboiled water. Terror pervaded the capital, for the disease was so sudden, so swift. One moment you were laughing and playing, and the next you had dropped writhing in the death throes of a convulsion.

Not a single case of cholera was registered at school. We were lectured and warned to take no chances outside where the plague raged. Our staff taught us overwhelming fear of the malady, even though we were permitted to go out on week-ends as usual, for our promenades. One day Vaslaw and I swung down Nevsky Prospekt, lighthearted over the promise of spring in the air, the joy of living tingling like a healthy race-stream through our veins. Before us a young student strode along, whistling his own rejoicing, a handsome young lad hardly less exuberant than we. Suddenly his step faltered and he dropped, wriggling in hideous contortions.

Without a thought of himself Nijinsky rushed forward so impetuously that he was almost too quick for me, for his speed was that of an arrow and his lightness that of the wind. I tore after him, clutching his arm at the moment he stooped above the student, already dying, it seemed to me.

"The plague! Nijinsky, it's cholera!" I gasped. "Come! You can't help him!"

Vaslaw's face was a blanched mask. About us, pedestrians were scattering, but still Nijinsky stood, his eyes filled with compassion, until I literally dragged him across the street. It was as far as he would go. From there he watched the ambulance with its white-robed doctor arrive with antiseptics which were sprinkled over the boy before they lifted him, unconscious, possibly dead, into the vehicle.

Nijinsky understood perfectly the danger he had run, the life he had risked, but he was so tenderhearted, so impressionable that no joke could raise his spirits. For days he was morbid and depressed. That incident and the revolution both left him in his youth with a permanent horror of suffering and death. He was becoming acquainted with catastrophe and anguish in the world about him, having already tasted the bitterness of both in his own life.

XIII

GOOD TIMES AND BAD

Not only did we boys provide "extras" for the ballet, but we did the same in opera, still in accordance with the school system which decreed a complete grounding in make-up, costuming, and drama. Thus it transpired that Nijinsky had an opportunity to distinguish himself in a series of ludicrous incidents before he ever enjoyed distinction as a soloist. *Lohengrin* presented insurmountable obstacles for a time, when destiny dogged Vaslaw's heels with errors. In the first and third acts, a small lad in the identical garb of Lohengrin, was used to "double" for the leading artist. Between the glued beard and the length of the wait between appearances, it was no favor to be assigned the double's role.

Nijinsky's initial difficulty occurred when he was playing a page and stood with three other boys under a tree near the throne in the first act. For some reason or other, Vaslaw found himself too fatigued to stand up and so, logically enough, he sat down! But the "prop" grass and tree were too comfortable. While the opera played on, Nijinsky slept peacefully, to the utter dismay of the director! A rude awakening and a lecture weren't enough to stave off disaster, however.

Our dressing room on the fifth floor offered an ideal retreat for study, and Nijinsky was perpetually at study! The governor had his own office on the first floor where he sat and rang us down in time for our cues. There were no elevators to save precious minutes when Nijinsky heard a voice shouting through the wings, "Nijinsky's entrance! On the stage, Nijinsky!" With only an instant to make his entrance, Vaslaw darted down the four flights of stairs and leaped into the swan-boat just before it took its first journey across the rear stage to create an illusion of distance.

There was stunned silence for a second before the theater rocked with laughter. Nijinsky, the diminutive Lohengrin, was without benefit of wig or helmet, sitting stiff and straight, a flowing golden beard surmounted by his own closely shaven brown poll! He was hauled before the governor and severely punished for a nap the regisseur had been stealing when the shout went through the theater!

To have had a situation of that sort recorded in one's history was bad enough without the complications that cropped up when Vaslaw grew a few years older and still contrived to get himself into scrapes. It was during the ballet *Bayadere,* in which Maria Petipa, the best character dancer on the Imperial stage, spun in the midst of frenzied Indians with such ardor that she became an incarnate fury among the dancers who formed gyrating figures in the group about her. Like most Russian stars, the great Petipa adored gems and made it her custom to wear them all in the Hindu Dance, turning faster and faster to a galloping rhythm until she whirled like a dervish, transformed into a pillar of glittering flame when the stage lights struck fire from the hearts of her diamonds. At the height of her stormy solo, one of her largest stones was torn loose; it rolled unnoticed to a crack in the floor and disappeared. Only Vaslaw had seen it as he had assumed his place on the stage as a part of the scenery!

After the dance, the frantic Petipa was rushing about like a madwoman searching for the fifteen-carat gem she had missed immediately. Meanwhile Vaslaw had run down under the stage, retrieved the stone, and climbed the four flights of stairs to our dressing room while a dozen secret-service men and special officers combed the stage before opening their cross-examination of the company. Upstairs, we were clustered about Vaslaw who held the jewel between his fingers.

"It is the biggest diamond Petipa wore tonight!" he announced. But we ridiculed him.

"That? A piece of glass and no more!" we scoffed.

On the instant the governor arrived. His eyes lit on the diamond.

"What!" he shouted. "The lost diamond up here while half Russia hunts it? Stupid boy, take it to Petipa!"

Nijinsky arrived in the midst of a storm of tears and anger, for the police had been unsuccessful, of course.

"Madame, your diamond!" he finally managed.

Before he could speak further, the great Petipa had clasped him in her arms. "My wonderful boy! You have returned a king's ransom!" she exclaimed. "The diamond is worth a fortune, and you, Vaslaw Nijinsky, shall have a great reward!"

That night Nijinsky and I speculated on the value of the reward a woman as rich and famous as Petipa should give to a boy as poor and as honest as Vaslaw. The next day it came, borne in state by a coachman—a one-pound box of chocolates!

Before long, a gala festival was on the calendar—a benefit presentation for Alexander Glazounov, one of the greatest pianists and composers in Russia and the director of the Imperial Russian Conservatory. The worthy musician had but one fault. Everyone knew his little weakness and understood that only when in high spirits was he completely the genius, and so no one minded at all when he arrived at his own benefit exuberant!

Vaslaw had been picked by our class to present a little silver medallion inscribed "With the best wishes of the boys of the ballet school," since he could not speak Russian well enough to deliver himself of a speech.

The moment arrived! We sat forward breathless to see how the idolized artist would accept our gift! Vaslaw fished in one pocket; then another and another, flushing crimson with embarrassment. Only a few people stood between him and Glazounov, delighted with it all. Vaslaw slid away from the line of artists waiting to congratulate the composer, and rushed to us.

"The medal! I have forgotten it!" he whispered. "It is in my other suit!"

In utter disgust, we appointed a substitute who could speak Russian fluently, and who dashed onto the stage and eulogized Glazounov so convincingly that the great man thanked him for a gift that was not given until the next day!

On another occasion, Chaliapin pulled Nijinsky's ears—and mine! It was in the opera *Mefistofele* by Boito. In the third act, Chaliapin played the title role at the Festival of the Damned, and Nijinsky, Babitch, Rozai, with the rest of us were appropriately demons and imps. The titanic basso began his aria, and we began our fun, poking, pinching, and tickling each other under cover of the half-darkness that shrouded us. There was a pause in the rich melody welling from the throat of Russia's mighty singer. He glared at us and muttered, "Shut up, you devils!"

In vain! What did we care for his temperament? His voice filled the theater with its volume and died into silence. The curtain dropped! And may the saints protect me from another experience like that! Chaliapin grabbed Nijinsky and me and three others as the chief disturbers, and pulled our ears until Morozov, the stage manager, shamed him by crying, "Feodor! Stop! How can you pull their ears from their heads? They are only little boys! Feodor! Stop!" We ran like deer, nursing ears that shone like ripe tomatoes, shamefaced and sheepish, for Chaliapin had been right! Later I met him in New York, and reminded him of my poor ears and Nijinsky's, but Chaliapin claimed he had forgotten his ear-pulling fracas.

Nijinsky was a devil incarnate when it came to thinking up amusements for the rest of us! I will never forget Verba, the gay Russian carnival preceding Easter, when Nijinsky prescribed itch and sneeze powder as potent "magic." He tried it out on us, and before five minutes had elapsed, he had us weeping from sneezing, and scratching as though the imps of hell were torturing us. We were due to appear in *Tannhäuser* that night, and there at the Marinsky we made our greatest sensation. We had every member of the company scratching through the opening acts, but we saved our coup for the tragic finale.

Yerschov, an artist with a divine voice and a great heart, was the soloist that night. Because he was fond of Nijinsky, it was Vaslaw who shook hands with him, covering Yerschov's hands with a combination of itch and sneeze powder, under pretext of tendering congratulations on the tremendous ovation he was scoring before a packed house. That still left the problem of trapping him into sniffing the sneeze powder.

Quick as thought, one of the boys remarked: "M. Yerschov! Your beard and make-up!"

There was time for no more, for the curtain was rising on the heart-rending finale of *Tannhäuser*. Yerschov nervously smoothed his mustache, patted his nose, and stepped before the audience, awaiting the dramatic moment of his song.

A tribute of absolute silence was accorded while Yerschov began to scratch his hands, not noticeably yet, but enough to reassure us! The moment came for his bell-like voice to play on heartstrings ready to break. He opened his mouth for the opening phrase and sneezed, loudly and lustily, as a Russian should sneeze! Before two minutes passed, Yerschov was scratching insanely, clutching one hand upon the other, tearing at his face and beard, and treating Russia's noblest titles to a divertissement supreme—the spectacle of Yerschov accompanying Wagner's vast music with a series of soul-stirring sneezes! Shrieks of laughter demoralized the house. For the first time in history, the curtain was rung down at the Marinsky, and an artist substituted to conclude the presentation, "because," as the director explained, "M. Yerschov is suffering from a sudden 'illness'!" None of us knew anything, as usual, thereby escaping unconditional expulsion.

Time was passing, and we were becoming perfected in the dance in the intervals when we were not disrupting operas. Finally, as we gathered for ballet under Obouchov's brilliant direction, a solemn clump of governors arrived with news of tremendous import! Isadora Duncan had arrived in St. Petersburg!

"One of the greatest dancers of history has asked to visit your class," we were told. "She has created a sensation wherever she has appeared, and now she wishes to see a class of boys work in Russia! It is against all precedent, but she is waiting to attend your class today!"

"Miss Isadora Duncan!" proclaimed the director, and the great woman stood before us, modestly smiling her friendship!

With profound respect, we bowed to her, while she was invited to sit and watch the class proceed without any change in routine. With our first exercise her eyes fixed on Nijinsky, and it was noticeable that when she complimented us on our work, she reserved her choicest expressions for Vaslaw! It was intimated that we might ask her to dance for us, and she graciously answered that she was giving a series of recitals in the Imperial Conservatory, and would be happy to provide boxes for us. We demurred. It was her work that we wished to see, we explained, and we offered our hall for the privilege of watching her exercises and preparation.

"Tomorrow, then, boys," she promised, "if your director will grant his permission!" That was done at once, and the next day we reported at our ballet hall to find the whole staff on hand, seated in chairs ranged across one end of the room. What a surprise was awaiting us!

First a French gentleman arrived and played some very beautiful but very serious music. We applauded, and a few moments later Miss Duncan stepped into the room attired only in a light blue Grecian tunic; her legs were bare! We stared thunderstruck! What had happened? Where were the billowy skirts, the toe slippers of a ballerina? We had never seen a bare-legged dancer. What kind of dancer was she? Nijinsky and I exchanged bewildered glances, and politely applauded the very elegant bow that she made.

The music began, but Isadora Duncan didn't! She hung her head, remaining motionless. Vaslaw's eyes were sympathetic. She had forgotten her steps! But no! At that moment she moved wearily and struck an attitude, standing still in her new position! It was more and more strange! She walked very slowly forward and made a little turn! She knelt; she raised her arms to the skies; then she laid herself down on the floor, wearing a very sorrowful face over that necessity. Of course, it was distressing, but no sooner did we commiserate with the predicament of a dancer who had to lie down in the midst of her dance, than she jumped up and took a position, the like of which we had never seen in this world! She finished this peculiar performance by kneeling on the floor, which she stared at instead of at us, and maintained her statuesque repose while the music played on!

We couldn't understand. Was this exhibition a *dance?* Was it an exercise, and would she suddenly begin to dance? Some of the school staff applauded, and we followed suit politely, baffled as we were by the weird offering. Then

Isadora Duncan—a mighty artist, we were told—blew kisses from her fingertips, instead of bowing! And as though she had performed a difficult dance, she sat down to rest!

Vaslaw's glances at me implied more than either of us dared voice. We sat in silence. One boy whispered, "She will dance soon and show us some technique!" But no! Four other eerie dances were endured. To our astonishment, she had no technique. We sat there glumly—so disappointed—for we had hoped to learn something splendid from the woman before us. Great? How was she great?

A few days later, she reserved boxes and sent us invitations to occupy them at her recital. Not a boy in the school would go until the director ordered it to save the great Duncan embarrassment and insult by the ballet boys! We were completely astounded to find the Conservatory packed, and the whole auditorium fragrant with perfume from the flowers that Russians had sent in tribute to an art that was past comprehension to us—so loyal to the traditions of our school that we had no eyes for a different art! We regretted our ignorance, and complimented the great Duncan politely always, but art? Where was it?

"You are too young!" the director observed. Meanwhile, the argument waxed hot and furious among the Russian masters of the dance.

"She has no art," said one group.

"She has given us a mighty dream to realize!" contradicted the other. Her visit to Russia precipitated a revolution, with Fokine at the head of the rebels.

"She has not given us technique," he admitted, although he was the first to acclaim her originality and to set ballet to classical music. "She has given us something as important as technique; she has given us the spirit of pure emotion, portraying it through her soul. She does not dance to trivial music, nor to music written especially for the dance. She is interpreting the Soul in the dance as Schumann, Beethoven, Bach, and Chopin expressed it with music, and she is using the music of the Soul that they expressed, to interpret her dance!"

Russians who are truly art lovers must pay an everlasting tribute of gratitude to Isadora Duncan for her interpretation and its success. In their hearts,

Russians who adore ballet must raise a deathless monument to the three Titans who have made the art an Art sublime—Duncan for her inspiration; Fokine for his tremendous adaptations of ballet forms and compositions to great music; Diaghilev for giving those creations of loveliness to a world starved for beauty!

XIV

EXPELLED AND TRIUMPHANT

For months we enjoyed a new sport without getting into difficulties. We took a rubber band, and using our fingers, contrived a slingshot, in which we used slim rolls of paper bent in the center for "bullets," dipping the bended ends in ink to make spots on the faces of our unsuspecting victims until we were capable of scoring a bull's-eye regularly. As usual, Vaslaw was our best marksman. We were being trundled along Morskoy Street in our Noah's Arks for rehearsal at the Marinsky Theater when the storm broke.

A grand gentleman in a rich carriage passed us. Traveling along at a smart pace, he was dumfounded to be hit precisely on the tip of his nose with a paper bullet. He was stopped by traffic, when along we came, our pockets filled with "ammunition," and our minds full of devilment. Nijinsky had chosen the red-faced gentleman for his own game, and drew back his slingshot to let fly one more "bullet" just as the man turned to stare at us. Vaslaw's last bit of paper caught one of St. Petersburg's most distinguished doctors squarely in the face!

In no time, the doctor had called the police and a mob was gathering. Vainly we protested a lack of knowledge; that nothing had been "shot" from our Ark, but alas! The doctor was gifted with an excellent memory, and unerringly picked Nijinsky as the offender despite our spirited denials. We rehearsed all afternoon with heavy hearts, for the doctor was a powerful man, and harsh punishment was a foregone conclusion. It was only our worst fears that were realized when we returned to find the whole school

73

staff waiting and ready for us. They demanded a sight of our "bullets," but we had safely rid ourselves of that evidence.

We were told that a special meeting had been held. In consideration of Nijinsky's great talent, it had been decided that he must be an example— enough of an example to teach both him and us that we were in school to study, not to disgrace ourselves and it!

They had devised a special penalty which was more of a punishment to Madame Nijinsky than to her son! "For three months Nijinsky will be conditionally expelled," we were told; "he will live at home, eat at home, and pay for his own books, slippers, and supplies."

Nijinsky went nearly mad at the unforeseen edict, weeping and shouting the injustice of the plan. "Do anything, anything to me," he screamed hysterically, "but not that! It will kill my mother. Punish me, not her! Beat me! Starve me, but not her!" He faced a jury that was adamant, and stood at bay for an instant before he leaped to a window. Only the quick action of us who had been with him in the carriage saved him from flinging himself from the window to certain death on Theater Street, three stories below! For weeks afterwards, one of us was constantly with him, watching lest he succeed in his threat to kill himself for the sorrow he had caused his mother, but then—it was Thursday, Visitors' Day, and Madame Nijinsky was waiting.

There were about twenty-five parents and friends of the ballet boys present when Madame Nijinsky was notified that she might see her son. She was obviously nervous and tense with anger, her eyes darting here and there in search of Vaslaw. Suddenly she saw him and he caught her glance, standing as still as a statue for the space of a second before he ran and stood before her without a word passing his lips while she spoke rapidly in a low, passionate voice. Unexpectedly, before us all, she slapped his face, again and again, first on one side and then on the other until it was scarlet from her blows. Nijinsky stood until her rage was vented and then he knelt before her, weeping and kissing her hands, totally unconscious of the onlookers while he begged forgiveness with all the anguish of a fifteen-year-old boy who had failed to live up to the ideal of the one person in the world whom he loved more than his life.

Officially, the school could do nothing for Madame Nijinsky or her son. It was announced that no uniforms, books, or food should be provided. Notwithstanding, immediately the school was dismissed, the man in charge of supplies was instructed to see that Nijinsky wanted for nothing, even though he lived at home, and Madame Nijinsky was saved from becoming more abject!

Once more we looked upon Vaslaw as our hero. There had been five of us in the carriage with him, and all of us were deprived of desserts for a month, but instead of resenting it, we rejoiced at the chance to share his punishment with him. Somehow, it seemed that he was not so thoroughly alone.

A year, however, can make much difference to a boy. It brought triumph to Nijinsky when he was sixteen. At that age, he was unusually matured and so the school sent him to the barber shop for his first shave. Nijinsky was a man!

Our friendship had grown with the years until we both found it something fine and clean and dependable in our lives. We were closer than brothers, sharing successes and failures, sorrows and happiness. His troubles were mine, and mine were his. Often we talked of graduation, of the future— and dreamed of what it might hold for us both. Neither of us ever visioned life beyond the Imperial stage, just as we never hoped beyond one hundred rubles a month! Paris, London, Monte Carlo, New York—we never talked of them, despite the fact that there was so much discussion of Vaslaw and his talents in the Big Ballet. It was freely prophesied that he was bound to be the greatest male dancer who had ever lived, and certainly the greatest the Imperial Russian Ballet School had ever trained.

I graduated a year before Vaslaw, for he failed at least one examination annually, while my marks had been high enough to pass me regularly. Nevertheless, I was with him daily, and so I was in on the secret of how his greatest triumph in school was scored, even though it defied every tradition of a custom-bound school!

It was in Obouchov's class, inevitably, that the plan was conceived, for

Obouchov, whose constant training had given Nijinsky's genius its perfect channel for physical expression, was so proud of his student that no sacrifice of himself was too great for the art that was Nijinsky's from the beginning.

"How would you like to dance with a group of great dancers like George Kyasht, Legat, and me?" suggested Obouchov, during one of his lessons.

Vaslaw was stunned. "It would be an impossible honor," he replied, "for they *are* great dancers, and I am only a schoolboy. No dancer would dream of appearing with a schoolboy!"

"Perhaps you are thinking that they are afraid because you are so good," pressed Obouchov, "or perhaps inside you know that they will dance better than you, and you are afraid that the world will learn that you are not so wonderful as it thinks you are?" I smiled, for Obouchov knew past doubt what the whole ballet hinted—that Nijinsky could outstrip any one of Russia's premier dancers without effort. It was the dream of Obouchov's life to show off the talent of his best pupil before graduation. I saw him look at Vaslaw with pride unbounded, while Vaslaw flushed with humiliation.

"You are the dearest and best teacher a boy ever had!" he burst out. "You are my master, and you will always be best and greatest. I can't bring myself to think that I ever could outstrip you in the dance. I don't want to! You are the master who taught me—how could I dream of being greater than you?" and Vaslaw's voice quivered with emotion.

"Dumbbell!" Obouchov cried, pounding Nijinsky's shoulders affectionately. I thought the affair ended, and only later did Vaslaw, ready to weep, relate how Obouchov had struggled with him to persuade him to appear; how Obouchov had trained and saved him for an anniversary celebration of Mozart's *Don Juan*.

The artists themselves had objected to the prospect of appearing with a student. They were unaware that the scheme threatened their own supremacy, and saw only a threat to their prestige as masters if they danced in public with a pupil. What Obouchov did—how he worked, how he overcame their prejudice, only he can reveal. Somehow, he must have succeeded on every hand, for it was announced that Director Teliakovsky had ordered

Nijinsky to dance with Kyasht, Obouchov, and Legat—and the school rejoiced for him.

I was perhaps happier than the rest, even though I turned the school topsy-turvy if he disappeared for an instant and followed him wherever he went for fear the jealousy aroused against him might result in an accident similar to that planned years before by Rozai. Nijinsky, on his part, practiced with more attention than ever before, until it seemed that his body was unbounded in its possibilities for dance expression.

Obouchov devoted all his knowledge, all his time, and all his power to Nijinsky's training. After each lesson, the master stood with Nijinsky until the rest of us had gone, practicing over and over once again the most difficult steps, drilling him until every muscle and sinew was like tempered steel rippling under the boy's skin. Obouchov ordered Vaslaw to keep absolutely silent about this special coaching, but Vaslaw broke his word to confide in me.

No one else knew how Obouchov was striving to make his student the most marvelous dancer of the age. It was at Obouchov's request that Nijinsky watched the three masters at rehearsal, for his teacher had said: "Watch, Vaslaw, how they dance, and when your turn comes, do not leap higher, or show more skill than they. Don't turn more pirouettes, nor attain more elevation than the masters. Watch, Vaslaw, and do as I have told you!"

I knew that Nijinsky was as nervous as a high-spirited horse before every rehearsal, for to me fell the task of calming him. He never entered the rehearsal hall but that I caught his arm and whispered: "Remember, Vaslaw! Remember your promise to Obouchov!" and Nijinsky would answer, "I will remember, Tola!"

When staff members looked in on him at work with the masters, they would remark, "Some day that lad will be as good as his teachers!" complimenting Nijinsky on his talent and Obouchov on his pupil, while both smiled their gratitude. Obouchov was charming! He accepted their congratulations graciously and, I have no doubt, laughed up his sleeve, for Obouchov had his plan! That was his secret!

After several weeks of waiting and rehearsing, we were given places in a special box at the Marinsky Theater. The great day had dawned. . . . Nijinsky, my comrade, was going to dance with Kyasht, Legat—and Obouchov! I was thrilled!

The three masters had beautiful dressing rooms under the stage, but Nijinsky was on the fifth floor as usual with the ballet boys! I flew up the long flights of steps to shake hands with him and join the rest of the boys who were wishing him success and assuring him of the pride we felt in him before we beat a retreat and left him to await his cue. I was almost downstairs when his voice arrested me. "Anatole! Come here!" Back I rushed, taking the stairs two at a time—what could have happened?

He ran out to meet me, grasping my hands in his, as cold as ice. He was shaking all over with nervousness. "Tola!" he exclaimed. "Maybe today will decide my fate! Obouchov has just told me to give my best—all I have —and I feel a devil force in me that makes me want to beat everyone of the masters—even Obouchov! He has told me to use all my power and I shall!" Vaslaw's face clouded. "There is no one here who cares, except you! My mother and sisters aren't here—they can't see me—they can't bless me! Tola, I will dance for you. Bless me!" and he bent his head, pressing the medals his mother had given him to his lips and whispering, "My mother gave them to me—and they are sacred and blessed," while I made the sign of the Cross above his bowed head and bent to kiss him gently upon both cheeks—the salute of a friend unto eternity. At that moment the bell rang for the curtain and I fled to the box where the boys were waiting excitedly, sure of Vaslaw's success, and certain, too, that his star would blaze its way to fame that day.

The four dancers were on the stage! We boys, according to custom, clenched our fists and teeth and concentrated as though with a single mind upon success for him, for we firmly believed that to do so would add to his power and help him to the success every one of us sincerely prayed for at that instant.

The dance had begun, and from the first step we knew—as did the whole audience—that before us was a genius, a Master among masters. His pirouettes, the flawless rhythm of his body, his leaps, his turns—every motion was a poem of unity and harmony blended with a perfection that was superhuman. He didn't jump—he flew like an eagle—and he was the boy we had hated—that dancer supreme! When he had done, he had scored, not success, but Triumph absolute!

The theater thundered and reverberated with applause. The three artists held hands and bowed again and again—and behind them stood Vaslaw, too modest to take credit for his own excellence. Suddenly Obouchov scanned the faces of Kyasht and Legat, and missed Nijinsky! Obviously the great teacher was amazed to discover that Vaslaw was alone behind them—and like the great man and master that he was, Obouchov went back, took Vaslaw by the hand and presented him to an audience that went wild with enthusiasm and acclaimed him with a mighty shout. Nijinsky bowed once, twice, three times, still like a bashful schoolboy while the tumult increased until it was deafening. We had lost our voices with shouting, and our hands were almost raw with the applause we had contributed.

When we passed through the foyer, on every hand we heard the comments of the connoisseurs of ballet, "He is the greatest dancer who ever lived!"

"We have witnessed the first success of a supreme genius!"

"He is born to fame!"

His praise was flying from tongue to tongue when we went up to the dressing room and found him, surrounded by artists, extras, the school staff, and the ballet boys. He, once more himself, was accepting congratulations with Obouchov happy and smiling beside him. Obouchov was more than his teacher, he was a friend, who, at the moment the whole city was afire with enthusiasm and praise for Nijinsky, remained true to form and said: "Yes, Vaslaw! It was pretty good, that dancing of yours! Pretty good! But don't think that you are great—or a star! You have plenty of time to work and improve your dance. I will help you, and one day you will dance better, much better than you did today! Steady practice, Vaslaw, steady practice!" and the man who had sacrificed his own supremacy for his pupil's was gone!

The first authority to acknowledge Nijinsky's genius publicly was Valerian Svetlov, a severe critic who knew the ballet as perhaps no other in Russia.

It was he who wrote his first comments on Nijinsky in a prophetic vein—
"That boy, Vaslaw Nijinsky, will one day eclipse every other dancer in the
world with his art!"—and Svetlov proved himself a true prophet.

Success, however, did not change Nijinsky, except to add an air of seriousness to his attitude, and lead him to attack his academic work with more
determination than ever before, while he practiced in every spare moment as
though his very life depended upon it, gradually improving his work in
every aspect.

Obouchov sought Nijinsky out a few days after his triumphant coup, and
it was a joy to see the delight of that generous-hearted man when he clapped
Nijinsky on the shoulder and laughingly remarked, "Well, Vaslaw, they
tell me you beat me, utterly, in the dance!"

"I could not! I could not!" Nijinsky cried. "It isn't true; it can't be! You
are my teacher; my master! I could not beat you! I won't believe what they
are saying!" Obouchov understood and smiled. If Vaslaw had believed that
he had, in truth, outstripped the dancing of the man who had taught him,
befriended him, and fought for him, Vaslaw's heart would have been
broken . . . and Obouchov, who knew, was silent.

XV

THE SCHOOL PERFORMANCE
AND PREPARATION FOR
GRADUATION

AFTER his first ovation, not a day passed but what I traveled through the familiar school corridors, a full-fledged member of the Imperial Russian Ballet, and sought Vaslaw to learn from his own lips just how things were with him. If I dared poke my nose into the ballet halls after classes, I was sure to find Kshessinskaya, Pavlowa, and Trefilova at practice, and once they set eyes on me, it was a foregone conclusion that I should be pressed into service to play for them while Vaslaw watched.

No longer was my reward for accompanying the ballerinas sweets, but, since I was a fellow member of the company, it was their thanks that repaid me, and a double portion of sweets that fell to Nijinsky, still my best friend. The ballerinas knew well enough that within a few months he would be their dancing partner, and yet, since he was still a student at the school, they showered him with gifts and treated him as a mere boy! Tradition!

Throughout the years of our training, we had been watched for special talents, since it was inevitable that not all could excel in every phase of dancing. Some would find character work or miming their forte, and others would remain always members of the corps de ballet. A few might be ballerinas, but how few! In many countries a dancer is honored by the unearned title "ballerina," an honorary designation which should never be applied to a merely good dancer. A ballerina is one who has been a *great* dancer for five or six years, whose technique is flawless, and whose art is close to genius.

Students were being picked for their parts in the annual Graduation Performance, given on the Marinsky stage, with the graduating class in premier roles, every member of the school taking part. Records were being scanned and only the testimony of years could determine which students might shine as fledgling stars in a presentation that would be witnessed by parents, the staff, teachers, artists from all of the Imperial theaters, and friends. No tickets were ever sold for that gala gathering; attendance was by invitation only.

It was to be expected that Nijinsky should draw the premier male role, with a few solos to display his tremendous power and genius. Ludmilla Schollar was his partner, and her inexperience accounted for the lengthy intermission that marked Nijinsky's Graduation Performance. Distracted with excitement, she danced in a costume glittering with spangles, and while she pirouetted and smiled, with the incomparable Vaslaw as her partner, her spangles ripped and tore his arms, until at the end of the adagio they were a mass of scratches and tears that made it necessary to call a surgeon to staunch Vaslaw's bleeding before the next act could go on!

High up in the balcony Madame Nijinsky and her husband watched their son with pride welling in their hearts. Some of us dared treason by thinking that, as the parents of the greatest dancer who ever graduated, they might have been accorded the recognition that an orchestra seat or a box would imply—but no! They peered at his splendor from the balcony section reserved for the parents of older students! It was the tradition!

Fokine had composed that ballet for Nijinsky's dancing, already departing from stilted forms in response to Isadora Duncan's far-reaching influence. Obouchov, too, had arranged dances for his pupil, and what dances! Obouchov contrived to display Vaslaw as the peer of peers in the Imperial Russian Ballet! He had especially worked out a divertissement which gave Vaslaw every opportunity to claim the laurels for the day, and those

Vaslaw won without effort. In *Don Juan* he had had to work to excel the mightiest dancers the age afforded, but to outshine the dancers in the school was mere child's play. Taking advantage of his gifts to humiliate his less talented fellows was contrary to Nijinsky's character, and so, I think he deliberately did well enough to make a one hundred per cent mark, but he did not attempt maliciously to overshadow his competitors. That he did excel was simply the result of innate genius.

At each intermission, the jewels of our ballet, Mesdames Trefilova, Karsavina, Sedova, Egorova, and Pavlowa flocked backstage to congratulate Nijinsky, who was beaming with happiness, and as usual modest to the point of bashfulness in the face of their perfectly justified compliments. At the last intermission, there was a stir in the knot of artists gathered in the corridor, and Madame Kshessinskaya, uncrowned but universally recognized queen of the Imperial ballet, swept into Vaslaw's presence with a wealth of compliment that made him flush with pleasure. "You are wonderful! A genius, Nijinsky!" She smiled. "I will take you for my partner this summer! and afterwards!" and she was gone, leaving Vaslaw unable to believe he had heard aright.

"Pinch me, Tola! I want to be sure that I am not dreaming!" he whispered, knowing better than anyone else that to dance with the all-powerful Kshessinskaya would spell immediate triumph.

"You heard the truth!" I answered, nudging him to return pleasantries with the host of male dancers who were waiting to wish him well. Guerdt, Legat, Kyasht, Fokine, Andrianov, and of course, Obouchov.

Nijinsky was the center of a kaleidoscopic group, colorful and gay, when word was passed that Gillert was coming! The great ones made way for him —Gillert, who had been mighty in pantomine, and had been the most glorious mazurka dancer of the past; Gillert, the friend of Thomas Nijinsky; Gillert, the ancient, patriotic Pole whose fame was still green in the memories of Russia's older dancers—Gillert was coming to pay homage to the youngest Polish genius at the School Performance! In tacit understanding, the ballet masters made way for Gillert until he stood facing Vaslaw. I watched them meet—the one whose fame was a dying flame on Time's horizon, the other whose sun had yet to rise, and blaze from midheaven. First the aged dancer kissed Vaslaw as though he were a son, and then he took Nijinsky's hand in his.

"I am proud of you today, Vaslaw," he said. "It is because I want you to enjoy both happiness and success all the days of your life that I have made a long journey to see you. I have a gift for you, my son!" Slowly Gillert's fingers were working at a green-gold ring set with a royal amethyst, loosening it on his old finger, wrinkled and stiff with age. "This ring brought me both happiness and success, but now, I am too old for both," and Gillert's eyes filled with fiery light. "I will give the gift of both to you, for there is no one else to leave them to but you with your genius. Swear, Vaslaw, the most solemn and sacred oath a man can swear that you will wear my ring as long as you live. Swear!"

It was as though I witnessed a rite past my understanding when Vaslaw swore his oath to Gillert, and the old dancer prophesied, "As long as you wear my ring, no sorrow or misfortune can touch you, but I warn you—the ring must stay on your hand!"

Nijinsky had the ring on his finger and was staring into its royal purple depths when we realized that Gillert had gone. It was almost uncanny, yet it was the first expensive gift Vaslaw had ever received, and we rejoiced together over it for a few minutes before he had to turn his attention to the big reception which was in progress in his honor, for Thomas Nijinsky had risen to the occasion and arranged a fete for his son.

The next day Nijinsky awoke famous, for Svetlov and all the critics of St. Petersburg had praised him to the skies. Wires were humming with the tidings that a new star of the dance had blazed into being for the greater glory of the Empire and its art.

That was all well enough, but there still remained the final academic exams, and Nijinsky's sudden fame meant little enough until he had passed them. Slow-witted he had been and slow-witted he remained, haunted by the thought of failure, until there was little room for joy left in him. Together we marked the days before his fate would be decided. We dragged out his textbooks, applying ourselves to the stupendous task of making his brain register names and dates and events, mathematics, languages. I drilled him with questions, backwards and forwards until it seemed that he must have committed every word to memory, before we turned some of our time towards graduation preparations.

Once exams were over and passed, the theater would give Vaslaw one hundred rubles, fifty dollars. That small sum was paid in recognition of the fact that the graduate was a member of the corps de ballet of the Imperial Russian Theater, but until it was paid his parents were required to spend their own money for the livery, overcoat, boots, shoes, and hats that were the tradititonal right of every graduate.

I had a tailor called Vassiliev to whom I paid fifteen rubles on account monthly, and who consequently would extend credit on request. I took Vaslaw off with me, explaining just how the dark-eyed Pole was, and because Vassiliev had read the papers, and my credit was good, Nijinsky was outfitted at Vassiliev's expense. How could a man lose money on Nijinsky? A few weeks and he would be dancing his way to fame, and teaching his way to wealth! The same attitude prevailed among the bootmakers and dealers in linen, for neither Vaslaw nor I mentioned his repeated failures in the final exams.

Oh, those examinations! They came in the springtime when I longed to let my fancy turn to lighter concerns than Vaslaw's eternal studying, but he must graduate! I labored with him, alternately rejoicing and despairing over him, for the lessons he knew best on one day were utterly new to him the next! If he failed them, there was one more chance offered in the fall, but failure meant tragedy that year. There was an imposing line of creditors, and unless he graduated, Nijinsky faced a summer without money from the school or from the theater, and without any chance of teaching, for only graduates of the school were accepted as ballet teachers by the wealthy and titled, who took pains to know the ability of the man who taught them!

After all our weeks of agonizing over names and dates and events, Vaslaw failed miserably in history! His mother wept, and he went about looking as though suicide were the answer to his hopes. There was no way out—and then the school performed a miracle for his benefit. Vaslaw was offered a fresh examination three days after his failure! Each official examination was judged by a jury of twelve instructors, ordinarily. However, the staff permitted his own teacher to give that last exam, and since his teacher was sporting enough to warn Vaslaw of what questions would be asked, Nijinsky finally passed history with flying colors—after two previous failures and an extra year at school!

He was going to graduate at last! We both heaved a sigh of relief and rushed off to tell Mother Nijinsky the good news.

XVI

GRADUATION DAY

It was a blue and golden morning that greeted Vaslaw Nijinsky as he donned his school uniform for the last time in preparation for graduation and at ten o'clock, took his place in line to march into chapel. What a scene it made—the boys dapper in their uniforms standing in their appointed places with the girls for Last Mass. In the chapel were the staff, directors, and officers, in full-dress uniforms, their orders gleaming on their breasts, as well as parents and friends garbed in their best. Every taper on the high altar and in the candelabra laved the scene in lambent golden light, while the picked choir, including many of Russia's opera stars, spilled melody through the great nave. Few heard the Last Mass; they were too intent upon the dreams that come with the realization that schooldays are done and the world—wealth, fame, romance—is waiting.

Every ear was strained for Father Pigulevsky's sermon and the blessing that closed his talk on the beckoning future. I watched Nijinsky—that Vaslaw Nijinsky who had grown great since the day that he had voiced his own name so fearfully. He passed down to the Great Altar and bent his close-cropped brown head to kiss the golden jeweled Cross—and then! Then we gathered around him—his friends, his family, the staff, even the little boys, wishing him well before he dashed off to the dining room for lunch.

For once we could talk and joke without fear of discipline in the dining room. We laughed and sang until benediction brought quiet, and the boys filed out, sobered and serious, to take their places in the first big hall of the Girls' School where graduation exercises were always held.

A mob opened a path for the graduates, the boys passing to one side, the girls to the other.

Under an enormous portrait of the Tsar stood a long table draped with heavy green velvet that fell in thick folds to the floor. It was covered with prizes for the most brilliant students, and diplomas for the graduates. A long blood-red rug stretched across the width of the hall, and when all was silent the voice of the inspector rose. It described the record of every boy and girl in the school in intimate and brutally frank detail, until the youngest and the oldest student had been publicly credited or discredited according to the year's record. At last the names of the graduates were reached and those who were graduating heard their names before they learned who among them had made the prize lists, or won special honor.

The room grew tense with expectancy. Beautifully bound editions of Russian or foreign authors were presented for scholarship or conduct, and one by one they were presented to the graduates, each of whom received an ovation. When Nijinsky's name was called, he marched forward to receive his diploma—and nothing more! All of the prize lists and awards meant nothing for the future, and with his hard-won diploma Nijinsky was content. For the first time in his life, he and his class were given the privilege of shaking hands with the director, Teliakovsky. The boys made an elegant bow, and the girls curtsied deeply before they flew off to hand their diplomas to their mothers, and begin the round of classrooms where each teacher waited to receive the new members of the ballet corps of the Imperial Russian Theater with congratulations and reminiscences of the pleasantest sort.

After that, I waited at the head of the great stairs for Vaslaw, and together we walked down the marble steps, lined on both sides by relatives and friends of the graduates, bearing flowers for them. The girls emerged carrying huge bouquets, but we boys were too old for that.

According to custom, Vaslaw had spent the last of his graduation money for a splendid equipage and, true to character, he had insisted that no one but me should accompany him on the pilgrimage before him. The first thing to do was to ride in state through the streets of St. Petersburg, and then it was imperative that every graduate visit his church and invoke God's blessing after giving thanks for the bounty he had received.

We went first to Spasitel—the Church of Jesus Christ—which Peter the Great had built with his own hands upon the bank of the River Neva, for after praying in his own church, Vaslaw had listened to my plea that he visit the two Orthodox churches which, tradition again decreed, must be visited by every graduate. So we prayed together in his church, and together in Spasitel, before I reminded him of his promise to visit Skorbiashey—the Mother of Sorrows.

Together still, we drove off to the Mother of Sorrows. His carriage had rolled along smoothly enough on the paved streets, but when we turned off by the glass factory, situated in the poorest section of the city, the carriage bumped and bounced ominously, until, at last, despite the fact that it was brand new, a spring snapped, and Nijinsky thumped down, while my side rose. We must have looked far from impressive in the richly upholstered vehicle, a caricature of itself, when we rolled up to the church and were surrounded instantly by legions of beggars who screamed for alms.

One old soul, wrinkled and haggard and half-witted with the sorrows of Vaslaw's laugh was louder than before when he answered, "On the side gazed at the carriage, a fearsome light in her eyes. "Whose carriage?" she demanded.

"Mine, old woman," laughed Vaslaw, standing straight and happy before her.

"Which side were you on?" she quavered.

Vaslaw's laugh was louder than before when he answered, "On the side that is down!!"

The old creature shrank from him for a second before she raised her face to his. Sadness seemed to have enveloped her when she muttered, "Poor boy! Poor boy!" but her eyes glittered oddly in the sunlight when she shook her toil-warped finger at him and pronounced: "It is a bad omen, my son. Always at the moment of your greatest triumphs, tragedy will spoil everything for you! At the height of your glory, tragedy will overshadow you!"

We laughed uneasily then, feeling the goose flesh creep over us despite the warm sun that poured over the whole world. I slapped Vaslaw on the back. "Don't think of it!" I laughed. "She's crazy, poor thing!"

But Nijinsky entered the shrine of the Mother of Sorrows with a shade of awe over him, and even after he reentered the carriage and ordered it off to my house, his eyes seemed less bright and joyous. The thought of the old woman and her words haunted me for a time. In spite of myself, their weight bore down on me, and I looked at Vaslaw wondering what he was thinking, until I grew indignant that the old woman could dare to spoil that great day for Nijinsky, my friend. It annoyed me for a few minutes more and then, as youth does, I forgot!

We went to my home where our parents, our brothers and sisters awaited our coming prepared to do homage to Nijinsky's genius. Our mothers and sisters and the maids were scurrying in and out of the kitchen and every one of Vaslaw's favorite dishes was included in the feast that was prepared. It was his day and his party, and we loved him so deeply that nothing, nothing could be too perfect if we were to express our admiration for him.

After coffee, our fathers proffered expensive cigars, and because Nijinsky was a little drunk with too much good wine, he took one and lighted it absently, puffing silently for a few moments before he turned a ghastly greenish-yellow—as he had when Rozai had nearly killed him. His head rolled, and his eyes glazed. He had never smoked before in his life! In no time, our mothers fluttered around, scolding our fathers, and working over Vaslaw, who lay back stupid and sick on his great day! They dosed him with home remedies and bicarbonate of soda until he was restored to something more like himself, and then a promenade in the Summer Garden was proposed to hasten forgetfulness that illness had marred Nijinsky's party.

Vaslaw turned the whole business into a travesty, suddenly beginning to laugh like one possessed, until he had us all convulsed with his declarations that everyone was looking at him, not because he was doubled up with laughter, but because he was in street clothes! Besides wearing street clothes for the first time, he carried a stick which was apparently unmanageable, for he used it as a blind man might, clumsily tapping it on the path before him until he did look the part of a clown! We laughed harder and harder, tears streaming

from our eyes, and still Nijinsky was uncontrollable. Realizing his hysteria, we headed homeward and ended the day with a party that lasted until dawn.

The first part of his tragic life was done, and laughing at the figure he cut in civilian dress, the world's most famous dancer faced the future—with a prophecy more dire than any in the past hanging over him while we laughed!

PART II

TRIUMPH AND DOWNFALL
IN RUSSIA

I

READJUSTMENT
WITH KSHESSINSKAYA'S AID

T HE day after graduation Nijinsky was in the repetizionnoe zalo practicing, with me at the piano to play his accompaniment. From May first until September first, all the Imperial theaters were closed and every artist took his vacation. A few rented homes near St. Petersburg and others scattered to enjoy woodland trails or the sea, while some among them sought the southern coasts of France and Italy for their holidays. Not all were able to afford the luxury of four months' idleness and so it happened that small ballet companies toured the lesser towns of Russia with a cast of fifteen or twenty Imperial artists, receiving from fifteen to twenty-five rubles for each appearance in ensemble and between fifty and one hundred rubles for solos. Generally, the corps de ballet included the most recent graduates whose insignificant salary from the school was insufficient to provide necessities and whose private classes were not yet under way to insure a respectable income.

It was this system that forced Nijinsky to two or three hours of intensive daily practice in preparation for the acceptance of whatever opportunities presented themselves. In the back of his mind the remembrance of Kshessinskaya's promise to take him as her partner encouraged him with hopes of Krasnoe Selo, where it was understood Kshessinskaya would dance during the army maneuvers.

After every day's practice we promenaded through St. Petersburg, sometimes seeking his home, sometimes mine. Night after night I sought my

club to gamble, for gambling had become habitual with me since one Christmastide when we boys had been introduced to the sport through the negative
influence of one of the poorer students in the school. Nijinsky called me a
fool for my gaming but was unable to dissuade me. Together we played in
little companies around the suburbs of St. Petersburg, and this Nijinsky
hated. There was no discipline; the theaters were small and mean. In his
words, they presented "nothing but grandmothers' parties." But Nijinsky
needed money and so he danced at grandmothers' parties for a hundred
rubles a show under an alias to protect his prestige at the Marinsky, while
his salary at the Imperial Russian Ballet remained at the customary fifty
rubles a month, his name appearing as "a member of the Corps de Ballet of
the Imperial Russian Theater."

That did not mean that Nijinsky appeared only in ensemble with sixty-
three other dancers, or that he was one of the eight coryphées, or even a second
dancer at the court theater! Far from it! He was a soloist from the day of his
graduation. The staff of the theater always made places for the most talented
dancers, even though they adhered strictly to tradition in being slow to raise
a boy or girl through the various rankings to acknowledged recognition as a
soloist or, for that matter, to raise their salaries a kopeck. Only dancing
lessons to the wealthy made it possible for us to live and have pocket money,
for society people rejoiced in engaging ballet artists as private instructors and
nurtured a cultural understanding of themselves through ballet.

"You will have plenty of students by winter," I chided, "you and your
fame with Obouchov, Legat, and Kyasht!"

"Oh, Anatole, it is bad enough to dance in those wretched little theaters!
It is worse, much worse, to teach."

Vaslaw managed to eke out his existence the same as the rest of us until
June, when he was transported with delight at learning that both of us had
been invited to take part in the performances at Krasnoe Selo, where Kshessinskaya would claim him as her partner. That could have but one meaning.
Vaslaw Nijinsky would never have to carve his own way to fame. The all-
powerful Kshessinskaya had chosen him for her partner and never again
would he be permitted to dance in Russia with any but a première ballerina,

though every male dancer in St. Petersburg burned with jealousy at his triumph over custom.

When we received the wonderful news of Kshessinskaya's favor, we decided to rent a small and inexpensive cottage at Dudergof, a summer resort near St. Petersburg. My family decamped for the country, leaving me with Madame Nijinsky, Vaslaw, and Bronia to look after me during the summer. Our furniture was poor, the walls were so thin that we could poke a finger through them, and yet, as I look back, we were happier that year than we have ever been before or since.

That summer Madame Nijinsky became Mother Nijinsky to me. We laughed all day, we ran over the grass with wings on our heels. We read scores of books, and talked and talked, while Mother Nijinsky cooked marvelous Polish dinners for us, the appetizing odors from the kitchen teasing our nostrils until we were as famished as Siberian wolves. When Mother Nijinsky stood in the sunshine shouting, "Tola! Bronia! Vatzo!" the last her pet name for Vaslaw, we ran like children, racing and tumbling in to destroy every vestige of a perfect repast while she smiled benignly at us. Her face was rosy and shiny from her cooking when she loaded our plates for second and third helpings until we were stuffed, almost too lazy to crowd into the kitchen to help with the dishes.

After dinner we sat down to discuss our futures, to plan for the wonderful day when Vaslaw would earn two hundred or two hundred and fifty rubles a month. Mother Nijinsky would wave her hands up and down in utter despair at our impossible imaginings, imploring: "Children, children! Don't talk about so much money. Be satisfied and don't dream of the impossible!" Then she would remind us: "Next year Bronia will graduate, and she will make fifty rubles. With Vaslaw's that will be a hundred rubles. It is big money!"

I broke in with a laugh. "Mother Nijinsky, one hundred rubles isn't big money. I made that much a week last winter and spent it all!" That angered her.

"You are no example for us to follow, Tola! You are a crazy boy to spend all that money on your cards and gambling!"

That fault of mine Mother Nijinsky never forgave. Often she scolded me for it. Meanwhile Bronia had learned how to manicure our nails and they shone like rosy mirrors all through that gay summer. Almost every evening was spent at home, sometimes taking Mother Nijinsky with us for a stroll along the country lanes at sunset where, from far off, the strains of orchestra music might come to us across the fields from the center of the village. Whenever we took part in any private performance, we might arrive home together, or, more frequently, I disappeared to my club for more cards while Vaslaw begged me not to go, walking beside me, filling my ears with reproaches and dire prophecies. It was useless. Gambling was as much of a habit with me then as any habit could be.

The next day would find me too tired to move when I came to play for his morning lesson. Vaslaw would treat me coldly, disapproval in every glance he leveled at me from under his heavy brows, for I was usually without a kopeck in my pockets after such an excursion. If I won, I tried to make my peace by buying pounds of chocolates, sweets, and fruits, but even this failed to appease Mother Nijinsky, who would exclaim: "Tola! Tola! I don't want your candy and your fruit! I would be the happiest woman alive if you would stop playing and never bring me a single chocolate! You will ruin your whole life!" As usual, her words were ineffectual and I continued my gambling.

The performances at Krasnoe Selo had no connection whatever with the Imperial Russian Theater but were given especially for the officers, their wives and children during the annual maneuvers. Colonel Kniajevitch directed the theater with Madame Klavdia Michailovna Koulitchevsky serving as ballet mistress, and Medalinsky as stage manager. The performers, never numbering more than forty, were all artists of the Imperial Russian Ballet who spent their summers near St. Petersburg. Each performance was in three parts, musical comedy, straight comedy, and the ballet divertissement, while discipline was as strict as that at the Marinsky.

Although the dancers were almost all stars, they received the smallest salaries paid in any theater, amounting to fifteen rubles for corps de ballet work and one hundred rubles for solos, the sum Nijinsky received. Besides this, all artists received passes entitling them to travel first class anywhere within a hundred-mile radius of the capital, and each might look forward to a gift from the Tsar bearing on it the crown and double eagle of the royal house. Between twelve and fifteen presentations took place during the summer, and each member of the company must take part in not less than three performances to receive a royal token, unless the artist was lucky enough to play in a production attended by the Tsar, in which case his gift was assured.

The presents were magnificent, the least among them being valued at not less than seventy-five rubles. For the women there was a pin, a bracelet, a brooch; for the men there were cigarette cases, cuff links, and similar gifts, all from Fabergé, the most exclusive jeweler in Russia, all bearing the royal insignia. The highest honor belonged to those who stopped the show in the royal presence, for they were presented with a gold watch by the Emperor. That was a dream to dream, and both Nijinsky and I longed for its fulfillment.

After Nijinsky's first performance, the newspapers and the summer colony were spreading news of his increasing popularity. I remember waiting at the station for our train to Dudergof after a wildly successful appearance. The crowds around us buzzed with excitement, exclaiming, "Nijinsky is a marvel! Ah, that Nijinsky!" completely unaware that he was among them until I committed an error that brought his rage down on my head.

The train pulled in, and I rushed to find seats; then, forgetful of the mob, I shouted: "Nijinsky! Nijinsky, hurry up! Here are places for us!"

In less time than it takes to tell, Nijinsky was surrounded by scores of women and girls, officers' wives and daughters, the officers themselves joining the crush and hailing, "Nijinsky! Nijinsky!"

By pushing and shoving and ducking, he reached me, disheveled and furious because he thoroughly believed that I had deliberately played what he was pleased to call "a muzhik's trick" on him. Not until long after we reached home did he deign to speak, and in spite of my assurances, he took a lot of convincing before he settled down and made me promise that I should never, so long as we were together, call him "Nijinsky" in public, but adopt the more familiar "Vaslaw" instead, in order that he might evade the crowds.

II

SAVIOR AND CONSPIRATOR

THE episode at Krasnoe Selo station had been enough to indicate Nijinsky's notability as an artist since his partnership with Kshessinskaya, but it had been more important to me, for I discovered that Vaslaw was, so far, unspoiled by acclaim and sought to keep his old friends rather than to trust himself to the vagaries of a changing public. As usual, we went to the repetizionnoe zalo for practice on the following day. I don't know what went wrong with my brain, but I conceived the notion that I must play a practical joke on Vaslaw that would scare the life out of him for a while. After assuring myself that he was occupied in conversation for a few minutes with the doorman, I ran upstairs and made for his dressing room. For a moment I stood indecisive, and then I hit upon the exact plan of campaign. I would hang myself!

With elaborate care, I selected one of the hooks upon which Vaslaw threw his street clothes while he practiced, and with great solemnity and deliberation I removed my heavy belt, fastening it on my chosen hook with a strong turn that formed a noose. I stood off to survey my handicraft and to wait until I heard Vaslaw nearing the door. Straining my ears, I detected his light step, rhythmically mounting the stairs, turning into the corridor—there! He was just outside the door, the knob was turning ever so slightly under the pressure of his hand. Quick as a flash, I thrust my neck into my lovely noose, and to my utter horror, I heard Vaslaw's steps retreating towards the lavatory!

He was going and I was being hanged! I wriggled helplessly, succeeding only in tightening the noose with every move. There was the sound of rush-

ing torrents in my ears, the taste of blood in my mouth, it was agony un-
bearable to breathe; my hands were powerless to reach my throat. I dangled,
fully conscious of the life that was ebbing away in labored gasps. With one
desperate spasm, I attempted to free myself. I dropped through what seemed
miles of space, and was dully aware of a frightful blow on the back of my
head before blackness swallowed me!

The sound of the doorknob squeaking roused me to the fact that Vaslaw
was standing before me! Beside me were splinters of rotten wood, and a
twisted hook. Vaslaw stared unbelievingly at the broken wood and the belt
before his glance traveled up the wall. I leaped to my feet.

"Fool! Idiot!" I screamed at him, half mad with mingled pain and fright.
"Why did you leave me to hang myself? Why did you run off to the lavatory and leave me to die? Why didn't you come in as you always do and let
me play my joke instead of leaving me to kill myself! As it is, I am nearly
scared to death! What are you staring at, imbecile!" To my disgust, Nijinsky was observing me calmly, with a great deal of pity in his eyes. At last
he spoke.

"Poor Tola! I know! You are always broke! Always spending your money!
Always discouraged! And so you tried to kill yourself—I understand," and
nothing I could say changed his mind. He firmly believed that I had attempted suicide.

"I'll never tell a soul," he promised and it became the first of a series of
confidences which, until now, have remained secrets. Nijinsky was not an
undependable madman. He was a loyal and good friend who never betrayed
my trust.

It is a fortunate thing that I chose the hook I did, else he might have been
one of the chief mourners at my funeral, for not another hook in the room
would yield to his tremendous strength! As it was, he brought me water
and rallied me with good-humored jokes until he was satisfied, in his own
mind at least, that he had saved me from any tendency to repeat my performance!

The simple pleasures of living claimed our attention wholeheartedly. We
usually arrived at the Krasnoe Selo Theater at eleven in the morning when

rehearsals were scheduled, to join a gay company of officers milling around the young ballet girls! We were allotted three rubles a day for food, but we rarely used it, for was not the great Kshessinskaya with her entourage of Grand Dukes and generals our especial friend? She had known us since we were boys. She had watched Nijinsky's training with an eye to his artistry that missed nothing, and she had pressed me into service as her accompanist at the piano since I had been old enough to play for her.

Our circle included the cousins of the Tsar, Grand Dukes Boris, Andrei, and Sergei. . . . They were unpretentious fellows and easy to know, hailing us by our first names, and dancing attendance upon the humblest member of the corps de ballet without condescension.

Their friends, the highest officers in military service, were likewise our friends, while Apelsin, Grand Duke Andrei's fox terrier, was a great help during rehearsals, which he nearly demoralized with his pranks. He jumped about our legs and barked, evoking nothing more ominous than our sympathy for his scarred side, laid open when the Grand Duke horsewhipped him in a moment of ungoverned frenzy. (Then, repenting his action, Andrei had had the little dog nursed back to health by the best veterinarian he could find.) Apelsin was the sort of dog everybody loved and was a favorite of Nijinsky's.

Chocolates and sandwiches, fruit punches and lemonades were always in demand during rehearsals. It became the custom for the Grand Dukes and Counts of the nation to see to it that there was a plentiful supply of everything at the theater. After rehearsals some of us went off in groups, celebrating our intermissions with drives through the countryside in company with Kshessinskaya and the laughing troupe of nobles, or rowing about on the glassy surface of a little lake near by. Still others started card games in the dressing rooms, and there I might be found unless a pretty girl stopped me or Nijinsky's anger grew hotter than I could bear. At five, we gravitated towards the restaurant across the street where the Grand Dukes played host to Kshessinskaya and her followers.

Those gatherings were like family reunions, with the Grand Dukes shooting a barrage of jokes from table to table, and listening to anecdotes as risqué

.nd fascinating as any they had in their repertoire, as soon as the company grew warmed with expensive wines and champagnes that flowed as freely as water. Immediately after dinner, we scrambled back to the theater to make up for the performance at eight, while the Grand Dukes scurried into the theater to await our appearance on the stage.

Those were great days! Grand Duke Nicolai Nicolaievitch was likely to arrive tardily, surrounded by his imposing staff of generals. We could tell the exact moment of his arrival, for his Romanov voice trumpeted through the theater unfailingly, and if anything displeased him, it thundered a stream of the most priceless and extraordinary oaths that ever fell on the ears of man or woman. If the Tsarina herself were there, the oaths lost none of their color, for Grand Duke Nicolai was not only the Tsar's uncle, he was the commander-in-chief of the Russian armies, and he feared neither God nor the devil!

Whenever we heard those wild words echoing through the theater, we knew that the performance was about to start! "The trumpet of Jericho," we called Grand Duke Nicolai, with his sunburned face, his short amber cigar-holder and tiny cigar, his short curly beard, his blue hussar's uniform, brilliant with gold braid, and his red officer's cap jauntily askew while he toyed with a silver cavalry stick. He often strode onto the stage after the show and talked informally with the artists in the same cordial and friendly manner that typified his nephews—only his eyes betrayed the dissipations that were a byword.

His generals, apparently molded after his prototype, were in perpetual attendance, among them Prince Vassiltchikov, General Ostrogradsky, and General Dubensky, making the same big noise that stormed around the Grand Duke, in love with life and living. His favorite artist was Maria Alexandrovna Pototskaya, a woman whose beauty was phenomenal, whose dramatic art was supreme on the Russian stage, whose love for expensive wine and gambling was famous, and whose vocabulary was second only to the Grand Duke's!

The theater was invariably jammed, with tickets at a premium, even then to be procured only by those under the protection of a titled or influential personage. Svetlov, Alexander Plestcheyev—a dozen equally famous critics from the best Russian newspapers were there with a host of Grand Dukes, generals, and colonels to do justice to the performance. After those presentations, hundreds of elegant carriages and cars filled the roads with elite of the country, while we ducked between equipages to Krasnoe Selo station where a special train waited with steam up, sometimes for three or four hours while we dined and wined. I always disappeared to seek parties and games of chance while Vaslaw returned home to tell Madame Nijinsky that I was gaming and living the high life of an artist. Only a saint could endure that treatment without complaint—and I was no saint. I determined that Vaslaw must join me on at least one excursion before he sprouted wings and a halo!

Mother Nijinsky and Bronia both feared my influence groundlessly. I never inveigled Nijinsky into accompanying me on my various adventures until the pressure of his reports at home, plus that brought to bear on me by several in the company, convinced me that Nijinsky must be persuaded to share my amusements. The younger girls dreamed of dancing with him, devising plans to worm semipromises from him, for he never had the power of refusal. I had made him give me his word of honor never to dance with any girl until he had told me about her and we had passed on her talent and her reputation. After dancing with Kshessinskaya or Pavlowa, it would have been an easy matter to ruin his career by an appearance with an ineffectual or unknown girl.

At that time, there was in our company a young woman who, having almost won the rank of ballerina, interpreting responsible roles with increasing frequency, was scheming to make Vaslaw her partner to assure her prestige. She haunted him at practice while I supervised from the piano stool.

"Isn't that beautiful, Bourman? Don't we work well together!"

Often enough I replied, "Yes, very beautiful, but heavy."

She simmered until she could see me alone and register her complaints. "Bourman, why do you always talk of my heaviness? Forget my weight, forget it!"

"Do you want me to see Vaslaw rupture himself with his lifts?" I'd counter.

A dinner at the Krasnoe Selo restaurant, when we were all feeling happy after plentiful drinking, afforded her the deus ex machina for her revenge. She devoted herself to being particularly gracious to me until between the wine and her eyes I was trapped into begging Vaslaw to join an intimate party at her apartment. Immediately he fussed about breaking the news to Mother Nijinsky and Bronia.

"Mother, mother, mother!" I blustered. "Are you a baby that you can't move without her? If you are with me, you know you can't meet with any harm and if we miss the train a coach will take us home!"

He mulled it over arduously and with the persuasion of several glasses of champagne decided to go. When we arrived at her apartment, our hostess met us alone. There were neither servants nor friends in evidence! She was clever, that one. Seeing our surprise, she immediately went into the next room to phone. Her voice drifted out to us, chiding and imploring our friends, in turn, to come to her party. Shortly, she returned to us, apologizing, "I am so sorry—everyone has gone to another party but I've persuaded them to drop in in a couple of hours. . . ."

At once I understood and raised my objections.

"All right, Bourman, if you don't expect to enjoy a threesome, you will enjoy cards! Run along to your club for a couple of hours and I will try to make Vaslaw happy."

I gave her no opportunity to repeat her proposition. "I have only ten rubles—if I lose, I'll be back at once—but if I win, don't expect me!"

Surely enough, luck favored me so unexpectedly that I played all night, winning steadily, quite forgetful of Vaslaw's dilemma. A barbershop and breakfast were in order before I reported to play for Vaslaw at ten that morning. To my amazement, his overweight partner was not with him and he tackled me.

"Through your foolishness, Tola, I haven't been home all night! My mother and sister have probably waited up for me. Why did you do it?"

"But the party . . . ." I sputtered.

"There wasn't any party. She fooled us. I spent the night with her alone!" The color mounted slowly in his face and he stammered: "I am sorry, Tola, but after last night I was powerless. I have promised her to dance a pas de deux!"

"Impossible!" I bellowed.

"Listen, fool," Vaslaw remarked in a very calm voice, "I may dance only once with her, but it's too late to change that!"

The next day we arrived home together to give battle to Mother Nijinsky and Bronia, who, as Vaslaw predicted, had waited up all night for him. Poor Vaslaw! He broke his heart with his lies that day. I heard, in the midst of his mother's reproaches, that we had been on a party with the boys and not a girl was present! I said nothing while Mother Nijinski and Bronia hurled accusations at me. Secretly, I rejoiced that Vaslaw, for once, was the wolf and I the lamb!

III

A GOLD WATCH
FROM THE TSAR

Shortening days harbingered the season's close with its warning that if we were ever going to win the coveted gold watch from Tsar Nicolai there was little time left to accomplish our purpose. Vaslaw and I lay prone on the grass, discussing the possibility.

"You are almost certain of getting your gold watch," I conceded, "but what chance have I? Who would ever dream of giving me a solo before the Tsar?"

Nijinsky popped into an upright position. "Why not ask Madame Koulitchevsky? She likes you so much that she'll give you a chance," he urged.

"I don't want to ask her unless I can feel sure of her consent," I worried; adding, "and if I do decide to ask anyone for that chance, there's only one person I'd go to—Malitchka," our pet name for Madame Kshessinskaya. "If she decided that I should have a solo, Vaslaw, you know her power! She would order Koulitchevsky to give me a chance and Koulitchevsky would obey!"

I proved, to my own satisfaction, that a special destiny heeds one's dreams. Next day Colonel Kniajevitch arrived to announce to the whole company at rehearsal: "Next week will bring the three final performances of the season before the Tsar. Make an especially good program!" He turned to Madame Koulitchevsky and remarked, "His Imperial Highness will be happy to see a typically Russian number in native costume on the stage."

As a rule we gave Russian numbers dressed up with spectacular finery but this time the Emperor had signified his wish to see something that meant peasant clothing and folk songs. Madame Koulitchevsky thought quickly.

"I have nothing of the sort in my whole repertoire, but I will try to arrange something new," she said. I had listened to the conversation delightedly.

The moment she stopped speaking, I rushed up to the colonel. "I have a wonderful idea for a simple Russian comedy number based on a scene I saw in the far country when I watched muzhik boys and girls at their dancing, singing folk songs to the music of balalaikas."

The colonel wheeled and pounded my back excitedly. "It is exactly what His Majesty wants! Exactly!"

Near us, Kshessinskaya was doing her bar work. I dragged the colonel along and explained the whole story to her, to her intense amusement. When I finished, she lifted her voice imperiously, calling Koulitchevsky.

"Klavdia," she said. "I want to see that number. Give Bourman the big hall for his private rehearsals," and there was nothing for Koulitchevsky to say but, "Of course."

Meanwhile Eugenia Lopokova, a dear friend of mine, had come from Paris, beautifully tanned and strikingly lovely. I asked Malitchka what she thought of Genia as a partner for me and Kshessinskaya never bothered to reply but beckoned Lopokova over, observing, "Genia, you will dance a number with Bourmanchik at the next performance."

Fortunately, Lopokova was both proud and happy over the arrangement. We began our rehearsal directly after the general rehearsal with only Nijinsky and Mischa Amatniak, the Marinsky drummer who served as conductor at Krasnoe Selo, present. I told him what music I wanted and he greeted my news with a roar, while Nijinsky, between spasms, puckered his lips to whistle tunes of the commonest variety.

Amatniak objected. "They are so common that no one has ever orchestrated them," he groaned, "I'll have to arrange a special orchestration myself!"

We finally decided on *Notchenka, Oukhar Koupetz,* and *Svetit-Mesiaz* which has since become popular in the United States under the title "Moonshine." Instead of rehearsing with the piano, we danced to the tunes Nijinsky and Amatniak whistled. I showed Lopokova her entrance and pantomime with flowers, taking the old theme, "He loves me, he loves me not." In half an hour the number was ready, so utterly ridiculous that Nijinsky was doubled up with laughter, declaring that we'd score a wild success with it and actually more elated over my chance to get the watch than he was over his own.

On the day of the performance, the orchestra accompanied us at a rehearsal attended by the Grand Dukes. Vaslaw was as excited as a schoolboy. "Tola, Tola! You will surely make a bis tonight!" he encouraged, bringing me the news that we were to be fourth on the program.

Surely enough, when I made my entrance that night with my balalaika, my red blouse, blue velvet pants tucked into high Russian boots, and started my comic pantomime, shoving Lopokova with my elbow in her ribs, the laughter began, the Tsar joining heartily. He sat in the center of the first row in front of Colonel Kniajevitch and what did I see after our dance but the Tsar lean towards the colonel and the colonel signal Amatniak while we bowed! The Tsar had requested a repeat performance of our number! They called us back again and again! We had stopped the show! My head pounded with excitement and my heart nearly jumped out of my blouse while Nijinsky ran to me in the wings, embracing me and whispering: "Anatole! Anatole, I am so happy for you! You will get your watch!"

My cue was given and I went on to the stage a second time. To this day I cannot remember how we finished the number. My first clear recollection is of Colonel Kniajevitch saying to me backstage: "His Majesty wishes to see your number in the next performance. I congratulate you, Bourman. It was a wonderful success, and you will get your watch."

I was too happy to speak and so was Vaslaw. Mother Nijinsky was so elated that she wept and stroked my hair as though I were her own son when she heard that His Majesty had ordered a third appearance, setting a record for the Krasnoe Selo Theater, which never before had witnessed the same number three times in succession.

Lopokova and I were the talk of the town and the newspapers as well. Very seldom did His Majesty present his gifts personally, generally giving an order that they should be delivered from his personal office two days before Christmas. When they arrived that year, of all the artists only Nijinsky and I were awarded the coveted gold watch, while Lopokova received a beautiful diamond brooch. St. Petersburg society rejoiced in the discovery that it might take lessons from two artists who had received His Majesty's highest honor, but what was equally important in our eyes was the assurance that the holder of a watch from the Tsar could never be arrested in St. Petersburg.

Summer was done and Nijinsky had, besides two hundred rubles from the Marinsky, two thousand rubles for his performances at Krasnoe Selo and a few private appearances. The first thing he and his mother and Bronia did was to move into a newer apartment, reestablishing his custom of an hour and a half's daily practice when the fall season opened. Seldom did he appear on the stage and never in opera, for he was in the category with Kshessinskaya and Pavlowa, who were always saved for gala ballets. St. Petersburg was fortunate, indeed, if it saw its idols ten times a year in title roles. Vaslaw did appear in duets and trios, always scoring a success whether he took part in small groups or performed variations of his own.

He rose in public favor with gigantic steps, winning the notice of everyone whose interest was caught by the theater. I remember his first presentation as an artist in Tchaikovsky's *Lake of the Swans* in the first scenes of which he danced a pas de deux. He was so nervous that he forgot his routine completely, and when his music played, improvised a startling pantomime.

"Dance! Dance! Nijinsky! Your music is playing!" the artists surrounding him whispered. Suddenly the meaning of the words registered and he flung himself into a series of the pirouettes that brought him fame, finishing with tremendous applause for the few amazingly spectacular turns he had had time to do. He was fined for his lapse and his name was posted on the official bulletin for all to see. That taught him care, though his success grew hourly with the adoration of St. Petersburg's society, while his rank remained stationary, at a salary of fifty rubles a month.

Once a year the corps de ballet of the Imperial theater gave a benefit performance, in which the whole company took part with the most famous
ballerinas and prima donnas, splitting the proceeds among whatever artists
made no more than nine hundred rubles per year. About one hundred fifty
members of the company were always in that class, among them, of course,
Nijinsky. Sometimes a benefit brought as high as twenty thousand rubles
and each dancer was given approximately one ruble for each performance to
his credit when the benefit split was made. Nijinsky's first receipt from this
source was seven rubles, since he had made only seven appearances in the
entire first year which followed his graduation. Every newspaper in the city
made a joke of the seven rubles per year with which Russia recognized his
genius, and the "member of the Imperial Russian Ballet" with which it
labeled its premier soloist!

IV

DANCING MASTERS
AND SOCIAL LIONS

Nijinsky's life is peppered with amusing incidents. He once showed me a letter inviting him to teach ballroom dancing to two children, a faux pas that made us howl with laughter. The missive was signed by Siniagin, the Russian multimillionaire wheat king, who could hardly be expected to differentiate between ballet and ballroom dancing.

"Vaslaw," I advised, "ask him a hundred rubles an hour for ballroom lessons. That will pay you for sacrificing art to your pocketbook and console you for suffering the agonies of a dancing lesson!"

Neither of us dreamed that anyone would give that amount, but to Nijinsky's disgust, a reply came the next day accepting the proposition and requesting Vaslaw to name the hour most convenient for him, in order that a carriage might be sent. So we started to give lessons to the Siniagins, Nijinsky teaching and I at the piano. It was a rich home that we entered, furnished in grandiose style at a cost of hundreds of thousands of rubles and in execrable taste. A concert grand piano of Beckstein's that had taken the first prize at the Paris Exposition in 1900 graced the Siniagin drawing room because the wheat king must have the best, even at twenty-five thousand rubles!

The family itself was typical of the Russian merchant class. We were met as though we had been born into the intimate family circle, our host and hostess bowing crudely, ignorant of the most rudimentary forms of etiquette. The children to take lessons were a boy of eight and a girl of nine, both extremely fat and even more clumsy. During the lesson, given in a spacious hall, the whole family and all of the servants congregated. Madame Siniagin, whose face was beautiful, even if she was fat and had short pudgy fingers covered with diamonds, the aunts and cousins, the cook, the grooms, the dishwashers, the laundresses, and the coachmen—they were all there to watch the Siniagin hopefuls at their dancing. After the lesson, we were slapped familiarly on the back by Mr. Siniagin, who invited us to dine and urged us to make his home ours while we were in it. Then we would be ushered into a huge dining room and placed in the seats of honor while everything expensive was heaped before us—apéritifs and conserves, mushrooms of all edible varieties, and caviar, the best that could be bought, would be served to us in silver pails holding pounds of it, while a soup spoon with which to eat it was provided! Russian vodka and beer were side by side with the rarest imported wines and liqueurs, the latter flanked with Russian kvass, a cheap light beer made from bread.

If the children were ill and unable to dance, their lessons were paid for, according to custom in Old Russia. Later, this amazing family decided on two lessons a week—two hundred rubles for ballroom dancing! In that house alone, Nijinsky made eight hundred rubles a month, while his work with the Imperial Russian Ballet netted him fifty. He also gave three or four other lessons weekly, besides passing many of his prospective students on to me.

After every session with the Siniagins, Nijinsky was moody and wretched, indulging the artist in him which could not be satisfied with money. I was spared the necessity of self-excuse since I had an entirely different clientele which I had started to teach immediately after graduation, although my days were made miserable by the family pride of my cousin who had forbidden me to use my own name and who considered that I had tarnished our family escutcheon by becoming a dancer. Hence it was as "Kouchinsky" that I taught the titled class in St. Petersburg, before whom I felt my alias an insult. Nevertheless, I was the dancing master chosen to teach among others at the homes of Count Tolstoy, Princess Ourusov, the Narishkin family, which once disputed the Russian throne with the Romanovs, the

Koushelev-Bezborodko line, another house as noble as the Romanovs';
Princess Hilkov; Princess Bieloselsky-Bielozersky; Princess Orlov; Countess
Zoubov; Prince Schirinsky-Shachmatov, in whose home I met Pourischek-
evitch, the man destined to kill Rasputin.

Not only the children of those houses took lessons, so also did their
mothers, in order to increase the natural grace of their carriage as well as
to reduce, for the value of a perfect figure was appreciated in Russia long
before faddists invaded the United States. No society matron would permit
herself to do gymnastics, because they were too rough and uncouth to contribute in any way to elegance, while ballet bar work and dancing provided
strenuous exercise neatly calculated to combine grace with symmetrical development and to reduce weight scientifically and naturally.

So it came about that Nijinsky and I found ourselves at tea with St.
Petersburg's most exclusive society, for all of our lessons were given in
magnificent homes where society women first took their lessons, and then,
exquisitely gowned, indulged in cultured and intelligent discussions of art,
music, literature, and ballet, sipping tea from fragile cups and nibbling tiny
sandwiches and pastries.

Elegance was the order in Old Russia, where the most dignified families
considered the convenience of others before their own and inquired whether
Ballet Master Nijinsky and Ballet Master Kouchinsky preferred a coach or
an automobile to call for them. Christmas was remembered with a choice and
appropriate gift from each family.

Lessons given before seven called for Prince Alberts, while full dress was
required for any after that hour, and it became incumbent upon Nijinsky
to pay great heed to his personal appearance.

Recalling those days with Vaslaw, I have yearned for five minutes to
describe to him the teaching that he hated in Russia as it is done in America
where one may be "high-hatted" for the price of a dollar!

Nijinsky spent most of his time teaching and practicing during the first
year. Later, he turned all his students over to me, for his heart was in the
Marinsky and not in the drawing rooms of Russia's great ones. It is easy to
understand, that passion of his for ballet, in a country where it was reserved

as the pièce de résistance for the cultivated and cultured. He was in a perfect environment where love for the dance was a national characteristic, and the ballet of which I speak was at the apex of the arts, performed by those to whom the title "artist" was worth more than the Tsar's glory!

Years and years of cultivation and appreciation had gone into ballet as an institution until it brought a breath of paradise into the more mundane affairs of living. Each presentation was a gem, its structure and its execution hardly less wonderful than the miracle of a flower unfolding its loveliness. It is not my intention to write a history of the ballet, but I do want to sketch its development.

First a family institution evolved in the homes of the titled as an aristo-cratic diversion, it gradually spread through the Empire until it reached the royal household and focused interest. Then it was that the court sponsored dancing as an art and instituted the Imperial Russian Ballet and its school to foster the exquisite strength and inspiration that dancing properly repre-sents. Thus every ballet became an achievement, and seats at the Marinsky Theater were held only by those who had originally sponsored the art. It was not uncommon in Old Russia to discover that the privilege of seats or a box at the Marinsky had been mentioned as a legacy, while if a mark of special favor was to be shown to one whose forefathers had failed to sponsor the ballet, an invitation to attend a presentation or the loan of a box was enough to cancel the most pressing social obligation!

In consequence, we played constantly to the same audience and came to know it almost as well as we were known. Years later, Nijinsky and I could sit down and recall the exact seats in the bel étage, balcony, and orchestra customarily occupied by Prince Youssoupov, Princess Orlov, M. Dandre, whose floral tributes to Pavlowa were once the talk of the capital, or of any other imposing name that came to mind.

When we were not taking part in the performance, Nijinsky and I strolled out into the foyer, certain of being guests of prominent boxholders who never failed to treat us as equals, for they considered it a privilege and were sure to reflect a certain pride of attainment when a recognized artist sat with them. Full evening dress was essential for everyone except those who sought places in the galleries—a tuxedo would have brought immediate censure. Tuxedos were fit for the smoking room—no more!

Not an officer but appeared with his full quota of orders glittering on his breast, for that, too, was an intrinsic part of the tradition. If it is understood that any officer of a crack regiment was required to support at least four thoroughbred mounts at an expense of thousands of rubles, it is more comprehensible when I say that only the wealthiest and most cultured houses were represented in the ranking posts of His Majesty's first regiments. The Hermitage Theater alone could outshine the Marinsky!

There was provocative luster and brilliancy to those gatherings. Here a hussar in his scarlet uniform bent over a woman swathed in rich furs and glowing silks, her jeweled ornaments luminous under the subdued lights; there it was a blue uhlan, a yellow cuirassier, or a white kavallergard who danced attendance upon women who symbolized the epitome of cultivation, poise, and charm.

During intermission, when a thousand lights sprang into life, the friendliness of the atmosphere was increased by the customary visits from box to box, while from every side formal bows were exchanged. Russian aristocracy held an informal reunion whenever the ballet presented a gem from its store.

In the tremendous foyer we beheld the grandes dames of Old Russia promenading with their escorts, making the foyer a fragrant garden with their rare perfumes. Around us, Nijinsky and I might hear scraps of conversation in Russian, French, and English. How often we stood there, smiling when a high title regretted in a subdued voice that disappointment was in store, "for Nijinsky will not dance tonight!" We would move aside unobtrusively rather than embarrass the personage with our eavesdropping.

The acceptance of a seat in a box signified our willingness to be whirled away at the end of the performance on one of the gay parties that always followed the spectacles of the ballet. Again, Nijinsky and I would be together in the colorful assembly congregated in the great Marinsky entrance. How many times we have watched the doorman, splendid in his red uniform, shouting for the carriages of the noblest names in the capital, his tricorn sedately in place despite the traffic which surged by the doors, and the Grand Dukes, Counts, Countesses, Princes, and titled ad infinitum that crowded about him awaiting their coaches. Ermine and sable wraps predominated as their owners pulled them close against the winter winds and rushed into the comparative warmth of carriages that dashed off, bound for the elite restaurants or for the luxury of a magnificent home.

St. Petersburg boasted several exclusive French-Russian restaurants that were more gorgeous in their appointments and service than any I have ever seen, even in self-indulgent America or in sophisticated France. We favored the Restaurant Cubat, which eventually provided the setting for the most epochal meeting of Nijinsky's career. There every doorman and waiter knew the name, the family history, and social standing of every customer, a fact that made it impossible for any stranger to pass the magic portals of the Cubat, or for that matter of the Donon, the Contan, the Ernest, or the Filisienne, the last two open only during the summer season.

Almire Cubat was in charge of the Tsar's cuisine. That lent him added prestige with St. Petersburg society which flocked to his restaurant en masse after every ballet performance, to be followed by scores of ballet stars. We danced and made merry to music by Oki-Albi, a Rumanian virtuoso. Not a table was to be found without a choice of the rarest imported wines ranged on it. Mumm, Roederer, Monopole, and Pommery were preferred although Mumm enjoyed the mightiest sale, for no matter how inebriated the most capacious customer was, he could always manage "m-m-m- . . ." which passed for Mumm!

The Cubat drew the brilliant parties staged for every ballerina after her success or her benefice. There the famous Svetlov sat and wrote his criticisms of whatever presentation he had witnessed, and woe betide the star who tried to influence him! He had been known to sit at the same table with a première ballerina, laughing and joking good-naturedly, and chatting most amiably with her at the very moment he was scribbling out a vitriolic criticism for his paper *Novoye Vremia*.[1] It was impossible to buy Svetlov.

Kshessinskaya and Pavlowa knew and loved the Cubat where the bills ran into thousands of rubles when they entertained or permitted themselves

[1] St. Petersburg *New Times*.

to be entertained. Their flowers were always crisp and fresh and lovely, for Russia adored her ballerinas passionately, and paid tribute with such a wealth of floral gifts that it was a foregone conclusion that trucks would have to be hired to transport the bowers of roses that surrounded the Marinsky favorites in coldest winter.

As for pocket money—Nijinsky and I learned shortly after our graduation that it was a fatal mistake to go to the Cubat with no more than twenty-five rubles in one's pocket! Once was enough, and so we were present as guests or saw to it that our rubles were counted in generous numbers before we entered its ostentatious portals!

V

VULTURES AND VAGARIES

At this period Nijinsky and I won for ourselves the nickname the "Two Ajaxes," for we were habitually together. We wore identical suits, making it a point to agree on what our costumes would be the next day before we went home at night. We had grown up together and our comradeship had become an accepted fact, save that it gave rise to incessant railing when our friends learned that I adored restaurant life and Nijinsky only tolerated it, preferring quiet evenings with Mother Nijinsky. We had few disagreements. My word had remained Nijinsky's law ever since that day, years ago in school, when he had given me his confidence. Artists and social leaders alike were quick to perceive that Nijinsky could be most easily persuaded to accept an invitation if I urged it. It was equally well known that I was a powerful major-domo in determining Nijinsky's attitude, since he was slow to realize that he was destined for fame greater than any ballet star had yet achieved in St. Petersburg, and that his reputation should be guarded with more than usual care.

A shade of misgiving disturbed me when I saw Alexandrov seeking Vaslaw out for confidential chats. Alexandrov was a fellow artist who, it was rumored, pulled thousands of rubles out of thin air, and Vaslaw, if his suspicions were not aroused, was easily led. Gossip labeled Alexandrov a glorified gigolo, but the allegation was never proved, and so he continued to move in most exclusive circles, despite evidences that whenever his attention was focused on our younger ballet girls, they inevitably arrived at the theater thereafter with diamonds, rubies, and sapphires in abundance. "More of Alexandrov's business" came to have a definite and not too savory sound in the wings of the Marinsky. He and one Gotch seemed to enjoy similar interests in life. What could he be planning with Vaslaw? Nothing, I decided. Vaslaw was a man. I stifled my misgivings.

No sooner had I dismissed my scruples than Alexandrov and Gotch approached me with an invitation to accompany themselves and Nijinsky to an exclusive restaurant in St. Petersburg. I was dumfounded and promptly refused their proposal, explaining that neither Vaslaw nor I enjoyed the company of men without the brightness of women's conversation.

On Theater Street, I tackled Nijinsky. "What's the idea, Vaslaw? We can't be friendly with men of that caliber—you know their reputation as well as I do!" He made no answer, but I determined to be on the alert once more and watched them buzzing away in Nijinsky's ear until I was forced into more questioning. "What in the world do they want, Vaslaw?"

"Oh, it's nothing to get excited about, Tola!" he replied. "They've been telling me of a certain Princess who is crazy about my dancing and wants to send me a present of diamonds without being discovered as the donor. It is to be kept secret, and Alexandrov is serving as an intermediary for her!"

That was reasonable, for every day Vaslaw had received perfumed letters, presents, and souvenirs from legions of admirers who were filling his ears with acclaim. "If she's really crazy about you," I remarked, "she can send you a gift on the stage easily enough without creating a scandal!"

Vaslaw squirmed. "All right, I'll tell you the whole story, Tola. She is the cousin of a certain Prince who has been observing me for some time. The plan is to meet him and through him to be presented to the Princess. You are in on it, Tola. All that remains to be done is to send word through Alexandrov to the Prince that we've no objection to meeting him at the Medvyed in a private dining room." That, too, was plausible. At seven o'clock the next evening we were taxiing to the most ornate and elite of St. Petersburg's select restaurants.

Alexandrov and Gotch met us enthusiastically, ushering us into a dining room where a richly appointed table and a supply of the finest wines in the whole Empire was waiting. The air was heavy with sweetness. I wheeled to

Alexandrov. "Are we entertaining Pavlowa?" I demanded, pointing to the wealth of flowers that flanked us.

There was time for no more, for the Prince—Prince Pavel Dmitrievitch Lvov—arrived. He was a typical aristocrat, tall, well proportioned, and handsome to look at, wearing his hair in a part that ran from the center of his forehead straight back to the nape of his neck. A monocle was skewered into one eye, and his voice was richly modulated when he explained, after an elegant bow, that for some months he and his cousin, the Princess, had been admiring us and planning a meeting. The Princess remained unnamed while Prince Lvov confided that she did not care in the least to send her gift through the usual channels.

"She has delegated me for the honor," smiled the Prince, slowly taking an exquisite miniature from his pocket. He handed it to Vaslaw, who showed it to me while the Prince talked on. "I beg you not to ask her name, but tell me—is she not beautiful?"

"You were born lucky, Vaslaw," I groaned after one look at the pictured face.

"I appreciate the influence you have with your friend, Mr. Bourman," the Prince continued, "and I think the situation is clear. What do you think?" His eyes bored into mine.

"I think Vaslaw is to be congratulated upon winning the favor of such a lady," I answered, laughing. "What can possibly be wrong in enjoying the admiration of a Princess with such obvious refinement and culture as hers?" I queried.

Prince Lvov was patently pleased. He turned to Nijinsky and extracted a promise to visit Fabergé's the very next day.

"The jeweler has instructions to measure your finger for a ring which the Princess wishes you to accept," he observed as we enjoyed an epicurean repast. We asked permission to leave a few hours later and Alexandrov and Gotch rode with us, dropping me at my home, before continuing on with Vaslaw who, with me, was riding in a Rolls-Royce for the first time in his life!

Lessons and the routine of living occupied me to the exclusion of everything else until the third day after our rendezvous with the Prince, when

Nijinsky and I exchanged opinions on the party. Vaslaw was wearing a beautiful platinum ring set with a sparkling four-carat diamond. I rejoiced with him over his excellent fortune, until, with a start, I realized that he had removed Gillert's ring! I was horrified! One does not break a vow such as Vaslaw's had been without thought!

"Vaslaw!" I exclaimed. "Where is your ring? Where is the ring Gillert gave to you and that you swore would never leave your hand?"

"That? Don't be a fool, Tola! It was nothing but a cheap amethyst. How could I wear it with a stone like this? His voice was impatient and a note of fear crept into it when he glanced at me. "There was no curse with it, so don't be superstitious!" In vain I reasoned with him. Something like terror for him had clamped itself around my heart.

It wasn't until everything else had failed that I burst out with my conviction. "You broke your life when you broke that promise!" I shot at him. "There is only trouble in store for you. Listen to me! Gillert's gift was more than a 'cheap amethyst'—it was success and happiness! You have flung it away for a glittering stone without meaning, and mark my words—you have brought tragedy on yourself! Don't ask me how I know. I know— and that knowledge is enough to make me sick for you and the future you've made for yourself!"

He was uneasy, but he chided me for my superstition, reminding me that it was characteristic of children and that neither of us was a child. What could I say? I went home and thought until my head was splitting and sleep impossible. I had experienced another of those rare moments when the veil of the future is rent asunder for a half-glimpse of what is to be, more terrifying than certain knowledge. I knew that tragedy was stalking the best friend any man could have—and I was powerless to do anything at all beyond knowing that Vaslaw had somehow broken a vow more sacred than either of us dreamed.

Superstition? Perhaps it was no more, and yet, from that moment on, Nijinsky's life was robbed of sincerity and simplicity. I knew past doubt that destiny was bound to overtake him with some ghastly fate—and nothing more. I tried to forget it.

Meanwhile Prince Lvov invited us to attend his parties with increasing frequency. Vaslaw no longer made-excuses. He was a regular attendant at lavish entertainments whenever the Prince played host, and although the name of his "Princess" was shrouded in ever-deepening mystery, the costliness of her gifts increased with Vaslaw's growing enjoyment of the Prince's gatherings. Rings, cuff links, and studded cigarette cases were showered upon him, always in my presence, by Prince Lvov, who was a most patient envoy for his cousin and who saw to it that there were always women present when I was. "My special concession to Bourman, who loves the ladies!" Prince Lvov would announce in presenting them to the company.

Vaslaw and the Prince would retire to discuss the merits of the unknown Princess, and I promptly forgot them to enjoy the charm of the feminine guests, all of whom were inordinately fond of music, and who, without exception, lived alone in palatial hotel suites.

Prince Lvov did his best to cultivate my friendship and one day requested the pleasure of meeting my family. I went home to prepare the household for a visit, describing in minute detail the splendor of the parties he had given in our honor.

Father's eyes narrowed. "I don't like that Prince, Anatole! He is too rich for you, but at the same time I'd like to see him. Bring him home with you." On the following Saturday, Prince Lvov arrived.

Father met him with frigid courtesy, ignoring the Prince's unconcealed delight with my mother and my sister, and the favorable impression my young brother's abilities as a linguist, and his smartness in uniform, had created. Converse in foreign languages with Father as he might, Prince Lvov could do nothing to thaw my father's coldness. He finally gave it up and invited my brother Mischa, my sister Nastia, and me to accompany him to the bicycle races at Michailovsky Manège, a tremendous coliseum accommodating thousands. We were seated in one of the best boxes and my sister was provided with roses and chocolates, while the Prince managed introductions for my brother and myself to the most famous personalities in the sporting world.

Nedela, the bicycle rider, won every honor that could be taken that night, and behold! he was among our guests! The Prince removed a great emerald from his own finger and presented it to the victor! We were thrilled over the whole evening, for none of our richest relatives could have afforded such entertainment! Prince Lvov left us with the promise of more box parties in the future, and we let ourselves into the house in high spirits.

Father met us like a thundercloud, fixing his gaze on me. "Anatole, I do not like your Prince. He is not to come to the house again, nor is Mischa or Nastia ever to be seen with him. You are big enough to look out for yourself. I am not interested in *what* you do."

"What is wrong with you? The Prince is a fine fellow!"

"I don't want a man of his type in my house! Out!—and don't speak to me again. If you are wise, you, too, will not be seen with him, but whatever you do is your affair!" Father was sterner than I had seen him for years, and even though I raged at him for denying hospitality to the Prince, I respected his decision.

On the following day I approached Vaslaw with an account of my father's attitude, but he was inclined to treat the matter lightly.

"Your father is old-fashioned, Tola, with his ideas of wealth. Why miss the Prince's entertainment for the sake of family prejudices?"

From that time on my comings and goings were unquestioned. With extreme diplomacy I permitted the Prince to guess that it would be best if he never visited my family.

Meanwhile I fell madly in love with Barbara Pavlowa, the most beautiful woman in St. Petersburg and the idol of a certain hussar in command of one of the best regiments stationed in the capital. Fortunately, his men revolted and were banished to an isolated province for three years as a disciplinary measure, and to my delight their commanding officer was ordered off with them! Despite the knowledge that all the money I could command would seem no more than a pinch of change to Barbara Pavlowa, I showed her my preferences, the company meanwhile railing me, "You are a fool, Bourman, to imagine that you can afford to flirt with a woman of her wealth!"

She held the whole company in a state of awe, for the treasure of her diamonds alone was enough to set her apart—and yet, lonely in the absence of her hussar, she seemed to welcome my attentions. Nijinsky was almost as fond of her as I, and was invited to her home with me until we both felt perfectly at ease in her apartment! Instead of staying with his family or mine, we frequently made for the home of Barbara Pavlowa, whom we called "Varvotchka."

She sent her carriage for us, and we dashed through winter nights behind a pair of sleek chestnuts, brilliant green and blue netting protecting us from the lumps of snow showered from their hooves. Fast driving was one of Varvotchka's favorite pastimes. Nijinsky used to leap in on one side of her, put his arm about her waist, and let her nestle down among her sables while through brittle nights we flew across the miles under moonlight so bright that it transformed the snow cloud enveloping us into a nebula of sparkling diamonds.

Often a sophisticated night club was our goal, until Varvotchka learned that we were unhappy about not being permitted to pay the bills, and then our visits became less frequent and our intimate threesomes more so. However, she permitted me to send her a single rose each day. Vaslaw was not slow in adopting her as his special inspiration, a circumstance that she recognized by meeting him for a few moments before his stage appearances to dissipate his misgivings with her faith. She was eight years older than we and took advantage of our devotion to exert a constructive influence on us. Through that interest she learned of our friendliness with Prince Lvov.

The cover was off! Her temper blazed and her voice shook with passion. She grew incoherent in her dismay. "I do not like him!" she pronounced flatly, and a week later she bade him to a surprise dinner! Truly the ways of women were beyond Vaslaw and me in those days. Prince Lvov accepted with alacrity and arrived bearing a great basket of roses, to dine with unconcealed delight in surroundings as richly appointed as his own.

During the dinner, Varvotchka sat near me, finally ensnaring my attention with a nudge. "Top, after the performance come back to me. Never mind the lateness. Promise!" she whispered. I nodded, and in due time the Prince departed after implanting many kisses on Varvotchka's white hand.

True to my word, I was back after midnight to find Varvotchka pacing the floor.

"Top," she began, "I am disturbed! I hate your Prince. I invited him here to watch his attitude towards you and Vaslaw!" She dropped into a chair and stared at me. "I am sure you are not in danger, but I am afraid Vaslaw is letting his head be turned by flattery. Too much wealth is not good for boys as young as you two, and I don't think Vaslaw has been honest with you."

"Vaslaw has been like my own brother. He wouldn't lie to me or about me," I protested. Impulsively, she grasped my hand.

"You don't understand. All over Russia today there are millionaires who cultivate art by sponsoring its geniuses and showering them with praise and gifts until their heads are turned, until they are spoiled for simple pleasures and are bored with opulence. Top, promise me! If Vaslaw has been your friend, be his now. If you cannot break his friendship with Prince Lvov, at least stay with Vaslaw and remind him that he isn't perfect. Don't let him be a sycophant! I trust you!"

It gradually dawned over me that Vaslaw was already suffering from a big head. I recounted the story of Gillert's ring, and Varvotchka shook her head sorrowfully. "Yes, it is as I thought. But Vaslaw's ideals are priceless—priceless, Top! He has a good head and a better heart and so we can help him."

From that day forward I reminded myself of the jester who sat behind Caesar at his victories to remind him that he was still less than a god—and our parties went on, with Vaslaw the center of attraction.

Money was of no more value to Prince Lvov and his cohorts than the snow that melted in the streets and was replenished from the heavens. Count Ribopierre was one of the Prince's closest friends. He was in the habit of spending enormous sums nightly at the private sporting clubs we haunted for wrestling matches, fencing tourneys, and every conceivable type of amusement, congregating the most talented athletes for our benefit.

After exhibiting their skill, they accompanied us on our perpetual rounds of the restaurants or to the Prince's palace, kept by a staff of twenty servants although he lived alone and was seldom at home. Every room in his mansion was hung with rich Gobelins and rare oils. Gold and silver knickknacks abounded.

I remember once taking an aspirin at one of his parties, and having the Prince rally me for carrying my remedy in such a poor box. He reached for a tiny container of gold, encrusted with his coronet, which I refused.

"Oh, well—give it to your Varvotchka for her pins!" he suggested.

I was insulted. "My Varvotchka can give you ten boxes like that. She doesn't need your box!"

"All right, keep it yourself," he laughed back, amused by my reaction, indubitably aware of Varvotchka's hate.

Besides a few society friends of the Prince who were always present, Prince Lvov encouraged groups of artists to attend his gatherings. Bohemianism reigned. Some of his guests sketched, some wrote, some wrestled, some sang and played, and all were happy when the Prince passed around hundred-ruble notes. The boys rejoiced in their pocket money and in their sponsor, and the fun went on.

Gradually it began to pall. I approached the Prince in a bored mood which I attempted to pass off as one of lightness. "Why not vary your holidays with a party of charming women?"

"Capital! Bourman, we'll do it!" he exclaimed, and the next day he presented me with dozens of photographs. "Take your pick, and we'll have a real party!" he promised while I glanced through the collection.

There were blondes and brunettes, and on the back of every picture was a description which furnished the age, height, coloring, weight, and more intimate details of the lady's character. Only three of the six I picked arrived for our party, and one of them was a famous French actress! All were cultured and clever. In no time, with the aid of Prince Lvov's champagne and abundant hospitality, we were old friends, ready for a trip to the restaurants.

That night we chose the Aquarium, an exclusive retreat, indeed, for a visit to pass on the presentation of foreign artists arranged cabaret-fashion.

Hopkins, an American Negro, was creating a furor with his tap dancing, a style novel to us, and one that gained him an invitation to dance for the

Prince, who was vastly amused at seeing the Negro throw sand on the floor for his dance. Stasia Oberbeck, too, joined us in our private room, since she was bringing St. Petersburg to her feet with her version of *Oyra, Oyra,* and necessarily added distinction to our party.

Nijinsky's eyes glinted with false, superficial brilliancy when he saw money scattered on the floor like scrap paper. Times were changing for him!

We toasted Mademoiselle Oberbeck and applauded.

VI

DIAGHILEV AND THE
PLAYBOY OF ST. PETERSBURG

THE following day found me accepting Prince Lvov's invitation to witness Nijinsky's dancing from the bel étage which was the Prince's hereditary right. I sent a note to the stage manager deploring my serious illness, regretting my inability to dance—and donned my dress suit for the ballet! During intermission we strolled in the foyer, the Prince greeting many as they passed. An exquisite creature in décolletage swept by, trailing an aura of subtle perfume. I stared after her spellbound.

"How do you like her type, Bourman?" chided the Prince when I remained glued to the spot. Blond she was, perfectly groomed and coiffured, with an officer dancing attendance on her. And then, I saw a brunette, vivid and delightful!

"Look more closely," advised Prince Lvov, and I did, somewhat disconcerted by his request. I noted the perfect rhythm and grace of carriage in both women, the brilliant collar of emeralds that shone on the one, the diamonds that glittered around the throat of the other.

Prince Lvov chuckled when I asked for an introduction. "Both of your ladies are gentlemen!"

"Impossible!" I exclaimed.

"Nevertheless it is so. The first you admired is 'Fifi,' which is the nickname of a rich Prince. The other is a nobleman who, as you know, has the best stable in Russia. That is one of St. Petersburg's amusements, for the lads enjoy fooling their best friends. There are at least eight here in feminine masquerade, besides the two you noted, both of whom will unquestionably win their wagers!"

Before I could reply, Prince Lvov moved away to speak to Diaghilev, a guest at the Marinsky that night. Returning, the Prince observed, "You probably know Diaghilev by sight. I've invited him to be with us at the Cubat after the performance."

As soon as he could jump out of his costume, Nijinsky joined us and we were off to the Cubat, to a private room where a table was set with every conceivable variety of wine, and caviar in generous silver barrels. Nijinsky had triumphed once more. He had been besieged by crowds, laden with gifts, and messages had been poured backstage on a flood of enthusiasm.

"Our supper is in honor of Nijinsky tonight!" proclaimed the Prince, while our feminine guests clustered around Vaslaw expressing their congratulations with abandoned avowals of affection.

They were not, as might be suspected, professional entertainers in the habit of throwing themselves at the head of any man; on the contrary, they were the wives of three of Moscow's most respected aristocrats! A few times annually they traveled to St. Petersburg for adventure, and that year they sought it with us. Nobody in the capital knew them, and so they devoted themselves to the enjoyment of life unrestricted. It was well known that our St. Petersburg matrons took trips to Moscow for the same purpose, returning home to be docile wives above reproach for another three or four months! There was nothing scandalizing in the situation—it was a part of sophisticated life!

Not more than fifteen minutes had passed when the head waiter announced Diaghilev's arrival. Prince Lvov turned to Nijinsky and me with a warning, "Be careful of your conversation, boys! Diaghilev is a big figure in the world, and his diplomacy is a byword!" Before he could manage more, the great man was with us, accompanied by Count Tischkevitch, the richest magnate in Poland, of whom fabulous tales were told. He lived, so it was said, in a castle where the doorknobs were of great jewels and he bathed in a tub of pure gold. Incredible as that sounds, it is not past the belief of any who knew the luxury and the folly that prevailed under the old regime. The Count owned almost the whole city of Vilna in addition to his other properties, and so he could easily have afforded jeweled doorknobs if the caprice took him—but introductions were going on.

Diaghilev met Nijinsky with marked cordiality. "How can I express my pleasure at meeting a dancer so gifted?" he asked when he held Nijinsky's hand.

Afterwards, whenever he looked at Vaslaw, compliments bubbled forth spontaneously in the short interims between the discussions of art, music, and dancing which the maestro permitted himself, relating the whole scope of his conversation by the thread of his ideas on dancing.

Whenever I glanced at Diaghilev, his monocle in place, his voice vying in culture with those of the nobles about him, I realized that before me was a man in whose veins flowed the blood of aristocrats and gentlemen, whose heritage was culminating in a brilliant mind and a grand manner. A moment's foresight linked his name to Nijinsky's in an eerie vision of fame that faded as swiftly as it had come. I weighed the man guardedly. He had the head of a Roman patrician, and his coal-black hair was marked by a broad white forelock, which had gained for him the cognomen of the "Silver Beaver," a fact that Diaghilev had been quick to capitalize. It was the Silver Beaver who was recognized in crowds wherever he went and won fame throughout Russia as an art patron.

The three women found him an admirable foil for their wit, the conversation became general, and the gaiety mounted until I precipitated something which ruined me and doused the spirits of the whole group.

Diaghilev was opening a new conquest to us with offhandedness that temporarily disarmed us. When Nijinsky and I became aware of the gist of his words he was saying: "I dream of carrying Russian ballet into every nation. I long to astonish the whole world with the talent, the grandeur and the beauty we Russians, alone, have as our own."

Silence fell as the gathering sensed the birth of an idée grande easily conceived as one which might turn the currents of individual destinies into broadened channels. Diaghilev continued, "I shall lay forever the ghost of

Russian barbarism that haunts Europe, and I plan to do my exorcism with
the proof of a culture so mighty in Russian hearts that it overshadows noble-
born and peasant-born alike with ardor and reverence in the presence of Art!"

Every one of us responded to the inspiration that vibrated in his voice
as he dreamed aloud. We knew that he was capable of carrying out the
immense project with typical opulence, when he crystallized his intention
by confessing that his execution of the campaign to educate Europe was
already under way.

"I have worked hard to interest the most progressive minds of the century," said the Silver Beaver. "I have succeeded in extracting promises of
help from Stravinsky, Roerich, Alexandre Benois, Leon Bakst, Golovin—"
His voice dropped to a whisper. "Soon now I shall talk with the artists I
have chosen—and with my ballet master who will make my dream of cultural conquest a triumphant reality!"

The most flagrant wastrels of Russia paid homage to him, leaning forward,
caught by the brilliancy of a goal offering satisfaction to connoisseur and
patriot alike. Diaghilev's voice rose with the consciousness that he had succeeded in capturing the hearts of his hearers. "In fact, my friends, I will have
two ballet masters! One will be the idol of St. Petersburg, Michail Fokine,
—and the other will be the Muscovite idol, Alexis Gorsky!"

When he pronounced the second name, Nijinsky leaped from his seat
and literally shouted, "Impossible, Mr. Diaghilev! How can you put those
two names together? The St. Petersburg ballet and Fokine are a hundred
times superior! That Muscovite school is not be compared with ours!"
It was an outcropping of the ancient feud between the two great Russian
schools, and Diaghilev seemed satisfied when Nijinsky rushed on. "No
great dancer has ever been great with a Muscovite training alone! Every one
of them has had to perfect his work under Fokine in St. Petersburg!" Vaslaw's eyes flashed with his passion. "You remember the mighty Theodor
Kosloff?" Diaghilev nodded and Nijinsky blurted out the truth. "He may
have graduated the premier dancer of his school, but he had to come to Legat
before he was an artist! He was tremendous, but he was made an artist with
technique and polish in St. Petersburg—not Moscow!"

"Don't worry." Diaghilev stemmed Nijinsky's turbulence with a sudden gesture and permitted a serene smile to wreath his patrician face. "I wanted to discover whether it was art or flattery that would guide you, Nijinsky! Don't you think I know Russia's mightiest geniuses—Pavlowa, Kshessinskaya, Karsavina, and you—all of you trained under Marius Petipa, Obouchov, and Fokine? Don't you think I know that the dancers I have named, and they alone, are the world's premiers? Only the cream of Russia's greatest will be in my ballet—not one from Moscow will find a place! My dancers will come from St. Petersburg and Warsaw! Everyone in my ensemble will have been a soloist in Russia!"

Nijinsky stood, leaning his hands on the table and peering at the Silver Beaver unbelievingly, until Diaghilev addressed himself directly to Vaslaw, a note of understanding in his tone. "You are a Pole, Nijinsky, and you have never seen Warsaw!"

Perhaps the memory of his mother's dream accounted for the tenderness in Vaslaw's expression as Diaghilev went on. "It is a tragedy that you have never seen that beautiful ballet with its lovely Polish girls! I am sorry our government has not seen fit to spend more money at Warsaw and less in Moscow, for the Polish seem more artistic than the Muscovites. But you will see for yourself what splendid work Warsaw is doing! And that, my friends, that dream of conquest is my greatest coup for the Empire!" Diaghilev concluded, "I will have the greatest artists in Russia in my company!"

"You will be a great entrepreneur!" I blundered unintentionally. An entrepreneur! No greater insult could have been offered than that, for to us an entrepreneur could be only a man who paid insignificant salaries to his artists after skinning the public alive and lining his own pockets. There was deathlike silence before the Silver Beaver deigned a reply very deliberately.

"Yes, Bourman! I will be an 'en-tre-pre-neur!' " That pause between syllables conveyed most clearly to me exactly what I had done, while a glance at Prince Lvov's ashen countenance clinched the matter. The Prince rallied to my rescue, plying the Silver Beaver with queries to cover up my faux pas. Notwithstanding, Diaghilev rose at the end of five minutes and shook hands all around with marked elegance until he reached me. There was an obvious halt, and then he spoke deliberately, staring into my face: "Goodbye, Bourman. I think you will soon hear of my en-ter-prise!" The pun was not lost. With a sense of foreboding, I watched the Silver Beaver exit with Count Tischkevitch. The moment the door closed, Prince Lvov attacked me.

"Bourman!" he said. "You have made a powerful enemy tonight! You have ruined yourself with one of the greatest patrons of art who ever lived —besides insulting him at my party! How could you speak to him like that? He is the last man on earth to profit at the expense of artists; he has spent a fortune on art and artists; he is a gentleman whose integrity is unquestioned from one end of Russia to the other! And you called him 'entrepreneur'! He chose my guests as the first to know of his mighty project to make Russian art supreme in the dance world—and you chose to insult him!" Prince Lvov shrugged at my humiliation. "Remember, Bourman! Diaghilev never forgets anything. He will make you pay for your little joke, and that soon!"

I understood without the Prince's reproof—and so deep was my embarrassment and regret for my stupidity that the company took on the color of my mood until the party ended more solemnly than a funeral. I had had my moment—everyone knew Diaghilev would have his.

VII

BEGINNINGS OF PROSPERITY

Prince Lvov's patronage continued, with the difference that Diaghilev was, almost without exception, one of the company and the Prince had proposed the great room of his palace for Nijinsky's practice instead of the Imperial ballet hall. I disapproved his working before scores of the Prince's guests who ranged themselves in the ballroom, commenting freely on the stature of an art already an epitome of perfection compared with that of other male dancers in Russia. Society women, too, were likely to attend, and once Prince Lvov sidled up to me, remarking, "That imposing woman there is the one who has been showering Vaslaw with diamonds, but don't tell him that I betrayed her to you!"

The Silver Beaver, meanwhile, had adopted a frigid but excessively polite air towards me which frayed my nerves until I said in exasperation: "Vaslaw, I am sick of this crowd and the life that we lead in it. This wealth—this flattery—we aren't used to it and I can't stand it. I prefer my own friends."

Nijinsky shook his head. "As you say, Tola. You know this isn't a matter of social life, only, with me. You heard Diaghilev's plans for his ballet. This may mean my career. You have your choice, and I have mine to make."

For long hours I talked with him, mustering courage to speak my mind, and then I left him to his choice. The revelry went on without me. I met Vaslaw daily and heard what news he had to offer before I sat down and from the piano stool watched him work out his routines. Expensive stones dropped into his open hands from the inexhaustible store of his unknown Princess, although he already had over forty rings—beautiful things set

with pearls, rubies, emeralds, and diamonds worth thousands of rubles. My
eyes nearly popped out of my head when he arrived at practice with a watch
chain of platinum stretched across his vest and set with nine blue-white
diamonds, each weighing over two carats, all of them beautifully matched.

The days of my rejoicing over his success were gone, for Vaslaw's ideas
were so different from what they had been. His head was turned with wealth.
It seemed that Barbara Pavlowa's fears had been realized. The high life
appealed to him and simple pleasures were past. Once he had reproached
me, and now he was deeper in folly than I had ever been. A hundred rubles
meant nothing. The tailor Vassiliev, who had trusted Vaslaw when he was
without a kopeck, no longer satisfied him; Nijinsky now imported his
clothes from London.

On one of the rare occasions that Vaslaw was at home with Mother Nijinsky and me, he broke the news of his growing affluence. The apartment
he lived in was a far cry from the early ones he had called "home," and as I
looked about in approval, Vaslaw broke in: "This apartment is so modest,
Tola! We are about to move into one better suited to our needs." I raised
my brows. What was there to say?

A few days later he invited me to inspect his new home located in the
aristocratic section of the capital. I stood at the door in astonishment. His
furniture had been imported from the most expensive house in Vienna.
Nijinsky had a desk of redwood which would have been imposing even in
America, where it is customary to impress one's visitors with imposing furniture. A Voltaire chair, into which one sank miles, flanked the desk on one
side; and the floor was hidden by Oriental rugs, exquisite in their subdued
colorings. Oils and tapestries in excellent taste concealed the walls.

I let myself into the big chair to recover. My head was in a whirl, for
where could Nijinsky raise the money that had been spent to furnish his
apartment like a royal palace? He grinned boyishly at my amazement, and
taking me by the hand led me into his room, where he flung open his wardrobe for my gaze. Dozens of suits for every occasion were hung in order.
There was everything any man could desire—boots, shoes, shirts, socks,

ties, fine underwear—everything, even the pajamas, bearing the mark of a famous Parisian house.

"Where did you get the fortune that is here?" I questioned with the right of years of friendship.

"Everything is simple, Tola," Vaslaw's voice was conciliatory. "Diaghilev is oragnizing a Ballet, you know, and he's proposed a five-year contract for me. The first year I'll draw sixty thousand rubles, and every year thereafter I shall have a raise of fifteen thousand. Don't imagine that I've no head on my shoulders! This is the time to take whatever Diaghilev can offer! Who knows what the future can offer? Who knows what the future holds for any of us? Just now, since he needs me badly, I have plenty!" He laughed, and then, struck by a vagrant thought: "But how about you? Can I share some of my good fortune with you?"

I refused. We went out for a walk, my brain reeling. I glanced at the man beside me, unable to realize that he, with his self-confidence, his wealth, and his palatial suite was the same Vaslaw Nijinsky who had been such an outcast that my friendship had meant nothing short of salvation during our schooldays.

Arriving at my house, he became once again the Vaslaw who had made our home his. He invited my mother and father and sister to celebrate an intimate housewarming with himself, Bronia, and Mother Nijinsky the next day, and my family accepted happily. He was like another son to Father and Mother.

Vaslaw met us at the door and ushered us to a table set with delicate glass, fragile china, and a rich silver service. With uncontrollable perversity, my mind flew back to that mournful celebration that had taken his last kopeck and ended without guests. My father looked at the luxury about him with patent misgivings. Not until we had eaten and Father was settled in a comfortable chair to smoke did he speak his thought, and then it was with all the polish and restrained pride of the old regime.

"You have done well, Vaslaw," he observed, "but I think you are too rich, now, for us. Perhaps too rich for yourself, but surely too rich for us!"

Shortly thereafter he pleaded illness and left. Mother, Nastia, and I stayed on with Mother Nijinsky, Bronia, and Vaslaw, doing our best to recapture the old friendliness despite Father's ultimatum, until the time came for Vaslaw and me to escort my mother and sister back to our house.

Vaslaw and I were free to seek diversion at the club, located in one of Prince Youssoupov's palaces, which had been turned over gratis to the artists of the Imperial Russian Ballet to use as they chose while the Prince defrayed its expenses.

It was only natural for me to take a place at the gaming tables and lose all I had. I turned to Nijinsky and requested a loan.

"I don't want to lend you money," he grumbled. "I'll give you a hundred rubles on condition that you spend whatever you win with me tonight—in the way I choose to spend it."

Lady Luck smiled, as she always did when Vaslaw backed me. In ten minutes I had five hundred rubles. It was my night! I reached forward to play again but Nijinsky's voice interrupted, "Enough, Tola!" He pulled out his watch and remarked that it was one o'clock in the morning as we left the club.

"I hate money won at cards," he began, "it isn't honest money. That's why I made you give me your word to help me dispose of it tonight. We are going to spend it on the beggars in the streets!"

I had visions of our progress down the boulevard, the two of us dressed like fashion plates, Vaslaw's hands blazing with diamonds, while we passed out largess to the flotsam and jetsam of the capital. I laughed until he proposed his plan. Then I was furious.

"You can't do it! I won't do it! You are crazy!" But Vaslaw was as stubborn as a stable goat.

"I will—and you will," he pronounced.

There was nothing to do but accompany him on one of the most fantastic excursions in our lives together. He had decided to go about St. Petersburg and collect the most degraded prostitutes in the city for the sole purpose of bringing some joy into their lives.

"We will bring them a few hours of happiness as innocent of taint as their childhood," said Vaslaw, "and perhaps more so, because I've heard that some of them had no childhood and never knew decent homes!"

I couldn't stop him. We strolled along Nevsky Prospekt to the arcade of the Café Andreyev, where the cheapest, most depraved women of St. Petersburg congregated after midnight to ply their trade while the respectable among the population walked on the opposite side of the street to avoid the insults and epithets bandied about noisily. We made for notorious restaurants.

Our lives were at stake in that quarter, where anyone might be murdered for less money than we had in our pockets, let alone the wealth that sparkled in the rings on Vaslaw's hands. An icy finger seemed to trace a line up my spine when I realized where his notion was leading us, but it was too late to turn back. More than a score of the painted creatures surrounded us. The rouge on their cheeks was brilliant even under the sickly lamplight. Their voices were husky with drink when they begged for cigarettes.

It was horrible to stand in their midst, but Vaslaw was adamant. Even when I whispered, "It isn't too late to call a cab and seek entertainment at the Cubat . . ." he shook his head. I tried once more: "How did this idea get into your head—you who have been used to cultured women all of your life! Have you no pride?"

"No! No!" he shouted passionately, fixing on the most frightful-looking derelict among women that haunted the unclean shadows of the arcade; then beckoning her to his side, he thrust a five-ruble note into her hand. She stared at it in disbelief, too overcome to smile, and Vaslaw spoke to her rapidly in Russian, "Call five or six of your best friends and tell them that they can make big money tonight!"

In less time than it takes to tell, half a dozen "beauties" from the half-world clustered around us.

Nijinsky hailed a cab for himself and me. Our guests screeched for other cabs and clambered in, two by two, cursing and shoving each other while they found places in the four cabs that followed ours. We stopped before the lowest of restaurants, where our guests would feel at ease, and entered it be-

tween two brutes who looked like Siberian bandits and greeted the women
with familiar and unsavory nicknames.

The sight of such abject misery and filth made me shiver, but Vaslaw
was intent upon playing host and his invitation rang above the hubbub filling
the sordid place, "Order anything and everything you want!"

A wild shriek greeted him. "Vodka! Vodka and pickles!" That was as
much as they dared expect. It marked the limit of their hopes.

There was nothing decent to offer them on the poverty-stricken menu,
but Vaslaw rose to that emergency. He delegated the Siberian bandits to
hunt up and down the section for caviar, cakes, snowy bread, wholesome
meats, luscious fruits, and good wines. When the tables were set, the
women forgot their benefactor—they forgot everything but the food. They
fell on it like a pack of starved wolves, tearing at chunks of steaming meat
with their bare hands while an accordionist wheezed out common tunes.
What a sight that was—with its pathos. . . .

Nijinsky and I sat watching. We couldn't eat. Everything was dirty. I
tried to get Vaslaw away, but his eyes were bottomless wells, and there was
in them a quality incomprehensible to me. He muttered something over
and over. I bent close to catch his words.

"Poor women! Poor women!" he was repeating.

Everything must end—even such a spectacle of degradation. The women
turned their attention to us as an expression of gratitude. I repulsed one, and
Nijinsky, leaping at her, caught the bottle in her fist just in time to save me
a smashed skull! His guests had indulged themselves with too much vodka
and started to strip. It was time to leave.

Four hundred rubles of my winnings remained. Two hundred dollars. It
was more than any one of them had hoped to set eyes on.

The woman I had refused burst into a stream of vitriolic language. "You
think you are fine gentlemen, you two!" she mocked. "I know your kind.
Once I dressed in silks and satins . . . and spent more money than you have
flung there! My father was General A—, my lover was Count X—, and
that is why I have a yellow ticket and you are too good to touch me!" The
names she mentioned were powerful, indeed.

"The money is to be divided among you equally," Vaslaw said, and sickened, we left them. Out on the street, the clean cold winds brought a new horror of what we had seen and heard. I turned to Vaslaw impulsively. "Why did you do it?" I begged, while the sounds of artificial hilarity drifted to us from the hole we had left.

He stood motionless when he answered very slowly: "I have been riding the crest of a wave, Tola—you cannot understand! I wanted to see with my own eyes how unhappy some are born to be! I wanted to experiment . . . to bring them a little happiness!"

He walked briskly for a few moments before he stopped and grasped my shoulder in a steely grip. "It has been too terrible for me, Tola! I shall never do it again! Swear that you will never repeat it to our friends!"

We went back to the theater the next day, and watched the splendid young bodies of our dancers spin in the figures of a dance, and the memory of those derelicts haunted us. Until now I have kept my word to Vaslaw, but this incident, alone, serves to show me better than anything else that, whatever of fame and wealth came to Vaslaw, he remained sensitive to the heartbreak and tragedy of others. His first success he celebrated in a pathetic attempt to brighten a few lives in St. Petersburg's slums. It was typical of him.

VIII

A SIBERIAN CROESUS

So QUICKLY had Nijinsky's fame spread over the Empire that the Imperial Theater of Moscow invited him to appear in a benefit performance with Kshessinskaya during the second year after his graduation. It was no more than logical that, since St. Petersburg was conquered, Nijinsky's art should subdue "the second capital" of Russia. Vaslaw invited me to accompany them, but Director Teliakovsky refused his sanction, and for the first time in my life I was unable to witness Vaslaw's triumph.

While Kshessinskaya's staff of servants was being stowed away in the train, scores of artists milled around our two stars, shouting good wishes and prayers that they might put the premiers of the rival theater to shame. Within a few days that hope was realized when our papers carried glowing accounts of an ovation that has taken its place in Moscow's theatrical history. The Muscovite press admitted the combination of Kshessinskaya and Nijinsky too overwhelming to brook denial and a revival of the ancient feud between St. Petersburg and Moscow.

While critics were lauding his genius, Nijinsky sent me his own account of his victory. "I enjoyed a pretty fair success," he wrote. "I have acquired more gifts—some rings, a dozen cigarette cases, and the usual presents. I am embarrassed by invitations to dinners and suppers tendered in such numbers that I don't know which to accept, and I have many floral tributes around me."

He ran on with the story of his visit to the Yar, a restaurant known from one end of Russia to the other for its Gypsy chorus and its excellent program of foreign artists. Tolstoy has effectively immortalized it. The letter closed with a brief description of the many Muscovites who had been presented to him and mentioned the name of Yarilov, "a Siberian millionaire who is twenty-two years old, whose money disappears like hot air in zero weather."

A day later, Nijinsky himself arrived back in St. Petersburg, bearing a case full of gifts, and half a dozen pieces of luggage which had been presented to him along with every conceivable memento that could have been given him. His own reaction was one of complete approval so far as Moscow was concerned.

The station was crammed with St. Petersburg notables and artists clamoring welcome to the first idols successful in winning acclaim from Moscow.

When I finally managed to make my way to Vaslaw, I discovered him accompanied by a round-faced, open-eyed boy whose sincerity was written all over his face. He looked precisely what he was, a good-natured Siberian baby, carefree and expansive, but a bit nervous and naïvely amazed at finding himself in company with the famous Nijinsky.

Vaslaw winked and presented me while Yarilov beamed admiration at Nijinsky and stood self-consciously staring down at me from his astonishing height. On an impulse he spoke when Vaslaw turned to greet other friends, "Mr. Bourman, Nijinsky tells me that you are his best friend! You are a lucky man! I should be honored if only he were my friend."

"Why not, Yarilov? Nijinsky needs every real friend he can find—and he's easy to know," I answered. With that Yarilov clapped his hands together after the manner of Russian peasants the world over.

"I will be his friend!" he bellowed like a bull on the steppes . . . and he kept his word.

He was the only son of the richest man in Siberia, who had made uncounted millions at Krasnoyarsk with a vodka factory, selling its output to the government. Yarilov had clustered a few dozen Siberian friends about him, and habitually entertained them in his apartment, the acme of luxury. Ostensibly a serious student at the university, Yarilov seemed incapable of anything like study, but enjoyed life by giving rein to his wild Tatar streak with no thought of restraint. He and his friends had money and spent it.

Their supply was never denied. Life was full of laughter and joy for them!

Mother and Father were delighted with Yarilov from the moment they set eyes on his round, fat face, ashine with good nature.

"He is so natural and unspoiled that his vast wealth is immaterial," Father declared. He visited us whenever the mood moved him, always loaded with presents for the whole family, effervescing with animal spirits, and thoroughly unable to appreciate the value of small portions. If he brought chocolates, it was at least ten pounds of the finest that he lugged in with him! If he sent flowers, there were never less than a hundred and fifty blooms to be distributed through the house!

Father scolded him. "You are mad! Why do you send so many chocolates and spend so much of your allowance? One pound would express as much, and you would have more for yourself!"

But Yarilov's hearty laugh would shatter our eardrums. "A pound! A pound! That is nothing! I'd be ashamed to come again," he'd protest. "If it spoils, throw it out, for I'll surely have another ten pounds to give to Madame Bourman when I return!"

Whenever Nijinsky danced, Yarilov saw to it that his idol was supplied with flowers. I shall never forget one massive piece he sent, so tall and so broad that it barely squeezed through the biggest stage entrance. Composed entirely of red roses woven into an intricate design centered by Vaslaw's initials, it created a sensation, for even the spendthrift Russians gaped at hundreds of long-stemmed roses in midwinter. That gesture probably cost Yarilov well over a thousand dollars, but he was as delighted as a baby with a new rattle over the success of his coup.

We knew the most side-splitting comedy would pall in comparison with Yarilov's entertainment, although if we refused an invitation, Yarilov, whose heart was as big as the earth and as sensitive as a child's, would weep openly. Great tears would stream down his ruddy round cheeks while he sobbed: "I know! You hate me because with all my money I'm nothing but a clumsy muzhik—and you—you are great artists!"

Only our acceptance would offer incontestable proof that we were his friends and stem his flood of tears; when we were too far on our way to change our minds, Yarilov would drag forth a handkerchief almost as big as a tent to dry his eyes, before he assumed his full responsibility as a host. And what a host!

Only those who have lived in Russia under the old regime—or perhaps only those who were born Russians—can understand the extravagant foibles that Russians indulged and the complete lack of common sense that prevailed when they staged entertainments. I know of a noble whose whim was to turn summer into winter and who spent thousands of rubles to cover an entire estate with sugar and salt in celebration of his wife's birthday!

What made us do things—everything and anything—on a grand scale? It is beyond comprehension, unless the tremendous expanse of our country prohibits the possibility of thinking in terms of self-limitation. We have never been able to understand the preference for a small house when a palace was available. Even our music is never merely light—it is either wildly abandoned or permeated with heart-tearing emotion.

Our love is the same. We cannot pretend. We will either give everything in us or we will hate with an intensity damning both to ourselves and to the object of our hate. There is no compromise. What we feel, we must express without conventional restrictions. The best proof of this is to be found in Russia, where the nation that once bent in utter allegiance to absolute autocracy is today bowing with profound devotion at the shrine of absolute Communism.

These incidents which may sound unbelievable to Anglo-Saxon ears, I solemnly vow are the ungarnished truth, for I have learned a little of restraint in my twenty years of travel in purely Occidental civilizations. Because I am certain of being accused of fabrication, I have purposely understated many occurrences for the sake of those who have never been able to penetrate beneath the veneer of Russia.

Yarilov was a true Tataric Russian, and Nijinsky and I have shared his bounty as Russians always did. We ate and drank with the same grand disregard for quantity that typified our host.

The Restaurant Samarkand and Villa Rodé were our favorite resorts. At the Samarkand, a Gypsy orchestra lilted its vivacious songs of love and gaiety to the noblest and wealthiest in St. Petersburg.

Yarilov's prodigality bought the management's loyalty for our bluff host, who engaged the biggest dining room for his parties. The Gypsies had only to catch a glimpse of him, or the echo of his blustering, to burst into a spirited tune improvised around his name, spurred to frenzied whirling about him by his childish pleasure in their praise.

Champagne flowed more freely than water at our tables, for Yarilov never ordered less than twelve bottles at a time, insisting upon the best that gold could buy. One order followed another with such rapidity that there was enough wine around us to supply a regiment before we had been at the Samarkand more than fifteen minutes. Our course was easy to follow through the dining rooms and corridors, blazed as it was by scores of empty bottles.

Sometimes our Siberian fell so madly in love with an orchestra that nothing would do but it must follow us from restaurant to restaurant while Yarilov silenced managements and clienteles alike with his inexhaustible rubles. Once he imported the entire Gypsy chorus from the Yar in Moscow and subsidized it in St. Petersburg for a week, insisting upon carrying it everywhere with our party.

On another occasion, he grew bored with the "sameness" of his amusements and started up from the depths of melancholy with a brilliant idea.

"Who wants to take a bath in champagne?" he thundered.

"I do!" a beautiful French girl from the Aquarium night club responded.

Yarilov beat his huge palms together delightedly for a moment before he discovered there was no tub available.

"No tub?" Yarilov's eyes crackled with furious little flames that stabbed into the bulging orbs of the manager. "Then get one!"

For half an hour the management bartered with the lord of the nearest manor for the purchase of his bathtub. How the baron was ever persuaded that the head waiter was not an escaped lunatic, Heaven alone may reveal. The Baron must have been convinced, for the head waiter arrived in due course nearly buried under a huge tub molded on true Russian proportions.

Yarilov solemnly inspected it before he helped the waiter heave it onto the center of our table, begging us to help fill it with champagne—at seven and a half dollars a bottle!

When the French damsel climbed in with Yarilov's assistance and emerged none the worse, he presented her with a thousand-ruble note and promptly forgot the incident!

It wasn't uncommon to discover that the Gypsies, the champagne, and the music were boring us. That was the signal for Yarilov to storm around until one of us thought up a scheme insane enough to intrigue interest.

We once systematically smashed all the candelabra and mirrors in the Samarkand, and Yarilov paid the bill, excitedly rushing after us to the Villa Rodé and other places which we demolished with equal thoroughness. We were happy and Yarilov was content! He paid the costs!

Occasionally oils and tapestries caught our eyes. Yarilov promptly supplied us with revolvers, offering prizes for the best marksmen and replacing the damaged portraits with new objets d'art!

Every one of Yarilov's extravagances was committed in the hope of amusing Nijinsky. Yarilov once discerned the suggestion of satiation on Vaslaw's face. That was enough. He decided that Vaslaw was tired of looking at the Gypsies, and ordered the latter ranged before him.

"You would look much better as Negroes," he observed. "I will give one hundred rubles to everyone who will let me work my magic transformation!" Every Gypsy stepped forward, and we became intent on a concoction of coffee that was used to stain the whole chorus. Still Yarilov was discontented with Nijinsky's reaction. He covered the waiter's face with a fiery mustard paste, and paid him well for the livid scarlet burn that resulted! It was money well spent. Nijinsky had smiled!! Our Siberian baby gurgled with pleasure.

After every party, he drove us home in sleighs and troikas,[1] standing and swaying dangerously while we dashed over the snow, and sending his voice trumpeting against the wind with his declaration that he hated "gasoline carts."

[1] Sleighs drawn by three horses.

"Give me a good horse . . . and you can have my cars!" he exulted, his great fur hat cocked over one ear.

The next day bills would roll in from every side. I have seen Yarilov charged for pianos, a dozen mirrors, glassware, champagne by the case— every conceivable item—most of them unquestionably added on by a management eager to make goodly profits for itself. That was easily enough accomplished, since Yarilov never spared a glance at the amounts. He simply signed the bills and tossed rolls of notes after each one, howling with mirth at his receding supply of cash!

Another of his pranks was played on one of the many islands near St. Petersburg, where the Krestovsky Restaurant was located. The owners sponsored a cabaret featuring famous European artists, presenting their performances in a great hall where only noble blood or a limitless fortune could gain admittance. Nijinsky asked Yarilov to control himself as we entered. "Kolia," begged Nijinsky, "forget you are a Siberian and be a gentleman for once!"

Yarilov promised, sheepish because his idol had reproached him. We took places at front tables while a finely staged presentation was in progress. Our Siberian sat like a strait-laced general. Everything went well except that Yarilov's voice rumbled like a heavy gun and its booming disturbed our neighbors. They tried to silence him. We tried to dam his thunderous protestations of innocence.

"What am I doing? Why should I stay as silent as a mummy?" cried Yarilov like a bull-calf wailing over the plains.

The truth of the matter dawned on us. Yarilov simply did not know how to lower his voice! The head waiter appeared with a subservient request for the gentleman to speak in a more subdued tone. In vain. Yarilov with the voice of Jove assured him that he was being natural and no more!

A policeman arrived on the scene with an ultimatum: "Either you stop your loud talking, or I'll arrest you and your whole company!" That was effective, since Yarilov was overcome by the fear of involving Vaslaw in difficulties. He called for the owner, whom he addressed by name.

"Mr. Yalishev, they have complained that I am noisy," he fretted, "and

I have done nothing but act like a gentleman. Send them home and I will pay you for your loss. I want to enjoy the program!"

Yalishev was indignant. He pointed out some of the dominating personalities in the government present and flatly refused Yarilov's request. It was too much for our ungovernable Tatar. He flew into a rage, shaking his fists at the elegant assembly, roaring imprecations at them while we edged him towards the door. A moment more and we should have succeeded, but in that instant Yarilov broke from us and shouted the length of the hall at Mr. Yalishev, superciliously watching our undignified exit.

"All right!" lustily proclaimed our unquenchable host. "You want them to stay here, do you, Yalishev? I'll fix it so they'll stay here until you long to throw them out! They'll stay!"

Yalishev smiled tolerantly. He had accepted the money for our bill before the storm broke. The spectacle of an insane Tatar threatening Russia's most powerful officers was merely amusing. What could he do? Yalishev's smile broadened, as Nijinsky thrust Yarilov through the door.

It was shortly after four in the morning when we stood outside the Krestovsky with a freezing wind biting into our faces. It was bitterly cold. Yarilov nodded his head and grinned, beckoning a coachman over.

"See here, my man," he said. "Take a good look at that line of taxis, sleighs, and troikas waiting for hire. Is any private carriage there?"

The man shook his head.

"Good! Tell every one of them that ten rubles are guaranteed every driver who follows my troikas in to St. Petersburg. It's between eight and ten miles to the city, and we are going to travel slowly. No one must pass us, and no one can accept a fare and be sure of my ten rubles. Tell them!"

Fully two hundred carriages waited for hire, since the Krestovsky was a restaurant large enough to accommodate a legion! As we stared behind us, every last vehicle swung into line until a long queue wound after us losing itself in the half-darkness before dawn.

When we entered Kamennoostrovsky Prospekt, I stood up to survey our cavalcade. It was no longer dark, yet I couldn't sight the end of the procession! Unquestionably every coachman along the ten-mile drive had faithfully followed for the sake of ten rubles!

Yarilov stamped around the capital until the banks opened, and then he filled my pockets and Nijinsky's, commandeering us as cashiers to pay off his army of drivers. All St. Petersburg gaped at the spectacle we made, Nijinsky and I doing our best to keep the men from returning for double wages while Yarilov, careless of being cheated, blustered cheerfully at the crowds surrounding us.

The next day we reaped bountifully! The whole story was printed in every St. Petersburg paper along with our names; the theater was unpleasantly stern about the scandal we had created; the nobles were not at all amused at their own discomfort, for they had had to stay at the restaurant until nearly noon before they could engage any kind of transportation!

Nijinsky and I were reprimanded, to Yarilov's dismay. He never again permitted himself to indulge his ungovernable temper when we were with him, but put himself in our hands until we had forced him to assimilate enough culture to prevent any more unreined Tataric impulses. We were forced to forget that we were Russians, to become gentlemen first!

IX

CALIPH FOR AN HOUR

GAMING was rife in the capital, a circumstance accounted for by the government policy of encouraging entertainment for a nation on the brink of revolution too frequently for comfort. Whenever the specter of dissatisfaction showed itself in the mass mind, a fresh issue of gambling permits flooded Russia in the hope of deflecting the stream of ambition into channels less dangerous to stability.

Such a period gave rise to the Elyseïév, a resort owned by Russia's fruit king. One hundred tables were centers of play that ranged in stakes from one ruble to heights unlimited. No matter how high the bet, the bank promptly covered it, offering a paradise to those, like myself, who found more excitement in the fall of a card than in the suspense of a race. Nijinsky, long since inured to more sophisticated pleasures than were to be found in his own living room, was no more averse to trying his luck than I, and with increasing regularity we made for the Elyseïév, keeping our destination from Mother Nijinsky and Bronia by common consent.

Vaslaw was thrilled by the fate that threw ten or twenty rubles into his pockets, and if he lost he simply stopped playing. That happy faculty was not mine. If I lost, I had more to win back, and if fortune was with me— who knew? That might be the time destiny marked for me to break the bank! In any case, I played on!

Vaslaw would stand watching me, shaking his head at my losses, smiling at my gains, consistently disapproving. On the day in question, I had lost all I possessed. As usual I asked him for a loan, expecting the terse refusal that was habitual. He was in a surprisingly tolerant mood.

"Here's twenty-five rubles," he observed, a hopeful twinkle in his eye. "You have it with a wish for real luck that comes from the bottom of my heart. Play, Tola, and if you win, I'll say no more, but if you lose, you do so with the understanding that never again, so long as I live, will I gamble with you!"

He had discerned my subtle cultivation of the gambler's urge within him. It was his way of telling me that he knew. Poor Vaslaw! All the years that I knew him, he did his best to break the fascination of the tables that had been fostered in me since the two of us were encouraged by a fellow student to gamble for pocket money.

Makao was the favorite game at Elyseiëv's resort. It was fast—faster than any other card game.

"I'll leave the twenty-five rubles to double itself three times. If I win, then luck is with me, not you!" I laughed, throwing my money onto the table while I spoke. Before my words were done, I had two hundred rubles to my credit, and Vaslaw was grinning waggishly.

I paid back his twenty-five rubles, once more ready to play. We walked from table to table as my winnings mounted and I became eligible to play for higher stakes. Placing my money more cautiously than ever, I found rubles showering into my hands with every turn of the card, though we could play only from the side, since every place at the tables was taken.

"A place at the gold table! A place at the gold table!"

The croupier was announcing a vacancy at the biggest table in play. That meant at least a hundred rubles for the bank, and nothing under five rubles on every card. Frantically I counted my money. More than enough! I looked at Vaslaw, uncertain of his attitude, but he met my glance with a nod.

"Better sit down, Tola! Today is your day!" he said.

One word of encouragement was enough. Before he could change his mind, I slid into my place with seven older men, one a long-whiskered admiral, another a notorious gambler, all of them smiling tolerantly at my youth. One old reprobate leaned over with a sneer twisting his mouth. "Baby-boy, can you shuffle the cards?" he cackled.

Incensed, I bided my time until my turn came to set the pace. Nijinsky was with me. I felt his hand clap my shoulder when he dropped a hundred rubles into my bank.

"I'll play with you, half and half," he remarked. Ten rubles, fifteen! I lost on the first card both times. Nijinsky's money was gone. I had begun on my own. I increased my bank. Every card fell my way! Luck had changed! Fortune was coming in on a flood tide!

Nijinsky was becoming nervous. He tried to distract my attention, but at the tables I was another man, taking either good luck or terrific losses with a calm exterior. Now our table was the focus of interest. Sensing Nijinsky's mounting worry, I kept my post, sure that his presence brought me favor with the gods.

Thousands of rubles were stacked before me and still I won! Inside, an inferno of excitement bubbled. Outwardly, I was master of myself. I played like the demon Nijinsky was when he danced. Vaslaw knew me so well! He realized, too late, that if I broke the bank, I was ruined . . . that the tables would shackle me more firmly than steel.

His decision was made. He staked our whole friendship to break my luck before it swept me into complete victory.

"Enough, Tola!" he commanded, but I ignored him.

"Stop, you devil!" he cried in despair. "Stop or I'll play against you! Do you hear? *I'll play against my best friend!*"

That cut through my concentration on the business before me. If Nijinsky played against me—he couldn't! I spared him a sharp glance and continued, undeterred.

There was no time to lose. In a few moments, I'd be too far towards breaking the bank to let the fires of Hades stop me! Impulsively, Nijinsky threw a hundred-ruble note against me. Only a hundred rubles, but for the first time my run broke! I raised my head and stared into his face, drawn and terribly intent.

"Will you stop!" asked his eyes.

"I will not!" replied mine.

He laid two hundred rubles against me and that time the other gamblers doubled their stakes. I lost, as I knew I would. An emptiness filled me. One more play, I promised myself. A loss, and I'd stop . . . a win, and I couldn't!

Nijinsky's eyes were black holes burnt into his head, pits of fury that swallowed my defiance. He was willing me with every atom of strength in him, with every fragment of power that could be focused against me through that stubborn brain of his. *"Lose, Tola, lose!"* he was commanding.

I felt his thought like a tangible thing! I lost!

My great pile of gold had melted into a miserable heap, not more than a fifth of what it had been. More than a hundred thousand rubles had been stacked at my place before Vaslaw turned against me. I stood up.

"Who wants the bank?" my voice was low and cold.

Behind me, a waiter swooped forward and swept my winnings into a cloth, following me into the restaurant. Nijinsky walked beside me in silence, but there were plenty of others to speak to me. Some chided me for playing after my luck had changed, others begged a loan "for luck." That I gave. There is honor among the men whose lives are spent hanging over a pack of cards, in that when they win they pay back their borrowings, but if they lose, not one will be reminded of the loan.

My winnings were thrown before me in the restaurant, and after distributing "luck largess" I counted it. There was a miscellany of notes and gold —in all well over eighteen thousand rubles. Eighteen thousand rubles in a few hours—and my salary was six hundred rubles a *year!*

The house changed my winnings into five-hundred and one-hundred ruble notes, and I celebrated by treating the gamblers to a dinner. My own appetite was gone. I sat, weak and shaken by the strain I had been under, and while my guests laughed and drank and ate huge servings, I drank glass after glass of cold water!

Vaslaw remained immovable, like a graven image, neither looking at me nor speaking. I had never seen him so implacable.

"This money isn't mine, Vaslaw. It's ours. You backed my first bank and brought me luck!" I offered.

"It's your money. I won seven hundred rubles from you myself! That's all I want!" No compromise could be looked for from a Nijinsky frozen with displeasure because I had forced him to use friendship against itself.

"At least help me to spend it," I begged.

"Why should I?" and there was nothing but indifference in his tone.

One tremendous regret overshadows the memory of my deportment. My father needed money desperately, but he never had a kopeck of my winnings. He had disapproved of Vaslaw, and I was too bitter to share my fortune with him!

Vaslaw, still as talkative as a sphinx, accompanied me to a florist's where I ordered flowers for the six or seven girls I danced with, choosing the most beautiful roses available for Varvotchka, then making straight for her home where I implored her to take my money and save it for me. If she only had! —but she sent me off to a bank with it.

The next day I went to Vassiliev and did the only smart thing to my credit. I paid my bill! Then I ordered suits, boots, shoes, and costumes, paying for them in advance.

Vassiliev stared thunderstruck. "Mr. Bourman, is anything wrong? You are not ill? Your head—it hasn't been struck? You know I have always trusted you." The poor man was unable to believe that I was sane. I had always paid him ten or fifteen rubles a month from the days I was in school. He had never before seen real money, and plenty of it, from me!

Nijinsky was a few days in readjusting himself after the scene at the Elyseïëv, so keenly had he been hurt by my refusal to listen to him. Finally, peace was established between us when, for the first time in my life, I asked him a personal favor.

"Vaslaw, this time *I* have money. Give me two weeks of your time," I asked.

"Two weeks? Great! What shall we do?" he demanded, and for a fortnight I showed him.

We were surrounded by carefree souls, while I flung money far and wide through St. Petersburg's restaurants. For once I was entertaining the girls I admired in company with men I had known as affluent friends, and I was no longer a guest. I was the host!

After rehearsal, I went to the club daily, Nijinsky faithfully trailing me and standing by while I played. My lesson seemed to have been learned, for if I won a few hundred rubles, I was satisfied, but if I lost up to a hundred rubles, I left at once.

Vaslaw was happy. He thumped me on the back whenever I rose from the table, congratulating me. "I thought you were weak, but you're not! It's good to have a friend with a will of iron. You can leave the tables like a real man!" I expanded under his unfamiliar praise until I felt like a millionaire, not because I had money, but because I was a man in the eyes of my best friend.

Vaslaw broached wise counsel, beginning tactfully. "Your father is looking worried these days, Tola. He hasn't much money and you could give him a hundred rubles, or better still a thousand rubles, without missing it. That would make him happy."

"I know what is best!" I snapped, and Nijinsky lapsed into silence. The spectacle of the man trying to help my father who had, by insinuation, forbidden our home to him, was humiliating. It served to increase my bitterness against my father whose formal attitude was responsible for Vaslaw's feeling unwelcome in our home. My father's stubbornness rankled.

It had been tacitly understood that Vaslaw was to accompany me whenever I sought the gaming resorts, but the day inevitably dawned when I sought the club without him and felt the old fever at work in my blood. My five hundred rubles went in a twinkling. I drew a thousand more from the bank—then three thousand! By five o'clock, I was without a kopeck of my fortune.

Guilty with the knowledge of a broken promise, I sought Vaslaw. He stared at me without recognition for several minutes, as though he were trying to place me as someone he had seen before. Suddenly he realized my identity.

"Tola, what have you done to yourself?" he exclaimed. What, indeed? My cheeks were sunken. My body trembled in every limb. My teeth chattered audibly. The strain of losing steadily had transformed me into a shattered wreck. Too late, I appreciated the friendship of the man before me, who had done everything in his power to save me from myself. He surveyed me with disgust, anger sweeping over him, sharpening his eyes until they were like polished flint.

He spoke, and his voice was like steel scraping steel. "You broke your word. You vowed that you wouldn't go to the club without me. You have your lesson—which is just."

He had delivered his judgment, and his voice lost its hardness when he added, "Oh, Tola—your poor fortune. I'm sorry—so sorry . . . ."

I lost what few wits I had left then, and like a madman, I begged him for three hundred rubles. It was a fatal mistake, for he laughed at me.

"Why should you win with three hundred rubles when you couldn't win with the thousands you lost?" My lesson was so short lived that I cursed him for those words. It was a month before I spoke to him again.

Gambling was never permitted to interfere with my work. My lessons went on and refilled my empty pockets with ten-ruble notes instead of hundred-ruble denominations, but far-reaching was the change in Nijinsky's life that month—a change that determined the course of his whole life.

Two agreements were made. One assured him of Kshessinskaya as his permanent partner in the Russian Ballet, and the other was a contract which he signed with Diaghilev.

"Nijinsky has finally signed on with the Silver Beaver," they told me. I had thought his contract already a fact, but I waited until I saw him, and we spoke as though I had never broken faith with him.

"I hear that you have just signed with Diaghilev," I said.

"It is true, I signed a few days ago," he replied.

"A few days ago"—my mind was prone to leap to conclusions. I thought of the story he told me about having received a twenty-five thousand ruble advance from Diaghilev weeks back to furnish his luxurious suite. I thought of the rugs which alone must have taken most of his twenty-five thousand rubles. There were many things to think of, but I never questioned Nijinsky. Vaslaw swore that Diaghilev voluntarily provided the cash with the promise of a contract. Perhaps he did. I never knew, and I felt that when I broke my word to Vaslaw I sacrificed the right to expect his confidence.

X

FOREIGN ACCLAIM

Every day brought news of new contracts concluded with Diaghilev. Fokine had signed up as ballet master and was rehearsing the pick of the Imperial theater with feverish haste. Diaghilev's Ballet Russe was no longer a dream. It was an established fact, assured by performances scheduled in Monte Carlo, Rome, Paris, and London during the two months' season planned by the Silver Beaver before he launched his more ambitious itineraries. Other artists might rejoice over their good fortune, but inevitably I could not. That was the price decreed for my "entrepreneur" insult.

Time and again, Nijinsky offered to serve as mediator between Diaghilev and me—only to be answered by my sullen "No!" The whole company rejoiced in its opportunity to see new countries and new capitals, while reports of Pavlowa's successes served to waken many with dreams of foreign conquest.

I recalled how Pavlowa had entranced us with her descriptions of strange lands and unfamiliar customs, of theatrical traditions that were unbelievable, of gala receptions that taxed our credence. Pavlowa had the trick of weaving tales that traversed vast space-gulfs on the wings of fantasy, without depending on exaggerations for her effects. It was going to be a high price I paid for my clumsy tongue—a price increased when I saw Nijinsky's preparations to explore far-off countries.

Pavlowa had said: "'Oh, my friends! I know in my own heart how you dream of conquering millions with your art, for I have had such dreams. They do not come true. That is the sad reality I have discovered. There is only money to be had in Europe and America. Only money, while your soul hungers for appreciation and your body is worked like a machine! The world has taken gold, not art, for its God!"

Rumor reached me that Diaghilev considered carrying his Ballet to the United States, and again Pavlowa's words leaped into my consciousness.

"Europe hasn't our appreciation," she had reminisced, "but it is paradise in comparison wth the United States. Believe me, my friends, the United States of America is nothing more than one great factory. There I was constantly asked, 'Where will you work next week?' and I laughed. Can you imagine the culture of a nation that would ask me of 'work' when I was going to *dance?* That is all Americans can understand. What art they have is 'work'!"

We had called her "liar" for her insistence that in America one gave both matinee and evening performances every day but Sunday, having to appear for a matinee in one city, and an evening performance in another, perhaps fifty miles distant. Either Pavlowa was lying, or the United States was a madhouse. There were no two ways about it from an artist's viewpoint!— And now, perhaps Nijinsky would have a chance to discover the truth of Pavlowa's stories for himself.

Pavlowa had ridiculed the two or three appearances required of her in Russia. As the curtain fell, ending her Russian career, she had broken down before us all and wept heartbrokenly.

"Goodbye, my Russians who love art—goodbye," she sobbed. "I am going back to America, not to dance, but to *work* for the money that will make my 'rainy days' comfortable!"

Her bow had been made with undignified flutterings and kiss-blowing, such as were expected in the United States, and her farewells had been blighted by knifelike criticisms from an outraged press which declared, "Americanisms have ruined one of Russia's greatest artists."

Pavlowa's departure had been tragic because of immaturities acquired in the United States. I prayed devoutly that if the gossip of a transatlantic voyage was well founded, and Nijinsky destined to be hailed by America, that Americans would at least spare him his art.

With mingled joy and despair, I stood on the station platform watching his train pull out, carrying him into a foreign career I might not share. St. Petersburg was as hollow as an empty rain barrel. For the first time in my life, I felt isolation, loneliness. There was not another human being with the breath of life in him who could share my follies and my sorrows as Vaslaw did. None other could proffer the camaraderie and loyalty that he had given freely—and I had only myself to blame for my undoing. There was no comfort in the thought.

Nothing assuaged the weariness and bleakness that possessed me as completely as the half-barren northern provinces to which I fled, self-exiled for the summer, unable to endure St. Petersburg with its reminders of the follies responsible for depriving me of a career with Diaghilev. Letters from Vaslaw were forwarded, every one of them pulsing with enthusiasm, while newspapers, ablaze with headlines, reached me with increasing proof of a world gone crazy over Nijinsky and the Ballet Russe.

Paris had greeted Nijinsky with an ovation! He was in London, where he had played a coronation performance for King George V, Nijinsky wrote. "London Conquered by Nijinsky's Art!" the press proclaimed.

After an infinity of waitng, Nijinsky returned to the capital, bearing expensive gifts of shirts, ties, and similar trappings for me from London's smartest tailors. He related to me the visit of a representative who had expressed the King's pleasure in his genius. He recounted the experience of the company, plunged into despair because the royal family had proffered no gifts, until it was explained that such was not the custom of English royalty. Vaslaw had been introduced to the highest London society and had dined at the most noble homes! In the flush of his first international success, he remained as natural as he had been when the applause of St. Petersburg alone rang in his ears during student days.

"The Convent Garden presentation reminded me of the command performance at the Hermitage," he remarked; "there was a royal audience that night, and it was much the same, except"—his eyes sparkled—"there were no gold knives and forks to hide in our pockets, and this is the best I could do for a souvenir!" He handed me a program printed in gold letters upon fine silk which had brought five pounds, chuckling, "Imagine the jealousy of other companies touring the Continent when they heard of the King's choice of Diaghilev's Ballet Russe for his coronation performance!" Then followed a glowing account of thousands of beautiful English girls who mobbed the stage door for his autograph after the show. Nijinsky grew more serious. He had had some purpose behind all his enthusiasm, then.

"Diaghilev has signed up scores of artists for next year, Tola," he said, his brown eyes boring their way into mine. "At the end of next year, I'll join his Ballet for good, but for this season—I have decided to stay at the Imperial theater."

"That's fine," said I skeptically, "except that the Imperial theaters will never give you permission to leave before your four years' service in the Ballet is over and your obligation to the school is discharged!" The reference was to a government regulation decreeing at least four years of dancing in the Imperial Russian Ballet in return for the sponsorship of the royal court for our seven or eight years of training at the school.

Vaslaw narrowed his eyes into thin slits, half-concealing his defiance. "I'll ask for no permission! They don't think much of me, you'll see, they'll fire me!"

"Fire you, idiot?" I exploded, glaring at him as I would at a man unbalanced. "You *are* perfectly crazy! How can you expect the Imperial theaters to fire the greatest dancer they have ever developed? Be sensible!"

"I am, Tola, that's the funny part of it!" He laughed, and I was too stupid to grasp the significance of his words.

XI

DISGRACE IN RUSSIA

$\mathbb{F}$ ROM the opening day of the season, Nijinsky practiced harder than ever, striving for increased elevation, concentrating on technique until every tiniest muscle was instantaneously responsive to his will, and his body perfectly coordinated. A few weeks fled by before it penetrated my consciousness that Nijinsky was no longer my friend. He was a man apart, barely speaking to artists who had once been his intimates. Where he had been humble, if not subservient, he became arrogant, lording himself on stage and off, until he succeeded in raising an insurmountable barrier around himself.

A fortnight or more might pass with scarcely half a dozen words between us. Where once we had shared hopes and fears, confiding loves and hates to each other with naïve trust, we became casual acquaintances. Nijinsky had passed his students on to me so rapidly that I was unable to teach half of them and perforce recommended them to fellow artists. Even then, there was little relief from the steady stream of lessons that followed on the heels of one another. Most of my profits were left in my clubs as usual, but Nijinsky no longer troubled himself over my welfare.

On rare occasions, when we attended parties in company with our old friends, Nijinsky's change of front became more understandable and, although it first precipitated my condemnation, it later served as a wellspring of pity for his predicament. If he had changed, he had not been alone. Everyone treated him as a soul apart. He was no longer a friend. Successes scored in Monte Carlo, Paris, and London had invested him with the air of a celebrity deferred to on every hand until the ease of an involuntary relationship became unnatural. Friendship was replaced by pride in a consciousness that Nijinsky might have been a comrade in the past, but he was, in the present at least, an international celebrity! He was universally treated as such.

Again and again he approached me with requests to play for him while he practiced, but I countered with superficial excuses that cut him to the quick. I suffered humiliation as well. It seemed farcical to play for a man who gave himself airs over triumphs that were only to be accepted since no one may depend on the whims of a multitude. No one knew his tempos, his dances, and the tricky details of his accompaniments as I did, a fact that accounts for his impotent rages against his pianists. It doesn't take a great musician to accompany a dancer, but it does take one with a sense of rhythm peculiarly responsive to the "feel" of the dance. More than one ballet has been killed by the greatest living conductors and musicians when some among them failed to rejoin with the one requisite of dance-accompanists—a sixth sense of rhythm. Nijinsky rapidly acquired a reputation for reckless "temperament" when news of his outbursts against his pianist began to trickle into the world. Vaslaw was helpless without an accompanist capable of the swift transitions of tempo imperative for successful dancing.

Nijinsky's boundless ego discovered its Waterloo in his hapless pianist and hauled down its fatal pride. He called me to him, with an infinitesimal trace of condescension in his manner, which, obviously, he tried to conceal.

"Anatole, you have been my best friend." I noted the use of the past tense silently and waited for him to continue. "Will you do me one favor—just one? I know, in spite of everything, that you want me to succeed. Give me a chance to triumph by playing my accompaniments properly just once before I dance at the Marinsky!"

Was it a command? I hesitated, and he rushed on: "You know that the right accompaniment is the greatest inspiration any dancer can have. I am lost! You know it! I can't dance as a dancer should, with my feet trying to keep up to the senseless drumming of a man so wrapped up in his music that he has no time for its adaptation! My fame—my whole career—is in your hands. I must have it! Give it to me! It is the last time I shall ever ask!"

"Why the last time?" I parried, startled by his intensity.

He simply shook his head. "I can't tell you, Tola. You will witness the reason and then you will know!" An air of discouragement settled over him like a black shroud. "Fame is a terrible thing, Tola!" His voice trembled. "It has driven me among people—people who stare—people who smile—people who clap their hands together—people who flatter me—strangers who cut me to pieces with demands on my time, on my art—crowds who have snatched away everything I care about—acquaintances who have deprived me of friends whom I could trust! That is fame, Tola!"

Sharper than acid was his tone when he glanced at me. "Fame and people have warped me until I don't know myself or my friends—even you are different! Help me, Tola, to be myself. Don't change because a brainless mob deafens me. Those same mobs are bent on giving me more fame. They'll grow and grow! It is horrible! Can't you see?—I have no sweetheart—I have no friend—I have no one. Sometimes I think it will drive me to madness, Tola! To madness where I can forget everything! But no—instead, I must forget everyone I loved and all I treasured in the success that has robbed me of everything. That is how I must forget! That is the price for fame!"

My heart ached for the man. The tragedy of trailing greatness bit deeply into my consciousness. There stood Vaslaw Nijinsky, my best friend, uncertain of a "favor" that had been part of an accepted routine less than a year ago. He was stripped of every pretense, naked in soul, when he implored the right to forget his dreams of content in a success already proven a mockery.

He interpreted my thoughtfulness as hesitation.

"Anatole, I think you understand how I feel—I have told you the truth no one else would believe. Can't *you* understand how alone I feel—and why I want you to play for me?"

"Of course—of course, I will play for you, Vaslaw!" I hastened to reassure him, sitting down to the piano and running my hands over the keys while he took his position, then following him without a signal, now increasing the tempo, now decreasing it, always conscious that Vaslaw was right.

Fame was a terrific testing time during which character and friendship, loyalty and faith might grow old and ready for discard. It was a crucible blazing with white heat that either discovered a man's grossness or refined his impulses and ideals until they were able to withstand the dazzling spotlight of public acclaim which left so little privacy for personal realization.

Vaslaw worked until the sweat ran off his body in rivulets. He smiled to himself all the time he practiced, certain that we would be friends again, while I played on, compassionate but incapable of tearing down the barrier his fame had thrust between us.

We practiced an hour and a half without interruption. He was so human, that lonely Vaslaw, that I spared him the humiliation of asking me to play for him. I was ready for his rehearsals when he came, and I played his music as long as he wanted it.

On the day destined to be his last as soloist at the Marinsky, he signaled abruptly. Pleading fatigue, he draped his towel around his neck and strolled over to me. He was dripping with perspiration, but it made no difference. He flung an arm across my shoulders.

"I'm sorry, Bourman, that you won't bring yourself to make peace with Diaghilev. Why not see him and apologize for your insult?" His nonchalant pose infurated me.

"I'd kill myself before I'd ask a favor of him! Besides, what difference does it make to you? I'm no longer your friend. Why concern yourself with my affairs now?" I challenged. "Here I am happy—with plenty of good friends, plenty of cultured students, and enough money for my needs. What can I want with Diaghilev? He can't pay me as much as I make here where at least I can enjoy my friends in peace!" Instantly I perceived that Vaslaw had cringed at the cut I had delivered. I tried conciliatory explanations. "Can't you see, Vaslaw? If I were without money, that would be one thing—but I'm not. Everyone welcomes me, even if I must wear a false name and let them call me 'Kouchinsky' to satisfy family pride—everyone knows I'm a 'Bourman' anyway. I've ruined my life with gambling, and my career is eaten up by a single insult; but if I lost pupils, money, friends, everything I possess—still I wouldn't apologize to the Silver Beaver!"

Nijinsky listened without comment.

I plunged on: "Maybe it is you who are making the mistake! Perhaps Diaghilev will be done in a year or two and then where will you be? I can stay with the Imperial Ballet twenty years to gain both pension and honor for my choice. Diaghilev will never send for me, and I'll never seek him out voluntarily. Let's have an end to this business and forget it, Vaslaw!"

The ballet *Giselle* was to be presented that night. Nijinsky as the premier male dancer and Karsavina, the première ballerina, as his partner. Together they were superb. Only two ballerinas in the world could do justice to *Giselle*, Pavlowa and Karsavina. One of the crowning triumphs of Pavlowa's repertoire, it brought Karsavina similar glory. It was universally adored. Nijinsky was the Prince—a royal and majestic Prince whose feather-lightness added subtle magic to the presentation. I was one of a group appearing only in the first act.

Without a peer in all the Empire, Nijinsky's interpretation of the first role had stirred interest in the Winter Palace. The Tsar and Tsarina with the royal family and staff had announced their intention of witnessing the superb genius of Nijinsky and Kassavina. The stage was set for Nijinsky's downfall!

During the first intermission, I donned my full-dress suit for a promenade in the foyer where, unexpectedly, I met Prince Lvov and Diaghilev. After brief greetings, both detained me with a series of questions. How was Vaslaw? Did he appear nervous? Excited?

"Of course not! Why should he?" I countered.

Diaghilev's chuckle was malignant. "Don't fence, Bourman! Of course you know why, and what is going to happen tonight!"

"Tonight? What's going to happen tonight?" They had caught me off guard and I had given them full evidence of my ignorance. The quality of their laughter sent me dashing backstage to Nijinsky. Two dressers were busy with his costumes when I ran in without knocking, a thing that I hadn't done for months.

I made a funnel of my hands and whispered into his ear, "Vaslaw! What are you going to do tonight? Diaghilev and Prince Lvov warned me of a big surprise. Tell me—what is it?

He ignored my attempt at secrecy and spoke aloud.

"They were fooling you, imbecile! Nothing is going to happen—except that I shall dance as I have never danced before! The whole royal family is waiting out there, along with every Grand Duke and Grand Duchess in the country! I shall give them something to remember, Tola! I feel like a lion!" To prove his words, Nijinsky sprang into the air before his mirror. "Tonight, I will leap twice as high," he crowed, "because all the royalty in the Empire is here to watch me and I am proud of myself!"

My eye fell on heaps of telegrams and letters piled on his dressing table. "Yes, look at them, Tola! They are from beautiful women and famous men abroad, all wishing me well! What good wishes! Life is beautiful!"

What sense could be made of his disjointed chatter? He pulled on his medieval jacket with its gold puffed sleeves that, with tights of golden tissue, and puffed trunks of heavy velvet, comprised his costume. To my astonishment, he paid no attenton to his trunks.

"Gospodin Nijinsky's trunks," reminded the dressers. He ignored them.

"Gospodin Nijinsky cannot go on the stage in tights alone!" one of the men remonstrated. Gospodin Nijinsky certainly could not. They were so thin that every hair on his legs was visible through them.

Diaghilev and Prince Lvov had obviously made a monkey of me. I shook hands with Nijinsky, remarking. "Don't forget the trunks, Vaslaw, or you'll make the little Princesses blush and shock the Grand Duchesses en masse!"

"Don't worry," he snickered. "They couldn't see anything wrong at that distance." The costume was Leon Bakst's latest creation.

"Of course, they could, you dumb-head, so don't forget your trunks!" And still shaking with laughter at the notion of Nijinsky in golden tissue tights, I closed the door and stepped on stage. The curtain was down. A few Grand Dukes chatted with Karsavina and the ballet girls costumed as sylphs. Nijinsky was the solo male performer called for in the act.

"Is Nijinsky ready?" shouted the stage manager. Then, "Off stage, everyone. He is ready!" and he signaled for the curtain. The Grand Dukes scurried into the wings, the dancers took their positions, Drigo started his music, and the curtain rose. I lingered near Nijinsky's dressing room, directly off stage to permit the star to wait until the last moment for his entrance.

Nijinsky's cue was playing when his door flew open. The assistant stage manager's tense whisper warned, "Nijinsky! Not on the stage like that!"

I spun around in time to see Nijinsky sail onto the stage with a tremendous bound, in tights so thin that his viens were visible—he was without trunks.

Apparently he had heard nothing. He had entered on the cemetery scene when the lights were dimmed. As they came up, I could hear whispering rising from the theater with a steadily increasing whir while Nijinsky mimed and danced.

Backstage the director, the stage manager, the assistants, the artists, the whole staff and company stood helpless watching Vaslaw scoring a success minus trunks!

The royal family had left its box immediately after Nijinsky's error was apparent, and as the scene continued scores of titled matrons rose and left the theater. When the curtain fell, it stayed down!

Director Teliakovsky led the rush to Nijinsky, who waited imperturbably. Teliakovsky had lost control of himself completely. "You have insulted the royal family," he yelled. "You are a disgrace to yourself and your art! You are expelled!"

If we had expected Nijinsky to beg pardon, we were disappointed. His eyes narrowed, his lips turned down at the corners. Wordlessly he turned on his heel and stalked past the infuriated director, raging incoherent accusations at him. I followed and closed the door behind us.

"How could you do that, Vaslaw?"

"Do what?" he adopted an aggrieved air. "I simply forgot my trunks, and instead of fining me, Teliakovsky has expelled me." A smile played around his lips. "He had no right to go that far—but I am happy, Tola! You remember I told you they would fire me? I was right—and now I am free!"

A knock interrupted us. It was Assistant Director Count Kankrin who entered. In his most suave manner he addressed Vaslaw: "Monsieur Nijinsky, we are profoundly sorry. We understand, now, that you forgot to complete your costume. It was an unfortunate coincidence that you insulted the royal family. According to the rules of the theater, Director Teliakovsky was forced to expel you, but you are needed! He invites you to visit his office tomorrow at ten, when you shall be reinstated and a satisfactory end to the affair arranged!"

Nijinsky bowed stiffly, replying, "I will speak with the director tomorrow!"

I paced the floor, relinquishing my resentment of Vaslaw's arrogance as though it had never been, my thoughts darting like lightning in an attempt to arrive at a solution which would spare Vaslaw humiliation and at the same time satisfy the director. If there was none, the matter would end in public disgrace and expulsion. It would mean, too, the loss of my best friend. In his adversity, I discovered that fame meant little. It was a man's need that determined the reality of comradeship—not what the world thought he needed. Common sense argued that Teliakovsky would propose an easy settlement, since he had overstepped his authority.

The following day I accompanied Vaslaw and waited in the general offices while he strode into the director's sanctum, where the first thing that met his eyes, he told me later, was an official document addressed to His Imperial Highness, the Emperor, and praying forgiveness. It needed only his signature to become a formal plea.

Director Teliakovsky chose to be gracious. "It has been arranged, Mr. Nijinsky," he announced, "if you will sign this petition, His Majesty will extend unconditional pardon in return for your apology. As for myself," he made a moué, "I regret the incident profoundly. It will be dismissed the moment your signature is affixed!"

Nijinsky's face was set. He was a Pole through and through at that moment. "I have never apologized to anyone but my mother. You have expelled me, and I find my freedom more desirable than any apology."

Teliakovsky's face blanched. "You have insulted the Emperor of Russia. The Emperor of Russia demands your apology!" The director was undoubtedly fearful for his own position in the event of Nijinsky's dismissal. "Sign the apology to His Imperial Highness!" commanded Teliakovsky in a perfect frenzy.

"I will sign nothing!" Nijinsky's voice was without anger, but it carried a sense of finality that was overwhelming. He pivoted on his heel and left. I rejoined him, listening to his story, half-numb with fear. Every day men and women were being exiled to Siberia for less effrontery.

A public scandal, which I have always laid at Diaghilev's door, was inevitable when news of Nijinsky's expulsion leaked out. Diaghilev deprived me of my friend and stole Russia's greatest terpsichorean genius from her, forcing him to leave the country within two days, completely disgraced.

Diaghilev was responsible for Nijinsky's first tragedy, and sometimes I have blamed him for the doom that ended Vaslaw's career. It is Teliakovsky who deserves the world's gratitude. Teliakovsky might have spoken the words which would have meant a traitor's death or a lifetime of agony in Siberia, but Teliakovsky was silent.

There was no witness to Vaslaw's revolt except the director. A new government in Russia relieves me of all responsibility in this revelation of "high treason" according to the autocratic code of Imperial Russia. For Diaghilev's sake, Nijinsky crept out of Russia, a traitor to his art and to the country which had loved him.

He faced the world, with discredit behind him and tragedy ahead—and again, he laughed!

PART III

LAURELS—GREEN AND SERE

I

FAREWELL AND REUNION

N<small>IJINSKY</small> forsook Russia with its ballet, its balls, and its interminable parties at the height of the January season. We had left comradeship behind us. Yet when I watched his train rumble into the distance and saw Vaslaw's vigorous waves of farewell to me, I thought, "There goes the one man who has been my friend . . . only this time he is being snatched out of my life forever!" Winter dragged on to a disappointing close, leaving me without money, tired—and without a solitary letter from Vaslaw. My parents did their best to coax me off to the provinces, but no!—the provinces offered no forgetfulness this time. I was determined on St. Petersburg for summer engagements.

They were plentiful. Krasnoe Selo saw me again, but Kshessinskaya and Vaslaw were not there and life had fled with them. My spirits rose temporarily when I transferred my gambling activities from cards to the races and discovered my winnings fairly consistent. A last fling "for luck" was just one too many, and so St. Petersburg found me with empty pockets and a discouraged outlook, while society students played away the tag ends of summer at their country homes and the Marinsky was still closed. What friends I had were so wealthy that it was impossible for me to seek them out without a supply of rubles to keep up the habitual rounds of restaurants with them. Mother did her best to help me with a handful of change when she could manage to supply me clandestinely, but her best was an empty joke in the mood I found myself.

A perpetual pass to the Alexandrinsky Theater was my sole consolation when, after a day of helpless wandering, I dressed like an affluent gentleman and attended the drama! There I might exchange social amenities without financial embarrassment and plead "business" when invitations to join gay and expensive gatherings were proffered. Friends in plenty and no money spelled apparently endless isolation that amply repaid Diaghilev for my insult if he had known it.

I sat in my seat at the Alexandrinsky, beset by regrets, when the lights went up for intermission, and I glanced at the boxes. Bronia Nijinsky! She saw me. She was actually beckoning me to her side! I was delighted, knowing as I did that she, too, had signed with Diaghilev and had traveled over the Continent with his company. She would be filled with news—news of Vaslaw, news of the Ballet Russe and dozens of old friends who danced in it. In less than two minutes, she had sensed my predicament, guessing that my gambling had resulted in fresh misfortune for me. Tactfully, she sympathized until she was sure. The truth of my situation was too obvious to conceal for long.

"Tola, why won't you join Diaghilev's company?" Her voice harbored more than a suggestion of exasperation. "He needs artists, and certainly you need the good money he can pay!"

Black despair reflected itself in my reply when I answered her gently, "You don't know anything of Vaslaw's life and mine—nor does Mother Nijinsky. You were too far away for our confidences. I can't go to Diaghilev!" I recounted the whole story, not forgetting Vaslaw's repeated offers to reinstate me in the Silver Beaver's good graces, adding: "But I didn't want his influence used for me, nor have I changed my mind. There is no way out. I must keep right on paying for a moment's lapse. I called him an 'entrepreneur' and *he's* treating *me* like one!"

"So that's it," Bronia sighed. "You know, I'm as far from my brother as is any common artist from the company's star, but Diaghilev has requested me to ask certain dancers to sign with him. I wondered why your name wasn't on the list. It's a shame for you both, Tola!" She puckered her brows into a thoughtful knot, then she brightened perceptibly. "I have it, Tola! I'll contrive everything while he's here contracting!" She tucked my arm

under hers and we went down to telephone the Silver Beaver. I watched
what seemed a rapid but agreeable conversation until she hung up the re-
ceiver and stepped out of the booth to face me.

"Diaghilev has told me to engage you, Tola, but there is one condition.
If you influence Vaslaw against the Silver Beaver, or if there is any trouble
whatever, I shall be held responsible. Your salary will be five hundred rubles
per month and you will sign your contract tomorrow."

My troubles were solved, and Diaghilev had invited me to sign with him!
I could hardly wait. Bright and early the next day I was at his office to find
him with my contract ready. While I signed, he smiled broadly, chuckling
audibly when I handed the contract to him.

"Now, Bourman, I am *your* entrepreneur!" he remarked, putting tickets
for London into my hand along with an advance of three hundred rubles.
For once the sarcasm that I was to know so well sounded agreeable in my
ears.

My feet barely touched the pavement between Diaghilev's office and
Director Teliakovsky's stronghold where I handed in my resignation. It was
the equivalent of touching off a bombshell. A babble of objections broke
over me from the Imperial Ballet company. "Bourman, you are crazy! You
have lost your pension, your students, and a dozen times the money
Diaghilev can pay you—for what?" they demanded.

Vain was my explanation that Monte Carlo, London, Paris, Vienna,
Berlin, New York—the whole cosmopolitan world that Diaghilev represented—called more imperiously than security, that its silent command was
imperative. I dropped a futile attempt to convey that idea in favor of an
invitation to attend a farewell party, my final gesture to the Imperial
company.

Impulsively, I had accomplished a release from Russia without conferring
with my parents, who were struck dumb with the news of my imminent
departure. Father understood, but Mother cried as though I were lying dead
before her, until my father exploded impatiently: "What difference does it
make where he goes? He will always be without a kopeck in his pockets, and
if he has a chance to see the world while he stays penniless, in the name of

Heaven, be glad for him!" A chance to rejoice for me was all Mother needed
to dry her eyes, embrace me, and grant her consent.

Two days later I was on my way to London with Bronia and Kostia Kobelev, today a ballet master in New York. A beautiful woman caught my interest on the train, and nothing would do when we reached Berlin but that I
must escort her to her hotel.

"How can a beautiful woman arrive at a hotel unescorted?" I protested to
silence Bronia's objections until she gave them up without ~n argument. I
accompanied my charming acquaintance and after leaving her promptly lost
myself in Berlin, without a word of German in my vocabulary. The name
of the station, the name of the street I had been on—everything flew out of
my head. I pulled out my watch. Only fifteen minutes remained to train-
time!

Suddenly the name of my acquaintance's hotel etched itself in my brain.
I leaped into a passing cab and somehow conveyed the necessity for speed by
jumping up and down and reiterating the name of the hotel in a loud voice.
Exactly one minute before the train started its grind to France my distracted
lady rushed me back to the station and placed me in the safekeeping of a
hysterical Bronia and a frantic Kobelev. In London I learned that my train
acquaintance had managed to make her way back to her hotel without mishap, despite her lack of an escort, but I didn't confide the fact to Bronia and
Kobelev, who watched me like a pair of cats until they presented me safe to
the Ballet Russe with a plea for release from the responsibility of my wander-
lust.

At the Premier Hotel at Russell Square, where they deposited me, I found
dozens of old friends together with a group of artists from Warsaw whom I
met impatiently, waiting for the moment when I might safely ask for
Vaslaw's address without rudeness. Bronia supplied it. He was at the Hotel
Savoy. My luggage was dropped hastily in the middle of my room while I
tore off in search of a taxi.

Eight months had passed since Vaslaw and I had exchanged a word. I
phoned him from the lobby with a jocular request for an interview.

"Anatole!!!!" he shouted. "Are you really here? Impossible! Quick! Take the elevator! Don't lose a second!"

A spurt of speed carried me to the lift, and when the door sprung back a thousand floors up, it seemed in my eagerness, there stood Vaslaw waiting for me. That was a meeting to remember! According to our custom, we pounded each other's backs and kissed, to the horror of the absolutely Anglo-Saxon bellboy whose eyes popped like ripe grapes as he slammed the doors.

In that moment we forgot the differences time and fame had worked between us. We were chattering like two magpies, exchanging news, reminiscing, sketching the future on a grand scale, and breaking into each other's conversation most of the time. It was good to be natural once more!

But Vaslaw grew serious and his eyes clouded. "I am still so utterly alone, Tola! My sole pleasure has been practicing in Covent Garden . . . ."

Before he could ask me, I was on my feet and thumping his back. "I will play for you tomorrow, Vaslaw! It will be like the old days!" His face lighted with happiness, the lines of weariness erased themselves instantly around his mouth and eyes. Vaslaw was my old comrade!

Diaghilev had remained in St. Petersburg, signing such artists as could meet his standards and were willing to leave Russia, relaying them posthaste to London. Vaslaw was warbling paeans in praise of Bronia and her political maneuvering. "She is more of a genius than I . . . she's managed to save Diaghilev's face and yours . . . and now we can all be happy! I have one friend and a sister I can trust . . . what more can I want? Fame has left me two treasures!" Vaslaw exulted, pirouetting into the air in his jubilance.

He collected a tie here, his coat there; then hooking his arm in mine he dashed into the Strand. We walked to Leicester Square before we dropped into a bar to sit down with London's commoners and drink beer while we talked over old times. We ordered a light supper at Lyon's, lingering over it; then tiring of our surroundings, we walked for hours through London's back streets and London's mews. Three o'clock in the morning struck before Nijinsky could be persuaded to leave me at my hotel.

"Until morning, Tola . . . only a few hours, and you will be playing for me as you did in Russia!" With a wave of his hand, Nijinsky was gone.

II

FIRST LONDON SEASON

FOKINE was rehearsing the company with headlong impetuosity when I arrived and was started on my quota of ensemble and solo routines. Only two weeks remained before the opening date at Covent Garden. Morning, noon, and night, Fokine—animated by his visions of figures and formations called into being by Stravinsky's *Fire-Bird* and *Petrouchka*, Chopin's *Sylphides,* Schumann's *Karnival,* and Rimsky-Korsakov's *Scheherazade*—rushed us and drilled us until we satisfied his gallant standards of art. The best known gems in Diaghilev's sparkling repertoire were developed by Fokine in those two mad weeks, while the Silver Beaver sent on strange dancers to be assimilated in the spectacular creations of the Ballet Russe.

My head was spinning with rhythms and steps and responsibility for my share in the kaleidoscopic formations that made Fokine's compositions as intricate as a mathematically perfect microcosmos. It was during those two weeks of precipitate haste that I learned to reverence Fokine's agility of mind and his masterly direction. From one complex score of Stravinsky's to the other he went without confusion, switching his attention to Schumann or Chopin with consummate ease until his diligence was repaid with five gorgeous ballets, each an artistic triumph in itself.

Nijinsky was present at every rehearsal, seeking me out for a chat on the rare occasions when we enjoyed simultaneous intermissions. The artists from Moscow and Warsaw stood amazed at the temerity of a man who not only addressed the star with disconcerting familiarity, but by a nickname as well. Neither Nijinsky nor I paid the slightest heed to them. We were reestablishing the friendship of a lifetime!—There was so much for us to say!

Fokine's welcome dismissal invariably was the signal for Vaslaw to carry me off to the Savoy for dinner. Often an intimate little restaurant or a tiny night club, such as the Harlequin off Regent Street, tucked unostentatiously out of sight, offered us a chance to discuss personalities and arts incidental to the ballet. A bar, where we might rub shoulders with the unpretentious, was a favorite goal for Nijinsky, beginning to yearn for simplicity and an end to the superficialities of a public career. The moment Diaghilev returned, however, our harmless excursions were stopped! We met only at the theater!

Our season opened in mid-November to an audience of English aristocrats who had journeyed from the shores for the winter social life. Leon Bakst, Tamara Karsavina, and Igor Stravinsky were the celebrities one ran into backstage where they were helping Diaghilev, while a glance at the boxes revealed such famous personalities as the English royal family, Lord Salisbury, Lord Montague, Lady Asquith, Lady Ripon, and Lady Gray.

"Sold Out" signs were posted for the first performance and set the pace for every presentation that followed. As extraordinary success piled on success, I discovered a truth that has seldom been voiced. The world has been told volumes about the British as a people of repressed emotions and coolheadedness, but rarely is it reminded that the English nation is one enthusiastically aware of beauty. It was as though we were in our beloved Russia, so understanding and hospitable were our admirers, who shortly made themselves acquainted with the name of every member of the company. Piles of telegrams, congratulatory messages, flowers, and gifts waited for us after every appearance.

I seldom saw Vaslaw out of full dress, except when he was on stage in costume. The fair daughters of cold Albion proved themselves charming. Regardless of birth, they crowded around the stage door for Nijinsky's autograph—or one of his smiles. He was sometimes half an hour traversing the few feet from the door to his car, which he reached on a path of roses scattered by his adorers. Drives in Hyde Park or Regent's Park with highborn ladies were pleasures accorded the personnel of the whole Ballet, a circumstance that laid forever rumors of unfriendliness on the part of the British, and one

which accounts for Pavlowa's choice of Golder's Green in London for the site
of her permanent home "Ivy House" with its Lake of Swans and its idyllic
name. There the brilliant ballerina was happy in the enjoyment of her brief
respites from "work" which should have been a soul-stirring joy.

Aristocrats with ancient names fought for the privilege of entertaining
Nijinsky, who used to stand in an agony of indecision—confronted by
scores of invitations, torn between the desire to accept every one of them and
the impossibility of such a plan. Love letters requesting appointments added
to his quandary, faced as he was with the necessity for some sort of reply to
the ones written on crested stationery, at least. At a formal dinner party, one
woman whose name was synonymous with power embarrassed him with
her insistence upon kissing his hand before the assemblage.

How often I have watched him patiently replying to the mighty women
who sought him backstage with unconcealed eagerness. Most of their names
have faded from my mind, but one of them stands out despite the years that
have passed since Nijinsky was the idol of millions. She was on the elderly
side, but beautiful with the mellow sweetness that age often brings to the
happy children of Time. Six feet tall, with gray hair and a grand manner,
the Marchioness of Ripon was among the most faithful devotees of the art
form Nijinsky had mastered.

She never missed a performance nor did she ever fail to pilgrimage backstage to express her appreciation in person, her sables and ermines adding a
subtle note of richness that bespoke unquestionable position. She found a
warm welcome extended by both Diaghilev and Vaslaw, while Vassily
Zuykov, their valet, grew well on the way towards opulence with the ten- and
twenty-pound notes she passed to him for his favor of delivering her
invitations to tea or dinner, or acting as personal messenger for the short
notes she frequently penned to Nijinsky.

Uncounted times our early morning practice was interrupted by Vassily,
entering to remark with an air of uncertainty, "Lady Ripon requests the
pleasure of watching you at practice . . . ."

"But of course! Why are you hesitating when you know she is at liberty
to visit me at any time?" Nijinsky would inevitably snap, watching Vassily

lumber around with clumsy steps, chortling the while he waved a twenty-pound note.

"See what I have earned for that hard work!" he would whisper gleefully before he adopted a more dignified deportment, and flung the door open, announcing solemnly, "Lady Ripon to see Monsieur Nijinsky!"

The lady would sweep onto our stage, smiling at Vaslaw when he bowed over her extended hand, sparing me a greeting when I kissed her hand after him. We would seat her, and continue our practice for the balance of the hour. When it was done, our guest would rise, shower us with compliments and depart, tossing a half-promise over her shoulder, "Perhaps tomorrow I will again request permission to watch Art in its preparation!"

We both enjoyed her visits and welcomed her from our hearts whenever she put in an appearance. I have heard that Lady Ripon's veins pulsed with royal blood so ancient that I think it wisest to hold my own counsel on the rumors of her birth that came to us, for I cannot vouch for their truth. I do know that her appreciative silence and her love for the poetry of motion Nijinsky created with his dancing was one of the rare compliments that added further inspiration to his interpretation during the London period.

Our final appearance evoked one of England's most generous tributes to the true beauty she has seldom failed to honor. For nearly an hour, her most powerful lords stood in their places applauding us, while the commoners clamored approval and demands for bows which kept us before the curtain for nearly an hour.

Our next presentation was scheduled to be seen in Berlin, but Messina had been rocked by a disastrous earthquake, and a benefit performance for the hapless victims of the cataclysm was planned at the Grand Opéra de Paris. Nijinsky and Karsavina canceled a week's holiday to sail for the French capital to volunteer their genius for charity.

III

GALA PERFORMANCE AT
THE GRAND OPÉRA DE PARIS

Arrived in Paris, Nijinsky and Karsavina found the whole Ballet Russe following in their train. Rehearsals were not overburdening to either, and Vaslaw was free to spend the greater part of his time with me. He had begun the perfection of his mightiest spectacle, *Le Spectre de la Rose,* to the music of the *Invitaton to the Waltz* by Weber. Beauty was a vibrant quality so completely permeating Nijinsky's every motion that his development of the brilliant duo was entrancing to watch, applying, as it did, classical principles of excellent ballet technique to the weaving of an exquisitely balanced and descriptive composition.

Diaghilev was so occupied by final business arrangements that he had neither time nor energy to direct Vaslaw's personal program. Escape from social life loomed for the two or three days intervening between our arrival in Paris and the presentation, tempting us to realize on every moment of it, traveling from one inexpensive restaurant to another, exploring Paris with the lightheartedness of schoolboys. Nijinsky found his favorite pastime sitting out on the terraces, sipping wine, and watching the world passing and repassing, too intent upon its own affairs to notice him, and willing to leave him in the peace he craved.

Evenings found us at the Place Pigalle with a gay congregation of Bohemians, laughing at the pranks of cabaret performers and delighting in the typically French show that was offered. The Moulin Rouge; the Cabaret

Mort, with its gruesome setting where one drank beer from coffin tops under
a flaccid green light and monks cursed their patrons until the scalp of the
most material-minded tingled with horror; the Cabaret of the Fallen Angel,
where angels with carmined lips waited to answer our prayers for good wine
and service; low-class cabarets where apaches glowered from under threatening brows—we visited them all!

Those were places that drew us into endless conversations over the simple
life that was gone for both of us. Nijinsky and I tacitly understood that our
few stolen days were no more than an ephemeral interlude between scenes
in the exhausting farce his life was becoming. He was a puppet of Fame
without opportunity to express any self-will—Diaghilev saw to that!

We strolled homewards down the grand boulevards, watching the night
moths flutter by, painted like pathetic butterflies who had somehow wandered
into nocturnal deeps and forgotten the way back to healthy sunshine. They
were not too different from the "guests" of our St. Petersburg's night. Both
of us pretended not to remember that occurrence and burst into spasmodic
outpourings of small talk.

Time is inexorable. Before we had more than tasted the froth of Parisian
delights, *Le Matin* and *Figaro* were screaming news of Nijinsky's participa-
tion in the gala event which would bring him in triumph this time before a
Paris already idolizing him! Philosophical acceptance, not regrets, was demanded of us.

"You must see me in *Le Spectre!*" Vaslaw asserted.

I tried to buy a ticket at the box office, but not one was available.

"Impossible, Tola," cried Nijinsky. "You must see me dance. There is
no one else to care whether I dance perfectly—no one else whom I can think
of as waiting for my success!" He was as helpless as I to coax a seat from the
wicket. He rushed off to Monsieur Rouché, director of the Opéra, begging
him for a seat as a special favor.

"C'est impossible, mon ami!" But Nijinsky threatened to fly into a rage.

"Non! Ce n'est pas impossible, monsieur!" he roared. "My best friend
must have a ticket. It *must* be. I demand it!"—and somewhere the frantic
director located a solitary seat for me in the midst of a box party. Nijinsky

was content, then, to face his audience, sure that there would be at least one friend among the thousands who stared at his magnificent dance.

I sat in my place, running over the program which had packed the tremendous auditorium to capacity. What a galaxy of stars had been assembled! The immortal Sarah Bernhardt, Ida Rubinstein, Sascha Guitry, Réjane, Felia Litvin, George Robey, Nijinsky, Karsavina—they were only a few of the celebrities who hastened to aid Messina with one of the most inspiring presentations ever planned.

My eye was next caught by an audience so brilliant that it recalled my thoughts of the Hermitage, except that the Tsar with his sparkling entourage was not present, nor were the splashes of color that meant dashing officers in Russia. Millions of gems glinted from the throats, the arms, the hair of fascinating and vivacious women, gowned, I knew past doubt, by Worth, Paquin, and other smart Parisian couturiers. The men's trim black evening dress and snowy shirts provided a contrasting note of soberness in that cosmopolitan gathering where French, German, English, American, Italian, Spanish, and Russian notables were drawn into cultivated concord by the supreme mystery of inspired art and inspired interpreters reveling in a masterly setting.

With the appearance of each international celebrity, the Opéra resounded with spontaneous applause until Bernhardt smiled before her adorers, and then the house rocked with reverberations that echoed and reechoed through it. That great heart of hers which beat for art alone must have thrilled to those plaudits! She played and scored an ovation that was unequaled until the curtain parted for *Le Spectre de la Rose*.

Who can describe the magic that focused itself in that scene?—a Colonial maiden reliving the love-dream of her first ball, finally dropping into slumber perfumed by a single ruddy rose—the token of her lover's smile. No ornamentation was needed to diffuse reality through that fantasy with its universal appeal—Karsavina slept!

Abruptly Nijinsky appeared in the great window of her room—an apparition clad in glowing red and brilliant green. He was Youth incarnate!

—Love, and the promise of supernal happiness! The audience recognized all that he was with a little gasp of delight, and then he danced!

That was fulfillment! He was Krishna expressing the agelong mystery of Life. He danced and the world shook with the power of his inspiration! His body was a delicately attuned instrument played upon by the rhythms of a cosmos. He was harmony of sound and motion and beauty. His body swayed with invisible chords, incarnating fleeting emotions. His feet pranced like winged spears, stabbing Time with their mastery until Time died and it was an immortal who leaped and spun in hypnotic cadences. He was tenderness and understanding, yearning over his beloved when he permitted Love to draw him to her side and take her hand.

Who can forget the somnolent Karsavina, swaying to the waltz with such grace that one's breath seemed to stop with the power of her loveliness? Then the sweeping nuances of a duo which translated the dream into transcendent reality vibrating like a clarion call through the surging sounds until Karsavina forgot her divinity and yielded once more to her drowsiness— and Nijinsky soothed her back to dreamlessness, with the touch of an entranced sprite, hardly skimming the stage with his flying feet. A few regretful farewells, fraught with the delicacy of elfin pantomime, a feather-kiss, a rush of music, and Nijinsky, hardly less heavy than the air that upbore him, stabbed the illusion of timelessness with his swift steps, and literally flew through the wndow on the dying vibrance of a masterly crescendo!

Karsavina woke and kissed her rose. Le Spectre divine was gone! The curtain closed.

Something uncanny gripped the thousands who watched a miracle captivated. There was a split instant of utter silence, and then that vast audience roared its release in a thunderous outburst. For ten minutes Karsavina and Nijinsky bowed, their breasts heaving with the effort of their dance, and still the tumult continued unabated.

Le Spectre took eight minutes to weave its glorious illusion of limitless life consummated with exquisite love, but in that eight minutes every muscle in the bodies of both dancers was called upon to contribute its part towards creating a deathless memory. Only absolute perfection could translate the poetry of invisible winds into a tangible expression of unbounded joyousness as did Nijinsky and Karsavina in their interpretation of *Le Spectre*. The physical effort demanded was terrific.

This last Karsavina explained in flawless French, only succeeding in stimulating the enthusiasm of the expectant hundreds who rent the air with shouts of *"Encore! Encore!"*—even though both dancers were exhausted. I sat forward in my place, cursing in Russian when I detected a query pass between the two. They couldn't re-create that vital spectacle that had symbolized all in all to whoever witnessed it—not at the price of eight minutes of heartbreaking dancing!

In mingled disbelief and terror, I saw Monsieur Pierre Monteux raise his baton—the inveigling notes of the *Invitation to the Waltz* were teasing me back into forgetfulness of everything but the unadorned triumph of Art.

I scarcely breathed at all, fearful that either Karsavina or Nijinsky would collapse, or failing that, give an inferior interpretation. I muttered encouragement under my breath while my neighbors twitched their shoulders impatiently, caught once more into that other-worldliness that was an actuality whenever Nijinsky danced. He exulted—and soared to greater heights than before with his final leap! He had achieved the physically impossible. His audience went mad!

Nothing mattered to me but Nijinsky's needs. I tore through the house, fear lending me incredible speed. As I guessed, Nijinsky lay as though he had suffered a knock-out blow in a boxing match. Perspiration ran off his body in little uneven rivers, his chest was heaving like a mighty bellows— and around him a dozen people crowded, waving turkish towels before him futilely. Diaghilev stood by, helpless.

"Quick—some water, before he dies from his exertion—please, please— water!" I shouted.

Vassily was off like an arrow for water. I poured it in small quantities between Vaslaw's parted lips, and turned his head to let it run out, lest he swallow any and do himself fatal harm. It was fifteen minutes before he signaled his willingness to stand, and then, half-carried by Vassily and me, he asked to be left alone with us to recover in his dressing room.

Fatigue had invaded every sinew of Nijinsky's body, taxed to its limit, when Diaghilev arrived, waving his monocle in nervous circles around his forefinger.

"Up and dressed, Vaslaw! I've promised you'll attend a gay and exclusive party to meet a hundred ready to acclaim you king!" asserted the Silver Beaver in a tone that brooked no denial.

Nijinsky unclosed his eyes, fixing Diaghilev with a distrustful stare. "Please, please," he begged, "leave me with Tola this time."

He saw Diaghilev's scowl and his impatient denial unmoved for once. "I am too tired to go. I cannot! Please make my excuses, and let me wear my oldest suit and go with Tola to forget that I am a slave! It is such a little thing to ask—a few hours of talking, and some sleep!"

Diaghilev flushed furiously, powerless to explode before a member of his company, pivoted on his heel, and slammed the door behind him.

"Quick, Tola, run and get into street clothes and get back here before too much of our precious time is gone!" Vaslaw implored.

Less than an hour later we slipped out a deserted entrance rather than face the transported crowds hunting him. By a devious route, we reached the Café de la Paix at the Place de l'Opéra and the Boulevard des Italiennes, where we sat on the terrace, listening to the people about us raving interminably over "Le Nijinsky" until Vaslaw plucked my sleeve and suggested a more quiet retreat before he should be recognized.

In a dingy place, too insignificant to draw Opéra patrons, Nijinsky stretched his legs out before him to relax them.

"Tonight I am happy, Anatole," he remarked. "If my whole life could be like these last few days, I should be happy always. Simple streets and simple people when I was not on the stage—and after a triumph, peace! No Countesses, no Princes, no Princesses—no ladies to bubble emptiness at me—no Savoy—no Plaza—I hate all that. It does something to me inside!" He considered me, his eyes twinkling.

"For the first time in my life, I'm jealous of you, Tola," he confided. "You're free to come and go as you please, enjoying the friends you choose and the pleasures you discover for yourself, while I—I am forced to do what

Diaghilev chooses and go where my public demands my presence! If I ever go mad—believe me, Tola, it will be the price I pay for the life I've been forced into! I was born for the dance—yes!—but society and the rest of it —no! Never was I born for that!"

IV

SUCCESS AND TRAVELS
IN GERMANY

Our first German success was scored at the Theater des Westens in Berlin, but our return engagement took place at Am Nollendorf Theater. The Royal Kroll Theater provided the setting for our final subjugation of prewar Germany, where our Ballet always scored a triumph with Nijinsky topping every ascent in favor with Schumann's *Karnival,* an offering which literally swept our German audiences off their feet with its flourish of classic charm.

There was less surcease from the crowds than ever. Nijinsky found that Germans, too, reverence art, and sought to express their enthusiasm by jamming the stage entrance and besieging him with invitations. He pleaded fatigue in vain to Diaghilev, who forced him into scintillating social life without regard for Vaslaw's personal comfort, making him miserable in the meanwhile by disapproving his choice of a tie or handkerchief, his manner of walking, or his hunger for simplicity.

Wilhelm and the royal entourage missed few performances; they injected an air of unwonted splendor with the sinecure of militarism reflected in colorful uniforms and burnished steel that attracted one's eyes from the wings. Wilhelm was considered the mightiest monarch in Europe at that period. His reputation for glory and might was based upon rumors of his power that penetrated even the politically disinterested group that we comprised. With distinct satisfaction Nijinsky told me of receiving a royal command for an interview, and hastened to seek the Imperial presence in company with Diaghilev—inevitably in company with Diaghilev!

"We sat and chatted with him as we would with any nice fellow," Vaslaw reported afterwards. "He liked my Harlequin in *Karnival* and certainly his conversation showed his understanding of art. He may be almighty with his power, but I don't think he's any ogre, personally!"

No present was forthcoming, however. The Kaiser had spoken with Nijinsky and invited him to the royal box. That in itself was the equivalent of a gift from the Tsar, we learned!

Berlin held us for six or eight weeks and patronized the Ballet Russe so faithfully that anything but a full house was impossible. Backstage life was made increasingly eventful by German newspapermen, cartoonists and artists, directors and producers who thronged the wings. Arthur Nikisch, Max Reinhardt, and the Adelheim brothers, whom we had met on their Russian tour, became staunch friends of the company.

At the peak of our Berlin season, a telegram notified Bronia and Vaslaw of the death of their father in a distant Russian province. They gave no sign of heartbreak, mutually explaining that Thomas Nijinsky had never found much time to spend with them—he was too intent on his own wandering existence. Together they had a Mass said for the repose of his soul, Diaghilev and I being the only ones to stand with them in the nave of an empty church when that lonely "In memoriam" was chanted.

Mother Nijinsky was living in peace and comfort in St. Petersburg, supplied with everything her heart could desire by Vaslaw and Bronia, who remembered still her years of self-sacrifice and penury while she struggled to make their education possible. The death of her husband marked an end to a long period of worry and uncertainty, occasioned by his unexpected disappearances. At last Mother Nijinsky was free to shower her wealth of affection on Vaslaw and his sister, both of whom had achieved prosperity far, far beyond her wildest hopes. A few days after the Mass, we started on our way through Germany and Austria.

Our journeyings would look like a snarled lump of yarn if they were traced on the map, for there was no logic in an itinerary providing jumps from Cologne to Stuttgart, from Munich to Frankfort, from Breslau to

Leipzig. These were only a few cities on a list that included every center of any size in the country. Vienna and Budapest were the sole stops we made in Austria and Hungary.

It was the accepted thing to count on playing theaters jammed with aristocrats and military leaders—to stumble over celebrities wherever we went backstage, or to trip over easels set up by the scores of artists who haunted Nijinsky for sittings whether he was at practice or at leisure. Much of our time was broken into one-week visits, with only the capitals persuading Diaghilev that a month or two might safely be risked.

Rehearsals were scheduled daily no matter where we were. After them, we flocked into the streets like any sightseers, invading cathedrals, castles, and historic spots—the ones we had had to break our young heads over in Russia! They were far more interesting to visit than they had been to worry over in a textbook!

Nijinsky and I added appreciably to our cultural background during those days, browsing through the museums and exploring the relics of an ancient past with delight, an occupation that restored his spirits like sparkling wine, except that it was not wine Nijinsky drank when he sought a terrace and liquid refreshment!

"This is my little Germany!" he would sigh, blowing the foam off the huge mug of beer that he lifted to his lips while a beatific smile of contentment spread over his features. His happiness accompanied him like a radiant aura, evoking a cheery response from whomever it touched. After beer at Aschinger's we had to forsake touring for our hotels.

How many times Vaslaw stood with me outside the Hotel Adlon distastefully surveying the bellboys who stood like wooden soldiers! With an air of despair, he'd hook his arm in mine and enter, striding up to the desk for handfuls of mail, running through the piles of letters for a familiar handwriting, and then dropping the lot with a scowl.

"It has begun again, Tola," he'd grumble. "My gilded cage has clanged on me and I'm shut into it until I can escape for another taste of life!"

If life was complicated for Nijinsky, it became well-nigh intolerable for Diaghilev shortly before we left Germany for Austria, owing to Karsavina's unwillingness to resign from the Imperial Russian Ballet. The Silver Beaver was perpetually faced with the possibility of playing without his première ballerina, who might be called back to Russia at any time by Director Teliakovsky, and being in St. Petersburg, might be ordered to stay there for weeks while Diaghilev pulled wires and laid siege to Teliakovsky in vain.

He tried to meet his emergencies by substituting another ballerina for Karsavina whenever she went speeding back to her adored Marinsky Theater. But that scheme was impossible to work in Vienna for the royal performance scheduled to honor Emperor Franz Josef—and Karsavina was in St. Petersburg with a Teliakovsky whose patience with Diaghilev's importunities was frazzled. He positively refused to permit her return to Diaghilev for the Austrian royal family—or for anyone else!

Kshessinskaya and Pavlowa were the only other premières Diaghilev considered worthy of the engagement, and both seemed impossible to secure: Kshessinskaya was happy, perfectly contented in Russia, besides having too much money to be persuaded by mere cash considerations; Pavlowa, who had her own company, was, naturally enough, unwilling to share her success with Diaghilev.

Diaghilev had protected himself and us, in a measure, by his policy of advertising "Diaghilev's Ballet Russe" rather than any soloist, further securing himself by his insistence that every member of his organization must be an accomplished soloist. The show had gone on several times since our departure from Berlin minus Karsavina, without occasioning worry, but a command performance! That was another story entirely!

Diaghilev was caught in his own trap when Karsavina's vacation was refused. Days sped by without making any impression on Teliakovsky. Whatever the Silver Beaver planned as a way out went awry until Kshessinskaya's favor was his only salvation. Day and night he dreamed of snaring her. Telegrams, letters, inducements of every conceivable order went off to the powerful Kshessinskaya. Diaghilev's aplomb deserted him entirely when those proved fruitless. He sat like a miniature Thor, heaving sarcastic hammers of criticisms that threatened to shatter our morale.

Nothing was right. The music was wrong. The dancers were imbeciles.

The Ballet Russe was a farce. No matter what we did, he persisted in promising annihilation until we were almost as discouraged as he. Apparently he had exhausted his last possibility. He sat glum and, to our unspeakable relief, silent.

A boy handed him a telegram which he tore open violently. He read it hastily. Instantly he was on his feet, beaming like benevolence incarnate!

"Boys and girls! Kshessinskaya is coming! Our greatest ballerina will actually be with us for the Viennese performance! Kshessinskaya is coming!"

We applauded. We shouted. We danced impromptu figures expressive of the elation that surged through us. Kshessinskaya was coming. Diaghilev's sanity was restored and all would be well. Nijinsky suspended himself in mid-air for a full second in the joy he felt.

Two days later the ballerina was due in Vienna, accompanied as usual by her full staff of servants. She engaged a whole floor of the best hotel in advance. Everything was in readiness for her arrival when I taxied to the station to meet her and Olga Evgenievna Borkengagen, my old friend and Kshessinskaya's companion for years.

"Bourmanchik! I am glad you came! Keep me from loneliness!" commanded the première the moment she set eyes on me, and then she embraced me before everyone. It was the equivalent of an imperial order and, nothing loth, I determined to dance attendance upon Kshessinskaya until she should leave us for the splendor of St. Petersburg—and as it turned out, it was lucky that I did!

I reassured her. "It's impossible that you can be lonely with so many of your old friends here! You've come for a reunion and a holiday—not for work!"

Diaghilev greeted her warmly, presenting her to the company with a graceful speech when she appeared for rehearsal. Her glance fixed on Nijinsky whom she had missed since his Russian disgrace.

"Vaslaw! Oh—but it is good to see you again!" And she folded him close in front of the whole assembly!

It was no mean triumph that the glorious Kshessinskaya attained in Vienna. The Viennese went insane over her magic when she pirouetted and waltzed. Front pages were devoted to unrestrained effusions over her witchery and technical skill. Franz Josef and his court paid homage by attending almost every performance and applauding her as enthusiastically as the most common peasant who shouted acclaim from the gallery.

Vienna! Its ovation, like the one in Paris, was indescribably great. I haunted the heroine of the day, accompanying her on long drives through the parks, out into the suburbs, and beyond into the rural districts close to the city. In the afternoon I was Kshessinskaya's escort on the interminable shopping tours that took us into every smart shop in the capital while the première bought cabloads of things that she needed once in a while and more cabloads that she needed not at all!

Vaslaw and the Silver Beaver joined us for luncheon and dinner in her gorgeous suite, perfumed by bowers of roses from her wealthy admirers. After every performance, Kshessinskaya was hostess at a night club, a cabaret, or a restaurant, surrounded by a host of elegant acquaintances until she grew bored and ended the party by carrying her old friends off to her apartment where we stayed smoking and drinking over Russia and our art until dawn grayed the east.

Our Viennese stay was over at last in a final breathless round of gaiety and dancing. We were off for Budapest! Our arrival there was distinguished by a reception attended, I veritably believe, by every man, woman, and child in the city. The press screamed news of Kshessinskaya's transcending art, of her famous collection of diamonds, of her Russian glories, of her mastery of the dance, and of Nijinsky's gallant interpretations of Terpsichore.

Every ticket was sold long before our train neared the packed station. With anticipation unbounded, we entered the Hungarian capital on air!

V

TEMPESTUOUS INTERLUDE

A WHOLE floor of the Hotel Danube provided haven for Kshessinskaya in Budapest where she lived in high spirits, her face constantly wreathed in smiles, for her performances were so inspired that, within a day, they were a byword. In the next to the last performance scheduled, Nijinsky and Kshessinkaya scored a fresh ovation with *Le Spectre de la Rose*. A dozen times the curtain parted and closed without quelling applause that thundered loudly enough to be heard in the street.

The première, tired and moody, decided against a repetition of the duo. "Let them pound their hands until morning if they choose!" she sputtered. "It will make no difference. I am going to get some sleep!" She consented to a final acknowledgment before she swept off to her dressing room, myself trailing her faithfully.

As we reached the door of her room, the acclaim reached another crescendo. Kshessinskaya threw her head up sharply. "Bourmanchik! Go and see if that Nijinsky was fool enough to take a bow without me!"

In the first wing I stood dumfounded, staring at Vaslaw, making a solitary bow against every tradition of the theater, receiving the plaudits of a packed house without his partner! It was unbelievable!

"Vaslaw, what in the name of Heaven are you doing?" I shot at him.

"Mala told me she didn't want to make any more bows. Someone ought to acknowledge the audience, and so I did. It is nothing! She will laugh when she hears about it!" and off he went to his own dressing room, humming a little song.

I made for Kshessinskaya's stronghold—and what a sight greeted me! One look told me that Russia's most temperamental ballerina knew exactly what had happened. She was in one of those rages which have made Russian temperament a phrase fraught with terror. Ballet skirts, tights, slippers, powder, perfume, stockings—everything she could lay her hands on was flying in md-air, while Kshessinskaya paced from one end of the place to the other like an enraged tiger, storming against Nijinsky as an imbecile!— a muzhik!—a dumbbell!— standing and stamping her feet up and down in a frenzy, starting the whole scene over again when she got to the point of screaming: "No one ever insulted me so! A bow by himself! A male dancer without his partner!"

A new thought struck her.

"Olga! Olga! The maid must pack! At once! We are going to St. Petersburg! Quick! We are leaving that miserable man and his Ballet!"

In the corridors near the star's dressing room, every member of the company had congregated, half-frightened, half-awed within hearing of such a splendid temper.

Diaghilev, urbanely sure of himself, made his way to her door and knocked.

"Who's there?"

With assurance absolute, he answered, "Diaghilev, Madame. May I enter?"

"You enter? To the devil with you and your insane pack of artists! No!" She flung herself at me, venting her outrage. "Did you hear? Diaghilev— against me like everyone else! And you too! You think I am wrong!"

There was only one way out and I took it without hesitation when I answered: "Mala, you are right! Go at once and leave Diaghilev and his unprincipled Ballet!"

Kshessinskaya smiled through the fog of powder that was slowly settling over her wardrobe, temporarily appeased. "Bourman, I will see only you. Go to my hotel and you may see me to the station!"

I beat my retreat without further invitation, closing her door to face the whole company. Diaghilev was wild-eyed, and Nijinsky lounged in his dressing robe looking mildly surprised. They crowded around.

"She's angry!" one boy remarked in a whisper.

"Angry!" I exclaimed. "Are you deaf? She is in a wonderful temper. It is marvelous to see her! She is leaving at once for St. Petersburg!"

"For St. Petersburg? Impossible!" It was Diaghilev who spoke, dropping his monocle out of his eye in amazement. He hooked his arm in mine, drawing me aside. "Listen, Bourman, she's insulted me before my company! She's ordered me around like a stage hand! She's screeched at me! But she mustn't go. Stay with her—do anything for her—and the moment she softens, come to me no matter what time it is! I shall wait up all night! Manage an interview with me or she'll leave the whole company stranded!"

Poor Diaghilev! For once the Silver Beaver was dependent and it was worth seeing. I promised and left him for the hotel to await Kshessinskaya, meanwhile watching the imperturbable Olga ordering every piece of luggage out, supervising the deft packing with unequaled skill. Diaghilev had reminded me that the first decent train to Russia left the following night. We had almost twenty-four hours.

Kshessinskaya arrived, still in high dudgeon, before I was more than comfortably settled. She pounced on me again, her words tumbling out white-hot with injured pride. "I won't stay! Don't ask me! Your best friend —that Nijinsky—he insulted me! He's betrayed every tradition of the theater! Stay? Never! Don't open your mouth to ask me!"

Oil on the troubled waters once more. "Of course, Mala, go! Go immediately where you are appreciated!" I counseled—and then we went through the whole scene time and again until I had every line by heart and had witnessed the grand Kshessinskaya in a perfect pyrotechnical display of ravening fury never to be repeated this side of Hades. She emptied the vials of her wrath over the entire company with splendid indiscrimination, her voice mounting shrilly with her choler.

Olga and I agreed with every word she sputtered, for it has been my experience that anger in a beautiful woman must be met with perfect agreement. A few moments later, the frenzy subsided and we ate supper in relative quiet. Only then did she discover that the first train left the next night.

"We will take it!" she decided and an empty discussion proceeded, Kshessinskaya animated by complete self-satisfaction.

Finally I took advantage of a lull and dared all.

"Perhaps there has been some mistake—I think that is it!" I offered.

"Mistake? A mistake, did you say, Bourman? Didn't that mad fool make a bow without me? Is that a mistake?" I had unleashed the Fury in her again!

"He probably thought you were behind him—nervous as he was, he was in the spotlight before he discovered his error. Mala, think! Nijinsky would never do a thing like that!"

"Don't be a baby! You think I don't know that Diaghilev was behind everything? It was his trick to promote his own interest! I know the success is his—and Nijinsky's. Of course, it was Diaghilev! For his meanhearted Ballet Russe and its profits! Poor Vaslaw, to have to listen to that spirit of Lucifer!"

"Let's call Diaghilev and invite him to explain!" I proposed.

"Diaghilev? Diaghilev, did you say?—I will never look at that man with his lock of white hair again! Never!"

"But think—Mala—think! Diaghilev wouldn't insult you! It was Vaslaw's stupidity! Nijinsky was the dumbbell! Give Diaghilev a chance to explain. Punish Nijinsky—but not the Silver Beaver and his company! Go—and you'll leave every one of us stranded in Budapest without a penny!"

Mala shook her head impetuously, crying: "But, Bourmanchik, that is not right! Why should the company suffer because Nijinsky is a madman?"

"We leave tomorrow for Monte Carlo. If we arrive there a day later without you, our contract will be broken—and Diaghilev, as usual, is without money until we earn it for him!"

"You are too smart—playing on my sympathies because I love the boys and girls!"

It was my cue and I plunged headlong, begging Kshessinskaya with every spark of eloquence at my command to ignore every thought but her own desire. "Don't worry about us, Mala! Every boy and girl in the company will be happy to suffer for an artist like the divine Kshessinskaya—what can hunger mean if you are happy! I think it is best for you to go, Mala."

"You devil!" she exploded. "Diaghilev graduated you from his own Machiavellian school. I will spend the night thinking. Maybe I will see him tomorrow!"

It was as nearly finished as I could make it, and with a wish of "Blessed dreams!" I left the première and dashed off to Diaghilev. He sat in full dress, although it was nearly four in the morning. When I entered, he rose, greeting me with his customary supercilious air. "And how did my lawyer arrange the matter?" he queried, only a trace of his concern apparent in his knitted brows.

My smile heartened him, and after a brief explanation, the two of us set out for Nijinsky's apartment, Diaghilev meanwhile congratulating me on my tact and promising me undying favor, a declaration that I valued as lightly as it was made.

Nijinsky hung his head like a schoolboy and refused to meet our eyes or to give any sign that he heard our tirade. We left him minus reassurance to seek a few hours' sleep before inveigling the irate Kshessinskaya into further capitulation.

At ten the next morning I called for her. What a sight greeted me when she invited me in. She was literally barricaded behind packed trunks!

I ignored them as tactfully as one can ignore a dozen trunks obviously on display, and we breakfasted to an accompaniment of trivial talk. Our usual drive followed without mention of her impending departure—and at one we returned to a suite filled with flowers, among them an enormous basket bearing a sentimental note signed by every member of the company except me.

"That Silver Beaver is behind all this!" muttered Kshessinskaya.

"Nonsense, Mala, it's the artists who have sympathized with you. They are merely expressing themselves!" I lied unhesitatingly, adding, "But it's useless to persuade you. Do me one favor—see Diaghilev and let him apologize for the insult Nijinsky offered. Say one little 'yes' and I'll call him at once!"

"And how do you know where he is? I don't want him for lunch. Tell him to come in an hour if you must!"

At that moment the head waiter announced luncheon, and I disappeared to call Diaghilev in person.

He was elated over the success of our coup.

"I'll be there in a few minutes," he promised. "What kind of flowers does she love most?"

Back I sped to Kshessinskaya, waiting to start luncheon in gay spirits, but keeping one eye on the clock ominously, her nervousness betraying her readiness to work up more temperament for Diaghilev. Within ten minutes, the Silver Beaver put in an appearance, smiling cheerily and twiddling his monocle.

"Good afternoon, beautiful angel," said he, stooping to kiss Kshessinskaya's hand, and sweeping her from head to foot with an approving glance. "Beautiful angel you are, indeed! And what a gown! A fitting one to set off the jewel of loveliness we adore. . . ."

That began a landslide of compliments that outdid themselves in grace and gallantry, melting Kshessinskaya into extending an invitation to eat with us. Diaghilev, meanwhile drew on an endless fund of jokes, reducing us to unaffected outbursts of laughter, and forcing Kshessinskaya to repeat her invitation. A knock sounded on the door before he could reply, and the head waiter entered eclipsed by the bouquet of roses he carried.

Kshessinskaya opened the tiny envelope with them and scanned it rapidly. "You devil!" she giggled. "You aren't eating with us! Eat!"

"Madame, I will—in exchange for exactly one minute's private conversation with you!"

They went into the next room while Borkengagen and I ate. "Perhaps you have been smart enough to keep her," Olga observed.

A half hour passed, punctuated at intervals by Kshessinskaya's high-pitched voice protesting, "No! No! Not for any money! No!" The last outcry was impassioned denial.

"Diaghilev has failed," I thought.

A few minutes ticked away. There were sounds of laughter and the groan of an opening door. Kshessinskaya entered on Diaghilev's arm!

"The world is saved!" said he. "Now I will eat!"—but everything was cold and Olga and I had to down another full luncheon to seal the pact!

"You are a poor lawyer, Bourman," Diaghilev chided, but Malitchka thought otherwise.

"He did everything—or you would be lost," she interrupted. Then, "Olga! My trunks!—Back to the theater with them—quickly!"

Diaghilev strolled to the phone and in less than five minutes Nijinsky was announced.

If you could have seen him at that moment, you would have forgotten his Spectre—and everything else, to laugh! His face was stained a deep mahogany shade with embarrassment. He stood first on one foot, and then on the other. He tried to speak and made an odd, stifled gurgle.

Kshessinskaya stared at him for the space of a half minute before she broke the painful silence with a shout of laughter.

"Vaslaw, come here!" she commanded, and when he stood before her, she was once more the siren who had won Russia's heart. "What can you say for yourself with the inspiration of a kiss?" and Malitchka embraced him.

He found his tongue at last and pleaded with her. "I was just a little crazy, Mala! Forgive me, for you are divine!" He bent his head over her hand.

"Forgive you?" cried Malitchka, gaily hooking her arm over his shoulders. "There is nothing to forgive! It is this temperament of ours, Vaslaw, that makes us great artists! You are forgiven—and you are lucky to have a friend at court! Come, let us laugh and forget!"—and for the balance of the tour Kshessinskaya's temper behaved itself.

That night I watched them do their *Spectre de la Rose* and share an ovation in perfect harmony, to the intense relief of the company. Monte Carlo loomed—and peace had been attained without a soul in the outer world aware that chaos had reigned!

VI

MADAME KSHESSINSKAYA

No LIFE of Nijinsky can be complete without a personal sketch of Matilda Felixovna Kshessinskaya [1]—the woman whose power was a more potent influence in his burst into fame than perhaps any other single personality who touched his. She placed the seal of success upon him when she sought him backstage at his graduation performance and announced that she would dance with him at Krasnoe Selo. So long as he had remained with the Imperial Russian Ballet, his supremacy was assured as her partner.

Favorite of the Tsar, friend of artists and nobles, and the idol of her audiences, Madame Kshessinskaya remained democratic and unaffected to any who knew her, despite the published accounts of her as an autocrat wielding heartless power. To be sure, her whims were laws irrevocable, and her word, once pronounced, carried little prospect of appeal, which may account adequately for those who failed to penetrate to the selflessness of her character and in consequence felt only her tremendous superiority in Kshessinskaya's presence.

I knew her well—better than most who have written about her, yet I never saw her use power meanly. On the contrary, I have seen her exert it on more than one occasion to assist unrecognized artists towards success that could hold no personal interest for the grand Kshessinskaya. Talent was bound to call forth her generous patronage.

The only thing I ever heard against her that I credited was the report that she was responsible for the resignation of Prince Volkonsky as the

[1] Princess Krasinsky.

director of the Imperial Russian Theaters. The story goes that Kshessinskaya was told to wear one costume and preferred another, which she wore.

Her name was posted on the official bulletin the following day, together with the amount of the fine imposed upon her, and on the day following that, Prince Volkonsky resigned. Rumor has it that Kshessinskaya's influence had reached far and above the head of Prince Volkonsky despite his position as one of Russia's foremost powers, and that he paid for insulting the mighty ballerina before the entire company. Whether or not Volkonsky proffered his post suddenly without pressure is one of those mysteries forever buried in the history of Imperial Russia, but it is generally admitted that Kshessinskaya, if she chose, could readly have forced his action.

Book after book and columns of space in the press have been devoted to Kshessinskaya and her art. As a ballerina her successes overshadowed those of every previous première in the history of the Marinsky. Even the superb Anna Pavlowa's record stands a shade under that set by Kshessinskaya. She was incomparable, and living quietly in Paris today she has the right to enjoy memories richer than those of any other living dancer—unless it might be Nijinsky, whose powers of memory have fled forever, according to renowned specialists.

Together, Kshessinskaya and Nijinsky set an unprecedented record for the ballet *Talisman* at the Marinsky when they were forced to repeat their duo three times before St. Petersburg connoisseurs permitted the presentation to continue. Kshessinskaya's technique in that variation placed it among the few perfect things on earth, and St. Petersburg was one spot where dance mastery was recognized. The ovation that brought the performance at the Marinsky to a standstill for the first time in history was a triumph that has never been equaled.

Gold and jewels poured into the première's overflowing coffers until she was the wealthiest woman in the Empire, with gorgeous palaces dotting the countryside—at Strelna, in the Crimea, in the Caucasian fastnesses, to furnish her with sequestered retirement when the vivacity of the capital and life in her white palace on the city's most enviable site bored the star.

Villas in France and Italy were awaiting the mood that sent her dashing across Europe in a private car as often as in a public conveyance. Her Villa Alam at Cap d'Aille was a center of gaiety when Monte Carlo offered a setting for her opulence. A few of us were permitted to call her Mala, and, occasionally, the more intimate diminutive, Malitchka.

She was universally adored for her wholehearted sponsorship of benefits, and for the presents she sent apparently without reason, sometimes to the entire ensemble, bombarding girls and boys alike with candy and fruits. Young dancers were thrilled into extravagant burblings when she sent an invitation to visit her at her palace or to attend one of her magnificent parties. She was never content to live for herself alone—life was barren then. It was only when she was sharing her bounty and happiness that she felt the fullness of life worth while to herself.

When Kshessinskaya entertained, rubles were spent by the thousands, and when she gambled she flung her money around like a feminine Midas. Sporting blood coursed in her veins strongly enough to thrill the most inveterate gambler when she brought out cards and proposed: "A good fast game of poker, with unlimited stakes!—or better yet, take me to Monte Carlo, or to a club for roulette!"

Bridge she despised. "That game?" she would ask. "Why should I play it? It is for doddering old matrons whose blood has dried up along with their brains!"

Monte Carlo acclaimed her as "Madame Dix-sept" for seventeen was her number and she played it with splendid abandon. She won or she lost, and she smiled regardless, though she knew herself the loser even when she won her grandest sums.

Her son, Vova, was only a few years old when we knew her best and we watched her run to fulfill his slightest wish. He was one of the handsomest boys I have ever seen, the refinement of his features betraying the dominating Russian blood that he might boast. Little lakes were laid out on his mother's estates so that he might ride in swan-boats. A miniature railroad was constructed in order that he might drive a tiny locomotive.

"I want to be King of the Monkeys!" he wept, and Kshessinskaya bought hundreds of stuffed monkeys for him to rule! There was no limit to her love or her extravagances if Vova's pleasure was at stake. While he was small, she carried him wherever she went.

Rehearsals were abruptly halted by his shrill voice commanding "Mamma! Vova wants a kiss!" Not another step did Kshessinskaya dance until Vova had been kissed!

Her stage appearances were veritable holidays, especially when she played Victor Hugo's *Notre Dame de Paris*.[2] Time and again I have watched Kshessinskaya's miming bring tears to her audiences, so tremendous was the emotion released by her playing.

Equally great were her interpretations in *The Lake of the Swans, Sleeping Beauty, Bayadere,* and *The Daughter of Pharaoh*. In the last-named ballet she never fell short of creating a sensation when the tomb of the mummy was opened and revealed the still-living daughter of Pharaoh—a daughter ablaze with diamonds from the crown of her gorgeous Egyptian headdress to the toes of her dainty sandals, ominous only when her enormous emeralds and rubies sent baleful shafts of color arcing through her scintillating costume.

That opulent character always astounded her audiences, unwilling to credit their eyes, yet unable to doubt that the gems clothing Kshessinskaya were authentic stones, since no paste jewels could glitter with such power, even under the artful glow of foot- and spot-lights.

Pearls, strung in tiny globes on metal wire, wrapped her exquisite body in yards of rich luster. Her costume reposed in her marble palace in St. Petersburg when it was not in use.

In 1922, I met her unexpectedly at Monte Carlo. After our first meeting, she burst out, "Do you know, I own nothing more than the clothes on my back?"

"What?" I gasped. "You are joking!"

"No, Bourmanchik! It is the truth, but it has made me laugh so often! I was dancing at the Marinsky—just practicing, and all I had with me was my practice suit and my ballet slippers in a little bag. You know how it was during the Revolution . . . there were no carriages as before. When I was

[2] This ballet is more familiar in Europe as *Esmeralda*.

done, I strolled back to my palace and—Bourmanchik! I couldn't get in for the crowds around it. I spoke to a woman in the crowd asking, 'What's going on here?' "

Kshessinskaya paused dramatically before she continued her story. "The woman looked at me without recognition, for she was poor, and I was dressed simply enough. 'Oh, madame, it is nothing exciting,' she said. 'Lenin and Trotsky are holding a meeting in a palace that has just been taken over by the government, and we are waiting to see them—they are such great men!' Such great men," Kshessinskaya laughed, "and all my jewels in the safe for Lenin and his Bolsheviki!"

I opened my lips to sympathize, but her face was wreathed in carefree smiles. "It was so funny! Imagine losing everything but your ballet slippers and tights! And now? I am having a grand time trying to teach girls how to do a proper pas de basque! I am a ballet mistress, if you please!"

Rapidly I contrasted her situation with what it had been when Nijinsky and I called on her at New Year's, and a supercilious butler had relieved us of our coats. After our visit with the Grand Dukes, Princes, generals, and celebrated artists in her salon, we had dropped ten rubles into the outstretched hand of the butler, observing a Prince contribute a paltry hundred-ruble note as a tip. Outside, Nijinsky had devoutly crossed himself and remarked, "Thank God, there is but one Kshessinskaya in St. Petersburg, for between providing her with a remembrance and giving her butler a tip, we should be penniless for life!"

That woman, a veritable goddess, with unlimited prestige and wealth, her devotion to her son and her imperial power, was the same who stood stripped of her wealth and was glorious still. She is the gallant spirit who saw Nijinsky dance and elevated him instantly to his true place as peer of all male dancers, without thought of her own reward.

Kshessinskaya gave her friendship to me, but when she said: "You are wonderful! A genius, Nijinsky! I will take you for my partner this summer —and afterwards!" she gave Vaslaw more assurance of fame and success than could the director himself, for she presented him with the inspiration of a technical mastery as brilliant as his own!

VII

MONTE CARLO AND
AGA KHAN

My DREAMS came true when we reached Monte Carlo and I for the first time gazed at that rich resort in its lovely setting. Great mountains bulked against a lapis lazuli sky, and a million million flowers bloomed in a garden of palms, scenting the air for miles aound, welcoming us with languorous charm—we who were used to the bitter north wind screaming down on us from a barren polar tundra! Even without the Casino, it would have been paradise. But the Casino was there—and the majority of us resolved to woo Madame la Roulette ardently!

It is a law that no permanent resident of Monaco nor any employee of the Casino may play, but we made it our business to sprint for the Casino and have cards issued to us before Diaghilev could take proper steps to put us on the "protected list." Nijinsky, no more prey to gaming fever in Monte Carlo than he was in St. Petersburg, was among the few latecomers to be denied a card.

He was consequently unruffled by the circumstance that deprived him of his gambler's rights, seldom borrowing a card for the privilege of winning or losing twenty francs, and becoming a model of virtue for the Silver Beaver, stripped of funds by our demands for advances on our salaries. Vaslaw had had my example before him too many years to enjoy high hazards.

Not so Kshessinskaya! She was among the worst offenders in the company, playing on a complimentary card issued by the Casino management, and deserting Madame la Roulette only for the Sporting Club with higher stakes in company with international celebrities and crowned heads who flocked around her.

Vaslaw and I were sauntering through les salles de jeux when Kshessinskaya arrived, beaming. Remarkably enough, she was alone.

"Come on, you two," she hailed. "Today isn't my day at all, but I want to lose my money in a hurry and get the sad business over!"

"Try trente et quarante," I advised; "the stakes are at least twice those permitted by roulette!"

"Splendid!" and we followed her to the table.

She played quietly, whispering her bets to the croupier in thousand-franc amounts, apparently immersed in her observations of bystanders with their few hundred-franc risks. In less than ten minutes, she lost sixty thousand francs!

I opened my eyes. It was the equivalent of nearly four years' salary for me, but the ballerina only smiled and remarked: "Bien! I told you it was not my day! But no matter—it was a small loss!"

There Nijinsky and I met some of the most famous persons alive. Members of the Russian royal family visited the resort annually, and we renewed acquaintanceship with them, meanwhile adding King Gustaf of Sweden; King Alexander of Montenegro, a graduate of the Russian Corps de Cadets; Basil Zaharov, owner of France's railways and coal mines, reputed to be the richest man in Europe and universally referred to as "the Mystery Man"; Camille Blanc, who with Zaharov owned the Casino; Gould, the American multimillionaire; and a host of others to those who were on more or less intimate terms wth Diaghilev and Nijinsky.

Nijinsky walked and talked with his London friends, Lady Ripon, Lady Salisbury, and Lady Montague under the warm Mediterranean sun, perfectly happy, apparently, to chat with them, and never permit a worry over the whir of a wheel to enter his head.

Occasionally he watched me play, often in company with the Silver

Beaver. I recall the two of them standing beside me while I played twenty-franc hazards.

Diaghilev smiled cynically. "You were playing beyond your pocketbook, Bourman! Watch those two old gentlemen risking only five-franc hazards on a spin of the wheel."

"They can't afford more," I scoffed. "They haven't as much in their pockets as you've put into mine!"

"Don't flatter me, Bourman," Diaghilev warned. "They are only Zaharov and Blanc who run the Casino! You're probably right about their poverty! Poor men—after all, they are only risking putting cash back into their own pockets!"

"No wonder they don't gamble! They have nothing to gain and nothing to lose—but I! Perhaps the wheel will toss a fortune into my lap in an hour!"

It was the best retort I could manage when I dropped my last twenty francs on the table, and Nijinsky smiled laconically, peering from under his heavy brows! That Vaslaw! He knew that fortune seldom rewarded me, and when she did I begged her to win back her favors!

Opposite our table a beautiful member of the Ballet Russe played, now winning, now losing, always hiding her face behind a heavy veil, and behind us a group of Orientals watched her, one in particular apparently amused at her attitude.

The dancer became self-conscious and moved to another table. The Orientals followed, politely, but still amused. I called Nijinsky's attention to her obvious discomfiture, pointing out the man who seemed most interested in her luck.

"He? Don't worry foolishly," advised Nijinsky. "It is Aga Khan, forty-ninth descendant from Mohamet in direct line, who watches. He is one of the richest maharajahs in all India and is an honored guest here at the moment!"

I watched him run up the steps of Monte Carlo's most palatial hotel the following day between eight turbaned servants who bowed to the ground, nearly upsetting their equilibrium, as he passed, and then fell in, two by two, and trotted up the steps behind him. A few days more, and our dancer wore an enormous blue-white diamond.

It was Klementowitsch who repeated to me gossip regarding the donor after the girl's boasts to artists in the company.

"I was walking past Cartier's and stopped to admire the marvelous jewels on display when Aga Khan walked past and stopped. 'Which do you admire most?' he asked—of course, he's been noticing me for two days! I pointed out this stone. 'Accept it as a little token,' he suggested, and when I answered, 'Why not?' he bought it!" exulted the happy girl, displaying her "token."

As a rule, she danced in the ensemble, and so when Aga Khan bowered the whole stage with flowers, she rejoiced anew, letting her imagination run riot.

"Aga Khan loves me," she cried, displaying gems and gowns rich in line and fabric. He happened to visit her native country. It was a fresh indication of his interest, she thought.

"I will be an Oriental Princess!" bragged the little star, and the words were ill-spoken. Aga Khan learned from someone among his numerous retinue that his little acquaintance claimed him as her suitor, and never again did he make a friendly gesture towards her.

"I'll sue him," she wept to Diaghilev, but Diaghilev was Aga Khan's good friend and knew the refinement of the Maharajah.

"Who knows who gave you all this?" questioned the Silver Beaver. "Be wise," he counseled; "if Aga Khan ever *was* your friend, he is no more. You have been empty-headed with your dreams. Enjoy the gifts the gods have placed on your fingers and around your throat! Rejoice in the sparkle of your diamonds—" and the little star listened, keeping her thoughts to herself until, at last, she left the company.

VIII

"L'APRÈS-MIDI D'UN FAUNE"

Paris was always our goal for the spring season when notables arrived from every corner of the earth for the Grand Prix races. Engagements were played either at the Grand Opéra or at the Théâtre du Châtelet, and a new ballet was inevitably required for our Parisian presentation. In 1912, it was Nijinsky's latest ballet composition, *L'Après-Midi d'un Faune,* set to music by Debussy, which was presented. Despite the many times I watched it in rehearsal, I couldn't find anything sensational in it, although the press had heralded the piece as a genuine creation bearing the signs of genius in its development. The only genius I could discover was that of Diaghilev who had prompted the extraordinary publicity!

I distinctly remember watching the premier from the first wing, with a crowd of curious visitors clustered about me, craning their necks for a glimpse of the latest marvel among a collection of priceless ballet gems. I knew every step of the ballet, for Klementowitsch, who is now my wife, was then my fiancée, and she was one of the seven girls who danced with Nijinsky.

Uneasily I waited in the wing, unable to discover anything wonderful at all in the show, wondering how Diaghilev had so far lost his senses as to bruit about the glory of an ordinary presentation! The story was so simple!

Seven nymphs were at play about a little lake, leaping and dancing happily when the curtain rose. At the top of a little hill, unseen by the girls, a faun stood observing their frolic. At last the girls decided to swim, and removed their tunics, an act which brought the faun leaping down from his vantage point to capture a nymph and carry her off to his stronghold, but the nymphs eluded him, and it was only the dress of one of them that remained in his hands. While the faun, madly in love with the nymphs, stroked and kissed the flimsy garment, retreating to his hillock with it, where he knelt in an ecstasy of sorrow, adoring and caressing it, the curtain descended by inches.

To my complete amazement, at the Paris opening Nijinsky placed the tunic on the grass at his side, and lay down with a series of suggestive movements, while women's screams echoed through the theater, mingled with applause and masculine growls of disapproval. Never have I seen such a scandal created! The curtain rose and fell to whistles, hisses—applause which created a chaos.

Diaghilev fluttered onto the stage like a butterfly, for the sensational ending was his way of making interest rise. Meanwhile, in the audience, gendarmes had been called to quell the disturbance. There were actual fistic encounters going on over the merit or demerit of Nijinsky's latest solo!

The critics disagreed, the audience disagreed, and inevitably there was but one way to know which camp was right, and that was to witness *L'Après-Midi d'un Faune*. All Paris felt called upon to make the decision, and once more the Ballet Russe was talked about from Montmartre to the Bois de Boulogne, while "Sold Out" placards dotted the lobby nightly. Diaghilev's scheme had worked! He was once more the sensation of the season, for the stage in 1912 was not the stage of today!

Nicolai Roerich stood beside me in the wings. He was interested in the sets by Bakst. Diaghilev rushed up to him, elated. "Isn't it wonderful beyond our dream, Nicolai?"

"Diaghilev, it is awful! God save me from a success like that!" responded the great artist in utter disgust.

So uncertain were Diaghilev and Nijinsky of their reception by the crowds mobbing the stage door that they left secretly. Front-page criticism emblazoned the battle in headlines. For days, censure and applause fought for supremacy. Press associations spread the scandal around the world until the names "Ballet Russe" and "Nijinsky" were spoken commonly in far-off America.

Meanwhile ticket speculators boosted the prices, so that it cost me four hundred francs for a balcony seat to take Mother Nijinsky to the second performance at Vaslaw's request. That night he danced as he had rehearsed, and immediately I understood why he had not secured tickets for his mother for the initial presentation. All of his life, Vaslaw showed his deepest tenderness to Madame Nijinsky, protecting her wherever possible from any unhappiness in connection with his art.

Those who saw the second show, saw nothing amazing at all, and again the fight waxed hot, making our month's stay assured, and a full house the inevitable conclusion.

London saw us for the summer season, with a *L'Après-Midi d'un Faune* minus scandal at the Covent Garden Theater, where the only change was in the orchestra, Sir Thomas Beecham or Eugene Goossens holding the baton at Diaghilev's invitation. Few rehearsals once more released us for visits to museums and historic shrines, while every afternoon at five the company gathered by common consent at Hyde Park for tea. As hot weather came on, the Ballet Russe sought the long white beaches of Deauville. Expenses were increased ten times above those of Paris, and were the cause for universal thanksgiving that our season lasted but two weeks. Notwithstanding, we left Deauville with empty pockets.

The theater was small but exclusive there, accommodating audiences of not more than five hundred. The stage was equally limited. In consequence, only the smallest ballets could be presented, but Diaghilev collected his regular twenty thousand francs for each performance regardless. The Casino counted its profits not in the theater but in the salles de jeux during intermissions! Besides the Ballet Russe, the Casino featured such names as those of Chaliapin, Smirnov, and Felia Litvin, and similar stars who played to those same small audiences of millionaires.

Nijinsky and Diaghilev were to depart for the Lido, and the whole company took two months' paid vacation. I gambled away every bit of money I possessed and then wandered around the deserted resort penniless. Some kind fate made Vaslaw the last to leave the watering place that year, and decreed that I should meet him on his way to the station.

"Tola! When are you going?" he exclaimed.

"I think I will have to fish for two months to earn carfare to join the company, Vaslaw!" I sighed. "I have left my money on the tables again!"

Without a word, Nijinsky handed me the price of my ticket to Russia, and off I went to serve my compulsory time with the army—four weeks, because I was an artist with influential friends!

IX

REHEARSALS FOR
"LE SACRE DU PRINTEMPS"

$\mathbb{F}$ROM all points of the compass, the company returned to play the fall season, meeting in Berlin; once more we visited the foremost cities of Germany and Austria. We heard that Nijinsky was composing a new ballet to Stravinsky's *Le Sacre du Printemps,* a name that excited visions of classic beauty in the mind of every one of us. I rushed off to question Vaslaw about the latest presentation, only to be assured that the ballet would be set in the Stone Age!

"Nonsense! You are joking," I commented and turned on my heel, positive that Vaslaw was enjoying a little entertainment at my expense.

At rehearsal my aplomb was shattered. True to his promise, Vaslaw exhibited himself in a series of clumsy steps, shortly thereafter transforming the whole company into a prehistoric clan! We had grown up with Rimsky-Korsakov, Schumann, Chopin, and Tchaikovsky, but Nijinsky cared not at all for our classicism. We were expected to enjoy the discordancy of Stravinsky, with its uneven rhythms and its angular pattern at an initial hearing!

Our first few rehearsals left us confounded and confused, although repeated performance enabled us to familiarize ourselves with a new beauty that the composer had somehow evolved through the use of weird harmonic progressions.

Stravinsky himself, small and wiry, sat like an intense focus of electric flame darting over the piano with such strength and vehemence that it seemed, despite his diminutive size, he must splinter the keyboard into infinitesimal fragments! He played as though the strength of Goliath possessed him, weaving his eerie thunders together with fragile cobwebs of sound until he eventually swept our prejudices away, driving us into incredible frenzies which we were directed to express in primitive steps and pantomime.

Nijinsky rehearsed like an inexhaustible demon until he nearly dropped in his tracks. Jumps were no longer completed on toes with slightly flexed knees, but flat-footed and straight-legged in a fashion to preclude the possibility of lightness, and to convey an impression of antediluvian festivity that nearly killed us. With every leap we landed heavily enough to jar every organ in us. Our heads throbbed with pain, leaving us continually with nerves that jangled and bodies that ached. Nijinsky had to rehearse with every single group, and danced hour after hour, pounding his feet onto the stage with mighty thumps that must have cost him untold agony, for he had been used to dancing with the lightness and freedom of a feather tossed by the wind.

Time after time I sought him out, my own head a fiery hell of jagged pain, and raved: "Vaslaw! You'll drive every one of us crazy with those jumps! And we have only half as many as you! Change them before you have us in the madhouse or in the grave!"

My reward was always the same. Nijinsky's face would flush, his eyes would shoot tiny jets of fire at me. "The steps are mine. They will stay. Go back and dance them and don't bother me with your complaints!"

Off I would go to rejoin my own group of aching, irritable dancers, ready to break under the strain of routine that defied every muscle and nerve with its bludgeoning. We relapsed into sullen resentment at the latest composition of that Vaslaw who could dance like a devil, and made the rest of us emulate him on figurative coals, since the soles of our feet were tender and sore from the outset.

The tempo drove us to distraction, with its sharp and unexpected accents.

We worked until we, too, were as ready to drop as was Nijinsky, and our heads spun with the interminable repetition of mathematical counts.

Nijinsky slumped on his feet. The whole company drooped. In desperation, I went up to him. "Nijinsky! I'm going insane with this barbaric music and wilder dancing. Do me a favor, for heaven's sake—release me!"

Just as groggy as I, Vaslaw stood with his towel flung over his shoulders, mopping his forehead every few minutes, and, of course, at that moment Diaghilev arrived! He fitted his monocle into place.

"What is wrong, gentlemen?" His suave tones sounded as though they had come from another sphere. "Bourman! Are you starting a revolution with your ideas? What's wrong?"

I turned on him, frantic with fatigue. "Nothing! Nothing except that I am going crazy with this insane dance! I want to get away from it, to leave the company!"

Diaghilev surveyed me coolly. "So! And that is the help Vaslaw can expect from his best friend! Interesting, Bourman! Do you realize that Nijinsky is doing ten times the work you are, by any chance? He isn't insane!"

I was goaded past reason. "No! He isn't crazy now! But if he continues this mad dance, he'll go crazy in the end! How can he help it?"

"Everybody rehearses, Bourman! Everybody must work, or leave the company, and that is impossible. You must do your routine with the rest of the company."

It was finished, and there was no second appeal for me. Back I went and danced, sickened with every leap, aware that Nijinsky must be more harassed than I with the dancing he had outlined for himself. No one who has not lived through such endless torments of jolting and jarring can appreciate our suffering, that finally numbed itself with its own pangs.

The Silver Beaver had not forgotten me, however. The moment rehearsal was over, Diaghilev called me to him, and stood with me before Nijinsky. "See here, Bourman! You act as though you were a privileged character, and wielded some mystic power over Vaslaw!

"Henceforth you will address him not by any nickname at all. You will call him Mr. Nijinsky, just as every other member of the company does!"

I stood dumfounded for an instant before I answered. "Impossible, Mr. Diaghilev, you may break your contract with me, but I will not call Vaslaw 'Mr. Nijinsky'!"

Vaslaw broke in, "I'll not consent to that either! Mr. Diaghilev, you don't understand! Bourman and I have been friends for years—ever since we were boys together at school. I will not be 'Mr. Nijinsky' to him!"

Diaghilev walked off, and within a fortnight Vaslaw and I were on our old friendly footing. As rehearsals proceeded, however, Nijinsky began to show the frightful strain, and for the first time in years he missed entrance cues, he forgot steps, and he lacked the verve which had distinguished his work.

As I look back through the years, it seems so clear to me now that Vaslaw's first indication of abnormality showed under the continued racking of those weeks. He was forced in the end to moderate his ceaseless rehearsing, and to sit down, correcting our mistakes with a word or a motion, instead of joining us in the dance and showing us step by step when we failed to master the routine.

He was no longer absolute master of himself and his dance, for he showed signs of nervousness and absentmindedness in matters relating to it.

At school he had been slow to absorb French, history, mathematics, and Russian, but he understood and assimilated ballet and its principles without effort. In Austria and Germany he was content at last to rest and relinquish his crown at intervals. We set it down to an outraged nervous system and fatigue, but in the light of what has since transpired, it appears that the single flaw in that body of tempered steel betrayed itself for the first time, and could we have seen it, might have revealed the tragic destiny of ultimate madness in store for our star. A wise destiny has shrouded the future in mystery. Totally unconscious of Vaslaw's future, we revolted, cursed the "sacre" as we called it, and danced on . . . to London, still preparing for the grande première in Paris when warm breezes and green bursting buds should harbinger spring in the French capital and *Le Sacre du Printemps* would enjoy its first presentation!

X

"THE LAKE OF THE SWANS"

WHILE the frightful rehearsals for *Le Sacre* persisted, we arrived in
London, half-dead with sleepless nights and nightmare days over that "sacre"
which blasphemed every law of our tradition and awakened our ire until
we were ready to fight at a look. At a psychological moment, our whole attitude was transfigured by a happy circumstance. Kshessinskaya joined us in
London for two weeks! As a mark of special favor, Diaghilev revived her
favorite ballet, *The Lake of the Swans,* which had been a triumph in Russia
for both Kshessinskaya and Nijinsky. We loved it! In the second act, the
première ballerina had danced an exquisite variation to music played by the
masterly Leopold Auer, and in London Sir Thomas Beecham had arranged
a perfect accompaniment. Perfect it might be for us, but not for Kshessinskaya!

She had heard that Mischa Elman was in London. It was enough! She
invited him to play her variation at her expense! The number lasted only
one and a half minutes, but it always stopped the show.

"All right! That is only three minutes!" she declared. Everyone knew that
on the day of our performance, Mischa Elman was giving his own concert
at the Royal Albert Hall, England's largest concert hall.

It made no difference to Kshessinskaya. Less than a minute before her
cue, Elman jumped into the orchestra pit, and swung his violin under his
chin. At the end of four minutes he was gone! To this day, no one knows
how much that caprice of Kshessinskaya's cost her, for Elman had arranged

219

his own concert intermission to coincide with his appearance at Covent Garden, and taxied back for his own next number before he was missed!

The day before the performance, Elman and his father arrived for rehearsal, and I chatted with him, reminding him of an appearance in Russia, when he was a student at the Imperial Russian Conservatory of Music and Nijinsky and I were students at the Imperial Ballet School. Mischa Elman, Leo Strok (now Strokov), Osia Urman, Vaslaw, myself, and a few other boys had appeared in an insignificant performance for the price of a few rubles, some chocolates, and a handful of fruit! Elman laughed heartily over it all. That genius of the violin had graduated from the Conservatory only a year before Nijinsky had graduated from the Ballet School, and Vaslaw had witnessed with me Elman's first triumph at the Pavlovsk, a few miles from St. Petersburg.

After her brief solo to Elman's accompaniment, Kshessinskaya announced a dinner party at the Savoy to celebrate her own success. Again it was the best apartment the Savoy afforded that Madame occupied! Her best friends were invited, among them Diaghilev, Nijinsky, Bronia, Baron Ginsburgh, Seraphima Astafieva, Leon Bakst, Adolph Bolm, a few others, and myself. There were no more than five of her old friends from the Russian Ballet left in the Diaghilev company, which at that time included artists from Moscow, Warsaw, and St. Petersburg, as well as from England, for Diaghilev maintained that English girls were the most beautiful and talented girls in Europe, and recruited a dozen or so in that belief.

Bakst, as always, moved from group to group, for he was among the most popular artists abroad. His appearances backstage were heralded by shouts of joy, and he was embraced as a long-lost and always welcome prodigal by every girl and boy in the company. Grand Duke Andrei assisted Kshessinskaya as host in a big dining room where we were served in typical English style under the supervision of the maître d'hôtel, instructed by the Grand Duke to prepare a typical Russian meal with the good things of Old Russia the Grand Duke had brought with him to celebrate Kshessinskaya's triumphant reunion with us.

Consternation wrote itself into our faces when the waiters served us, not as Russians but as Englishmen! There were small glasses of water, small portions of meat, small portions of caviar! Seeing the company convulsed at the English notion of a Russian meal, the Grand Duke did his best to spare the pride of the maître d'hôtel at Kshessinskaya's request.

"Our customs are different," he stated. "May I call my own Russian head waiter to explain?"

The maître d'hôtel acceded at once, and the Grand Duke's voice thundered "Luka! Kuzma! Show them how you serve wine!" In no time huge tumblers were before us filled with wine. "The little wine glasses are for liqueurs with coffee," His Highness pointed out to the amazed English, who stood by in holy horror while we ladled huge tablespoonfuls of caviar onto our plates, and heaped them high with meat! We drank our "vodka" minus water or ginger ale and survived, to the undying astonishment of the Savoy waiters!

After an intermission of informal talk and smoking, Kshessinskaya brought forth her cards, and we played poker. I was without more than a few pounds and as ignorant as Nijinsky of how one played poker, but we declared ourselves ready to learn. With every cent Bakst had, plus all I could borrow from Vaslaw, I started instructions under Kshessinskaya's expert guidance.

One loss, enough to put Vaslaw out of the game, was precisely what I needed to whet my appetite. Nijinsky sat near by, watching, while Diaghilev insisted that my sole aim in life was to ruin Vaslaw's life and fortune with my infernal gambling. They watched my stupid plays and heavy losses tolerantly. A few wins were likewise sufficient for me. I insisted that I could play poker like a veteran, but Vaslaw only laughed and tossed his money to me. "If you're so lucky, here's some money to make my fortune on, but you play for me!" With Vaslaw's faith and Kshessinskaya's help, we won over two hundred pounds. Grand Duke Andrei changed our chips for real gold pieces, an act that delighted Nijinsky, who became feverishly excited as the money clinked back and forth across the table.

Hours of conversation and light drinking followed, until we broke up in the early morning, Grand Duke Andrei's invitation to visit Windsor Castle on the following Sunday echoing in our ears.

Like all of the Romanovs, Grand Duke Andrei was affable and friendly, boasting hundreds of enthusiastic friends willing to swear that he was a prince among men, even had he been born a peasant. During our rehearsals he frequently wandered into the theater, dressed in the simplest fashion, insisting that the rehearsal go on and that he be permitted to find a seat for himself without attendants. Often Madame Kshessinskaya grew thirsty, and then Grand Duke Andrei dashed off to the nearest bar, returning not only with Kshessinskaya's drink, but with punches and fruit juices for the whole company, along with sandwiches enough for all.

On Sunday, as prearranged, we met at Paddington and boarded a special car ordered by His Imperial Highness for the trip to Windsor Castle. Arrived at the station, he took a provincial carriage and ordered others for the company, laughing and joking at the coachmen perched like great blackbirds high above our heads, indolently swinging long whips over their horses whenever the thought occurred to them. Off we went in these amazing equipages to the Castle, ready to invade it en masse and discover its splendor for ourselves. The thought of being turned away never occurred to us. The Grand Duke demanded entrance from a guard, who stood adamant. "None may enter on Sunday without a special permit, sir," he insisted, while Grand Duke Andrei paced up and down nervously, conscious of the twelve guests who watched.

"See here," he stormed, "I am the cousin of the Russian Tsar. I am a Prince of the royal Russian line. I am Grand Duke Andrei Vladimirovitch!"

The soldier saluted. "Perhaps I believe you, sir, but it is impossible for you to enter without a permit. What proof have you of your title?" His Highness was losing his temper when an officer strode up, again addressing him as "sir," and assuring him that, without credentials, entrance to the Castle was out of the question. Completely blocked by English stolidity, Grand Duke Andrei conceded defeat, when the officer raised his brows and observed, "Of course, sir, if you do happen to be the Grand Duke, the Russian ambassador could relieve the situation in five minutes."

We tried to explain to our host that the soldier merely followed orders and that a visit to the ambassador would set things to rights in no time, but he was crestfallen.

"You see," he explained, "I am so tired of being surrounded by pomp! I thought I might visit Windsor Castle without formality. I see it was a hopeless thought. Next Sunday you will visit it as my guests, and I will be officially recognized as the cousin of the Tsar, the Grand Duke Andrei of Russia! It is too bad!" And shaking his head mournfully, he climbed to his place and rode back to the station at Windsor, the guard and his officer smiling owlishly.

On our way we saw boys from Eton, with short jackets, big white collars, and tall silk hats, which made them look to us like boys playing at being men. In an ancient tavern, a typical Englishman served us generous slabs of roast beef with mild and bitter ale that repaid us for our empty call at the Castle. All the way to London, the Grand Duke seemed humiliated, his mood brightened only temporarily by the suggestion that we occupy ourselves by recounting the most risqué jokes in our repertoires.

Count Benckendorff, Russia's ambassador to Great Britain, received orders without delay. The following Sunday we departed once more for Windsor Castle in a royal train! At the station our party was met by a guard of honor. A red carpet was spread for us from the train to the carriage. When we arrived at Windsor Castle, the guards stood at attention in full-dress uniform, their officers splendid in gold braid, themselves at attention before the royal equipages ranged to greet us in the court. The gates were flung wide, and the Castle, closed against us the previous Sunday, was courteously thrown open "at the disposal of His Imperial Highness, the Grand Duke Andrei of Russia!"

Through miles of galleries we wandered, inspecting presents that had been tendered to Queen Elizabeth, and coronation gifts acquired through ages, down to the last, presented by the Tsar to King George V, a tremendous vase made of malachite.

I recall the Grand Duke's mannerisms, his courtesy, his democratic attitude devoid of artificiality. Anyone who came near him was his friend.

I cannot resist the temptation to compare him often with the pitifully in-adequate pretensions of "born democrats" who seek to impress one with—what? I cannot understand! A few days later, he left, asking us for the addresses of our relatives and requesting the privilege of making presents to our families. I gave him the name of my brother at the Military Cadet School of Alexander II, which was thrown into a furor when the Grand Duke telephoned to present my brother with a plum pudding!

XI

"LE SACRE DU PRINTEMPS"
IN PARIS

After rehearsing our "sacre" until we had mastered every detail of its technique, it was evident that its originality of concept was startling enough to guarantee a sensation in Paris. An appearance in Monte Carlo left us disappointed so far as the Casino was concerned, for we were perpetually at the "sacre" in preparation for our expected triumph in the Théâtre des Champs-Elysées, which we were to have the honor of opening.

Diaghilev was a center of activity. He directed the press, the printers, the artists, the costumers—the thousand details that went into an opening presentation. Around the world our programs were noted as works of art prepared by Diaghilev without thought of expense to provide every ticket holder with a worthy remembrance of whatever ballet he witnessed.

Jean Cocteau, Claude Debussy, Paul Dukas, Maurice Ravel, Igor Stravinsky, Sergei Prokofiev, Leon Bakst, Alexandre Benois, and Nicolai Roerich were among the world-renowned artists and musicians who haunted Diaghilev. They became familiar to us likewise, mingling with us at rehearsals, for they were employed to bend every effort towards making Diaghilev's ballets supreme in every artistic detail. Later, as the modern movement gained prestige, Picasso, Matisse, Sert, and Durand were often working on and bizarre atmosphere that the Silver Beaver insisted upon as a fit setting problems with Diaghilev and his whole company, providing the splendor for his "jewels." Fame and glory were the certain rewards of whatever "moderns" Diaghilev discovered for sponsorship.

The conductors engaged were as well known as the composers and artists who gave their genius. Albert Coates, Rhené-Baton, and Ernest Ansermet have all held the baton for the Ballet Russe.

Diaghilev cultivated them all as personal friends, and each contributed his own thoughts and ideas to produce the harmonious whole that made Diaghilev's presentations more than originations, inevitably establishing his reputation as a creator par excellence. Madame Edwards, with her highly developed sense of discrimination, often criticized the Silver Beaver's plans until they were nothing but shadowy ghosts of glory. Without exception her opinion triumphed, scoring anther compliment for Diaghilev's "artistic perception." Beautiful Mademoiselle Chanel gave her time and inspiration to create gorgeous costumes, culling ever fresh distinction for the Ballet Russe. Let adversity deprive Diaghilev of every cent, it was still Gabrielle Chanel who came to his rescue—and Diaghilev whose laurels were increased by his legions of admirers.

To the surprise of most of us, *Le Sacre du Printemps* achieved an ovation without too much censure for its primordial appeal in Paris. The feminine lead had been given to Hilda Munnings, an English girl who later was billed as "Lydia Sokolova." Her role would have challenged the strength and art of a man with its reiterated emphasis on sensational leaps and turns. Certainly it was impossible to find another girl able to execute the powerful routine with the same sureness and brilliancy that characterized Sokolova's work.

Her initial success in the "sacre" justly placed her as a ranking première in the ultra-modern productions which followed. The whole range of modern ballets by Picasso and Matisse, including *Parade, The Three-Cornered Hat,* and *Le Sacre du Printemps,* introduced the type of dancing which seems to be enjoying a revival by the Germans. During the past few years, it has been bruited about that the German Moderns have opened a new era in dancing. Most of the world seems to have forgotten what I know; almost twenty years ago, the movement began, not in Germany, but in Paris with Diaghilev's first modern ballet!

We made our success then with real modern work, unmixed with the principles of classical ballet, unmarred by steps which are an integral part of the classical dance, and are defended by the "new moderns" on the grounds of "public appeal." Then we were frankly and completely "modern" without borrowing from Fokine or any other ballet master to add the semblance and sanction of convention. Today's "moderns" have worked from a ballet foundation. In the past few years I have watched them dancing steps, with slight variations, taught to me years ago in St. Petersburg by Legat and Obouchov. That alone effectively eliminates the interminable argument that ballet is artificial, for the very exponents of the primitive have obviously built upon ballet fundamentals which have equipped them for the whole gamut of dance interpretation, group formation, and figure compositions.

XII

FIRST TOUR
OF SOUTH AMERICA

In July, 1913, Diaghilev called the company together to notify us of our departure for South America in the fall. For two months we salved every irritation with the prospect of twenty-one days of absolute rest while we sailed from Southampton to Buenos Aires. On September 17, we stood at the rail of the *Avon,* Vaslaw and I, watching Cherbourg recede, Nijinsky's face an implacable mask hiding his thoughts. We rolled in wealth, while our salaries piled up without an opportunity to spend money. Inevitably we played cards; we took our daily exercise without too much effort and shelved every concern for the Neptune Ball that claimed us as we crossed the equator.

Diaghilev had remained in London—once more Vaslaw relaxed. Like a boy on a holiday he joined in our fun, practicing with the company, completely forgetful of the "position" and prestige he commanded as star of the Ballet Russe, since Diaghilev was not present to remind him of it.

Vaslaw hooked his arm in mine as in years past, remarking, "For a little time I am free to do as I wish; but it won't be for long, so let's talk as we used to, before I have to begin my role of star!" In no time we acquainted ourselves with the passengers, Nijinsky often promenading, immersed in conversation with a young woman who seemed familiar to me. I watched them swinging past my deck chair, vainly trying to place his companion. I had seen her before—but where? I gave it up.

One night shortly afterwards, we sat on deck, gazing off into infinities of space, dreaming in silence. Suddenly Vaslaw moved nervously. "Tola! Can you understand how it feels to rest? *Really to rest* in the midst of this peace, without Diaghilev's objections, without the need for formal compliments with society people who have become almost my sole companions? It is a taste of Paradise, this trip that takes us gliding through the stillness!" His eyes traveled astern where a silver fan spread out on a smooth sea, under the vast night curtain folding noise and trouble away in its beauty. "Yes, it is a taste of Paradise!" he repeated.

The magical quality was gone an instant later, and our talk turned to women, to flirtations, and to love.

"You see, Vaslaw," I began, "I am happy, now. This trip to South America is an interlude only. When I return to Europe, I will be married to Loda Klementowitsch. Why don't you marry, too, and be happy with someone to care more for you than for anyone else in all the world?" But Nijinsky was staring into the night, and I hardly knew whether or not he heard me as I rambled ahead. "There are many women who would accept your proposal—wherever you go! But, Vaslaw," I warned, "when you marry, remember how you have hated society life all down the years I have known you. It will be wise for you to choose a Russian dancer for a wife, a woman who knows your language and your heart, who loves the dance as you love it. That is what will bring you happiness! You have made enough money, so it isn't necessary for you to marry wealth, or anything but love. Think of the beautiful girls with the company!"

"You're right, Tola, but the girl I wanted is engaged now," he remarked.

That was a surprise. I started in astonishment. "The girl is in our ballet? But I never saw you flirt with anyone, or pay any attention to any of the ballet girls!"

He laughed shortly. "You are in love, Tola! You have no eyes for what is going on! Besides, I can't talk with whomever I please as you can. If I speak to any girl in the company, there is a buzz of gossip. Diaghilev has me more firmly chained than you can understand. For the sake of the girl I loved, how could I show my attentions?" He swung one leg over the other and settled back into silence.

"All right! But who is the girl you wanted to talk to?" I persisted.

Furiously he turned on me. "She's *your* fiancée now!"

"My fiancée! I never saw you talk to her except on business! Are you trying to joke at my expense?" My indignant reply ended in blank amazement as the import of his anger thrust itself upon me.

A moment later Nijinsky was defending himself in a tone half-bitter, half-reminiscent. "Think back to Prague, Tola! Remember the big fight I had there with Diaghilev when I shouted at him, 'Either Klementowitsch goes or I will! She leaves the company or I do'? Do you remember how I'd shout, 'All right, Bourman. This is no time to flirt! It's time to work!'— and you flirted with Klementowitsch before my eyes! How many times did that happen? Answer me!" he commanded.

"Why didn't you tell me?" I groaned. "Why didn't you?"

"Why should I?" he countered. "I watched you until I was sure you were both in love. I never spoke to Klementowitsch of it at all. I tried to fire her from the company rather than endure your flirtation with her—then I saw that she loved you! What could I do—except to forget about it? Do you remember my Faun? Do you remember that not a single man was permitted to watch rehearsals except Diaghilev and Grigorieff? Yes? That was at my order." His voice had risen with his recollections. It sank almost to a whisper. "That was my order so that I could rehearse with Klementowitsch and six other girls—without your watching her! That was to keep you out of my sight! I didn't make her my première because she wasn't quite tall enough to play the leading role. Otherwise she would have been my partner—and you might have waited outside longer than you ever did! When I had pictures taken of the group—who was it I ordered to step forward? Klementowitsch! Didn't I spend more than thirty pounds on the picture I gave to her? What more could I do? How else could I show her? I who am spied upon and watched and ordered about for the sake of 'my public'? Do you believe me now? If you hadn't been so blind with your love, you would have seen when I closed rehearsals to the boys!" He flung his last words at me viciously.

For long moments we sat, until he broke the silence between us. Everything had become so plain to me. I understood why he had shut himself away from me—why he avoided me—why he ceased sharing the old confidences. "Forget all about it, Tola," he sighed. "You love her, and you are happy. Maybe, very soon, I will be happy too. I'll tell you first, but don't worry about me!"

There was nothing more to be said. I went to my cabin, feeling guilty. I might have deprived Nijinsky, the mighty artist, of the heart of his inspiration, I thought, reproaching myself for stupidity, for blindness, until, whichever way I turned, one fact emerged, I was in love with Klementowitsch myself! What could I do? Nothing!

I threw myself on my bed, thinking, thinking—and arriving always at the same conclusion. There was nothing to do. Klementowitsch knew nothing of his love, and I was in love with her. It was better to forget everything but our happiness and pray that Nijinsky, too, would find happiness.

Two weeks remained of our voyage. Day after day I watched him walking with the same young woman, speaking French with her, joking at the mistakes he made, for his French and English were always poor.

He rarely chose my company after his outburst, although it became my habit to walk the deck until long after everyone aboard had sought his bed. It must have been past one in the morning when I retired. Hardly was I in bed when someone knocked on my door, and I opened to Vassily, Nijinsky's valet!

"Mr. Bourman, Mr. Nijinsky wishes to see you now—in his cabin."

"Vaslaw wants me?" I questioned.

What could Vaslaw want at that hour? I speculated on a dozen possibilities while I dressed, unable to satisfy myself as to what could persuade him to stir me out of bed at that hour. Nothing short of an emergency. While I worried, I sprinted through the passage, until, at last, I was pounding on his door for admittance.

He sat in his pajamas, rising to greet me with a broad smile. In front of him, on the table, stood a bottle of champagne. He poured a glass for me, smiling enigmatically when he said: "All right, Anatole! Drink now to my happiness! I'm going to marry, and my wedding will take place in Buenos Aires!"

"Wait, wait!" I broke in. "Before I drink I want to know all about it!"

"You know her, Tola! The young woman whom I have been with constantly. I didn't tell you the other night—I have fallen in love with her. Her name is Romola de Pulszki. I shall be happy with her! Even if she is not a Russian dancer," he chided, "she is refined—she comes from a splendid family. Her mother is the greatest dramatic actress in Vienna. She loves me and I love her! It is more than I deserve!"

Only then did I actually realize why his companion had been familiar to me. I had seen her in Monte Carlo, in London, in Paris. "Oh! Yes!" Then I remembered.

"Have you thought over the differences of language and background?" I queried. "If she comes from an excellent background, have you thought of your own beginnings? Are you sure you can understand each other and be happy?"

He laughed. "Thanks for your consideration! You went over all that the other night. I'm no schoolboy! I have a mind of my own." His manner softened. "You see, Tola, I'm *really* in love, and that explains everything! I am inviting you, my only friend, and the guest of honor at my wedding, to announce my engagement. I am not consulting my mother or my sister, or anyone else but you. Come! Drink to my happiness!" We finished the champagne together.

The next morning, at Vaslaw's direction, I announced his marriage engagement. Vaslaw's wedding took place in Buenos Aires shortly after our arrival, and was followed by a splendid wedding party at the hotel where Vaslaw had placed me at his left at the head table with his personal friends, Adolph Bolm, Madame Karsavina, Baron and Baroness Ginsburgh, Monsieur and Madame Rhené-Baton, Grigorieff and Tchernicheva—all gaily proposing toasts, while I rejoiced in Vaslaw's happiness, even though I wished he might have married a graduate of our school.

Ten weeks concluded our stay in South America. We played Buenos Aires, Montevideo, and Rio de Janeiro to packed houses which had never witnessed a ballet of any sort. In amazement, the whole audience rose to its feet, craning to understand just what the dancers were doing on the tips of their toes. Neither untutored nor discourteous, our audiences represented South America's most prominent and wealthy families. It was simply because our presentation was something utterly unexpected, and their interest sincere, self-forgetful interest, that they peered at us so frankly. Our second appearances and Pavlowa's tour were accepted in the orthodox fashion, but Nijinsky and the Diaghilev Ballet enjoyed the unique experience of instructing an unprepared public in the exquisiteness of ballet.

XIII

BALLET RUSSE MINUS NIJINSKY

AT THE end of our South American experience, we sailed for Europe, Nijinsky and his wife to visit Vienna, while I traveled to Russia for my own marriage to Klementowitsch. After vacations, we gathered in Berlin, where we were bowled over by the announcement Diaghilev made, "My friends, Nijinsky will never dance with us again. He has organized his own company in London."

With that, the Silver Beaver left us buzzing with surprise bordering on disbelief. How could Vaslaw conduct his own company with a temperament that had begun to be too noticeable for happy organization?—Even with the diligence and cunning of the Silver Beaver, peace was established with difficulty.

Bronia Nijinsky had left us to join her brother, and my contact with him appeared likely to be lost for the balance of our lives. Michail and Vera Fokine replaced him, scoring success after success. A triumph was likewise claimed by Karsavina when they were absent. Once more Diaghilev was dependent upon the whims of St. Petersburg for his dancers. His nervousness and distraction mounted whenever we were due to play a big capital— there was always a chance that Fokine and Fokina might not come, or if Karsavina were scheduled, that she might be recalled. Poor Silver Beaver! He had built well, but he counted upon current glory to stay the flood of

unpopularity that might momentarily engulf him if ever he was accused of degenerating into a second-rate producer.

He hunted Europe and Russia to engage a permanent male soloist in Nijinsky's place, but the best dancers he tried out were dull shades in comparison with the transcendent Nijinsky. The company felt the difference, and sulked. There was but one Vaslaw, universally loved despite the occasional fits of temperament which marked his genius. Without him, life was gone from the Ballet Russe, as it had fled with him in the old days following Rozai's attempt to kill him.

After bleak disappointments and thankless struggles with second-rate soloists, Diaghilev turned his back on us all and went off to St. Petersburg, Moscow, and Warsaw in search of a new student who might be to the public and the company all that the incomparable Nijinsky had been. Leonide Massine, a student at the Imperial Dramatic School at Moscow, who had deserted ballet for the drama, was Diaghilev's find.

Diaghilev returned with him, only to decide that without study under the teacher of Pavlowa, Enrico Cecchetti, the first mime and permanent teacher of the Ballet Russe, Massine was incapable of dancing a solo role! One season's study advanced him until he was an artist capable of achieving a noteworthy success as the premier of *Joseph* in Paris, where we interpreted the Biblical legend of Joseph and his brothers to music by Richard Strauss. Diaghilev immediately established Massine as first soloist of our company, devoting his own genius to the task of extolling Massine's virtues as a dancer.

Meanwhile Nijinsky had, in theatrical parlance, "made a big flop" in London. The self-assurance engendered by his tremendous genius led him into the fatal folly of assuming complete responsibility for every phase of his ballet. Rumor, later confirmed by Sir Alfred Butt, millionaire art patron, when I met him personally in London, brought us news of Nijinsky's broken contract. It seems that Nijinsky, on being requested to come to the office of Sir Alfred, the theatrical manager, sent counter orders for Sir Alfred to report to him on the stage. Sir Alfred declined, asserting that Nijinsky had shown inexcusable discourtesy. With no delay their contract was terminated and both Nijinsky and Sir Alfred lost thousands of dollars. Nijinsky was minus an engagement, besides having gained an unenviable reputation.

Our company continued its tour, playing Paris, Monte Carlo, and London, while Vaslaw journeyed to Vienna. It was while we were in Paris that our Silver Beaver appeared on the stage. "Boys and girls!" he said, "the last Empress of France wishes to see our rehearsal!" and Eugénie, swathed in black, her face obscured by a heavy veil, was before us. For the first time in my life I beheld Diaghilev unnatural in manner. Touched by the majesty and age of the Empress, he stood like a soldier before her, according her every deference, until with a brief and gracious expression of appreciation, she left us to return to her own sequestered life.

As news of Nijinsky's misfortunes reached us, we rejoiced. It was a foregone conclusion that Diaghilev would invite him to join the company. But Diaghilev was implacable. "I do not need Nijinsky. I have a wonderful soloist!" he declared, while the company buzzed with comment. Who, after all, could better the king of all dancers?

Memories of Vaslaw began to occupy our conversations, as reports dribbled through concerning the one-time star of the Ballet Russe and his catastrophic financial reverses. Nijinsky's wild disagreement with Cecchetti was recollected. Cecchetti, an Italian, had lived his whole life in Russia, originating his own version of the language. It took concentration, almost the power of a mind reader, to understand him, supreme master of the old school that he was. Wherever he worked there was trouble, for Cecchetti was stubborn and temperamental, once his rage was aroused, firing the greatest star with the same indifference as the clumsiest nonentity in his classes.

After violent battles in Warsaw and St. Petersburg, which had resulted in Cecchetti's dismissal, Diaghilev rescued him from disgrace with an invitation to join his company. What if he had slapped the faces of little children under his tutelage?—and insulted celebrities? It was simply because he was a genius!—and Diaghilev specialized in geniuses. Cecchetti had practiced daily with Vaslaw, directing him constantly in the grind of polishing an already perfect technique. Often I played for them, watching Cecchetti's strictness and stubbornness with misgivings. Were Pavlowa, Kyasht, or the most unimpressive members of the corps de ballet two minutes late, the maestro's voice shattered the atmosphere with his edict: "Out! Out! Have you no respect for time and the master? Out! You are through!"

Yet it was Cecchetti who trained the Ballet Russe in ballet fundamentals until its technique was the envy of dancers from St. Petersburg to San Francisco. Modern dancing meant nothing to him, but the ballet he loved with his whole heart and understood from its inception. He was too old for us. We belonged to the generation which had allied itself with Fokine in his revolt against the old school. We were those who had finally caught the new vision Isadora Duncan had opened to us, while Cecchetti never deigned to consider Fokine's achievements. Our technique we recognized as Cecchetti's, but our souls were Fokine's! Fokine owned allegiance from the greatest ballerinas of the age even though they had passed through Cecchetti's school, reverenced his teaching, and had heard him dismiss them over and over before the applause of thousands ever thundered for them. He had the face of a recluse and a soul of fire.

Such was the maestro we remembered for his tremendous battle with Nijinsky. Vaslaw had failed to follow exact instructions, and like a skyrocket Cecchetti flared. Throwing a baton at Nijinsky and stamping his feet in ungovernable fury, he opened the scene by shrieking his opinion of Diaghilev's star before the entire company.

"Salami!" he screamed. "Do you think you are great? You idle, uncouth schoolboy! Out! Out!" and Nijinsky, white to his lips, silent as a sphinx, left Cecchetti's class, never again to dance with him, or for him!

Recollections of Nijinsky and Fokine offered us food for more gossip when we gathered for discussions. Nijinsky was miles from us, but he lived in our thoughts constantly. Fokine's name was then and is now the name of a giant in the dance world—a titan, who created ballet history, besides attaining his own tremendous triumphs as an artist. The world will be richer if Fokine some day writes his own memoirs, for I can only describe my memories of him with Nijinsky.

Backstage, while the company rehearsed, my mind went traveling back
to the years when Vaslaw and I danced together at school. We had heard
of the close friendship between Obouchov, Nijinsky's master, and Fokine,
who had graduated in the same class. From the first year of our entrance at
school, Fokine had habitually visited Obouchov's classes and had witnessed
Obouchov's dream of Vaslaw's brilliancy evolve into a dazzling reality.
Fokine had patiently awaited the day when Nijinsky could interpret the
ethereal creations that crowded his own mind with beauty—a beauty of
ravishing dance compositions wedded to the overpowering magnitude of
inspired classics, until each was the setting and revelation of the other.

Without Fokine's dreams, and their culmination in Nijinsky's inimitable
miming and leaping, Diaghilev's Ballet Russe must have been simply
another company of dancers. With them, the splendor of *Scheherazade, Le
Spectre de la Rose, Sylphides,* and *Karnival* bloomed into joyous art, fraught
with the inspiration of realms beyond our ken. It approximated a religious
experience to behold Fokine, his eyes focused in that other world of the
creator, watching Nijinsky dance. Suddenly he would cry out, "Not that,
Nijinsky! More soul!" The ringing tones of Fokine's voice, thrilling to
a soaring fantasy, lent new strength to Nijinsky, who would apparently defy
physical law in his attempt to touch the vision that was real to Fokine.
Together, they made an unforgettable tableau of creative power!

Moreover, if Nijinsky reaped inspiration, Fokine was stimulated to renewed daring by his knowledge that in Diaghilev's Ballet Russe were to be
found the foremost artists of Russia. He was sure of his dancers. He knew
every member of the Imperial Russian Ballet. Their limitations, their talents,
their genius, if genius they boasted, were indelibly engraved upon that finely
tuned brain which to this day can work wonders with gifted dancers, provided only that it is given scope for its vast creations.

Those who seek to discredit Fokine's art speak without understanding,
without knowledge of the man who is, without doubt, the greatest creative
artist of the dance who has lived in the nineteenth and twentieth centuries.
Many may disagree with him personally, but none can question the mighty

art flaming within him. It will be America's tragedy if Fokine leaves his work undone. Within him is a wealth of beauty unexpressed.

Nijinsky felt towards him as a student feels towards the master who deigns to reveal the secrets of an immortal heritage. Often Vaslaw has said, "I have seen Ballet So-and-so. Tola! How can they steal from the genius of Fokine!"

Then we would laugh at our own fears for his grandeur, and as one cry out the inevitable answer, "But who can steal from a creative genius? They can, after all, no more than copy!"

If Vaslaw could understand how Fokine's treasure has been undervalued, he, too, would be quick to acknowledge the master as the greatest of ballet teachers. All over the world, we who had the privilege of working with him are adapting his ideas, a fact which, I am sure, adds a measure of pride to Fokine, who can credit to himself whatever successes we, who worked with him and danced for him, attain because he taught us well.

Only once did trouble occur between Nijinsky and Fokine. Unquestionably the outgrowth of jealousy, the affair split the company, many artists following Nijinsky, who represented the power of Diaghilev and the payroll, a few clustering loyally about Fokine's standard. Few there were who would not admit, to themselves at least, that Fokine was right. The schism lasted only a few days before harmony was reestablished, Nijinsky inspiring Fokine to more courageous pioneering in his supreme endeavor, and Fokine provoking Nijinsky to excel his impressive interpretations with increasing delicacy and effectiveness. Together they transmuted their fleeting moments of vision into sparkling presentations, alive with the priceless essence of their rich imaginings. A mystic quality animated Fokine and Nijinsky, summoning forth sheer loveliness in which all might share while Time stayed itself to permit an endless vista, a transitory glimpse of eternity.

When the news of Nijinsky's final insanity reached Fokine, it must have shocked him past expression. At that moment he lost a friend, a genius, a fellow worshiper of infinite beauty as it is reflected on the earth, and an inspiration. He must have mourned the fate of the only other who could open the very gates of Fantasia for those who had the divine spark of appreciation within them. Fokine was responsible for successes that have made Nijinsky's name immortal. Yet even Fokine's titanic imagery, without Nijinsky's imperial interpretation and his impassioned faith, has gone unsung for nearly a decade. The world seems unable to appreciate his glorious creations enough to sponsor them. It is as though Fokine and Nijinsky were inseparable as masters of the dance and its translation into a universal language of Art. It is impossible to crown either with a victor's laurels. Both have well earned the tribute of fame that the world gave to them together, and a taste of the happiness it seems forever to deny those brave enough to portray truth in the Vale of Illusion.

XIV

THE GREAT WAR

A few days before the war cloud loosed its ruddy rain, we closed our season in the Royal Drury Lane Theater, London, feeling an uneasy spirit of farewell engulfing us. Audiences no longer applauded and left. Instead, they stood for hours, giving us an unprecedented reception, sometimes demanding speeches, and thrusting a celebrity to the stage for impromptu expressions of appreciation for the Ballet Russe. Two days before the war swirled us into its maelstrom of horror, I arrived in Russia, and immediately war was declared the army claimed me for two months' service before I was discharged for defective vision.

Meanwhile Nijinsky had lingered in Vienna, where he was a veritable prisoner of war. Only the influence of his wife's mother kept him from the further ignominy of a prisoner's camp, but even that privilege of living at home was conditional. He was obliged to report daily to the military with his credentials in order. Later he told me of his humiliating trips to the police to prove he was not engaged in plans for escape or in the service of the Russian Intelligence Department. For nearly two years his life was under constant surveillance, forcing him into the indolence of reading or halfheartedly practicing his beloved dancing, until his spirit all but lost its vital spark. The press brought reports of terrific struggles and heartbreaking tragedies. He watched long ambulance trains winding through the streets, filling the air with the burr of machinery and the screams of the dying. He stood helpless, tormented by the sight of young men minus arms, legs, eyes, hands, tottering unsteadily along in the heyday of their youth. With that sensitive soul of his, he suffered unspeakable agonies over the hideous waste and cruelty of war, until morbidity obscured his thoughts and his reason wavered.

In June, 1915, the Russian government issued my passport for Switzerland, where with Klementowitsch, my wife, I joined Diaghilev's company. The trip was fraught with trials and difficulties. There were rigid military laws to satisfy, and the North Sea with its hidden mines and submarines to traverse. Somehow, after days of confusion and uncertainty, I joined Diaghilev in Lausanne on Lake Geneva, where he was occupying a villa through the courtesy of an American family. Massine and his valet, the faithful Vassily, lived near by. The boat I had taken passage on was sunk on its return trip, but Diaghilev had thought us on it, and so it was in the role of prodigies that we returned, unexpectedly confronted by the responsibility of proving that we were no ghosts!

Diaghilev questioned me minutely, accounting for every Russian artist one way or another. "I have signed a contract to appear in New York in January, Bourman," he observed. "So far I have about six artists, but we will be there!"

Wires hummed across Europe, and from the four points of the compass dancers appeared in answer to their summons. Cecchetti started his classes, and day after day we worked under him, our number increasing as the weeks passed, and Massine practiced adagios with Klementowitsch as his partner.

Diaghilev, driven to desperation by the absence of Fokine, conceived the notion of creating his own ballet. An interval of humor dawned, despite the tragedy surrounding us. The Silver Beaver worked diligently but, after all, he was not a creator of ballet. He was merely a brilliant producer. He chose a modern theme, and half killed us with frightful mistakes in technique and composition, forcing us into farcical steps and humiliating figures. We were experienced artists, used to the glory of a Fokine, not the folly of a Diaghilev gone mad with the necessity of producing something, anything which might pass for a ballet. We tried to point out his errors, but he turned on us. "You are being paid to work. Do, then, as I order you!"

We collapsed in utter horror when Diaghilev announced that our contortions were to be featured in a modern version of the Annunciation, the Birth of Christ, and His Ministry. In the first place, Diaghilev's blasphemy was astounding. His ballet was more obscene than the most unbelievable "modern" version of anything I have ever heard of, and I was to have the pleasure of playing one of the Apostles. The Annunciation was depicted in a disgustingly suggestive series of posturings. After that exhibition, the Apostles were required to make their entrance on all fours, in single file, the head of each Apostle between the legs of the preceding Apostle.

In dismay I stood beside Diaghilev watching the Entrance of the Apostles. "Do you really think, Mr. Diaghilev, that you will present *that?*" I asked.

He screwed his monocle deeper into his eye. "Yes! Yes! I have a notion to crucify Christ in a similar fashion. It ought to make an effective scene— the Master upside down on the cross, or something of the sort!" He squinted a critical eye at the Apostles crawling around like beasts. "Uh— ah—there's only one drawback, Bourman. We are due to play some—ah —religious countries. I—ah—I wonder, now, if they would let us live if we produced the Crucifixion, and the Birth, and the rest of it just as I'd planned!"

Inwardly I decided if he ever presented the horror we watched, with its insane travesty of the holiest of stories, we would all be crucified upside down—and that justly enough! Fortunately, some of his friends had more balance than he, and persuaded him to cancel the whole thing, arguing that if it was ever presented, especially at a time when religious fervor was the sole recourse of a stricken world, he would be insulting the finest instincts of every nation.

To our unspeakable relief, rehearsals for *The Midnight Sun* by Rimsky-Korsakov began, the whole an adaptation to the music of Rimsky-Korsakov's *Snow Maiden.*

In those days Massine was taking his first steps as a choreographer. No one dreamed then that he would achieve mastery and score the success that he has, for he has developed into an excellent dancer, teacher, and ballet master.

Only half of our new company was Russian, the balance being made up of French and English boys and girls, signed on for an appearance in New York City. We had heard enough from Pavlowa to fear the experience, since it was understood that in America one worked incessantly. At the same time we longed to see this "terrible America" for ourselves.

Diaghilev was receiving letters and telegrams from the United States in bunches. Photographers and correspondents haunted our rehearsals. Surely going to America was something big in the life of an artist! We felt a lack of resilience, of vitality, for neither Karsavina nor Nijinsky was with us. Instead of Karsavina, Ksenia Makletzova had joined us, journeying from Moscow, unflattered by Diaghilev's extravagances when she found a company yearning for the reappearance of its beloved Karsavina.

We pestered Diaghilev with questions about Nijinsky and the prospect of his joining us, unaware that the Silver Beaver was working day and night towards that end, as uncertain of his success as were we. War raged between us and our dancing king. Vienna and Lausanne were only a few hours apart, yet they might as well have been on separate worlds. No Russian could speak sanely with a German or Austrian during those fevered days, and so despite the scores of friends in Germany and Austria whose loss he mourned, Diaghilev was forced to rely upon his Spanish and American acquaintances, for they were neutral.

Especially helpful to him was King Alfonso of Spain, who was credited by Diaghilev himself with providing the assistance which eventually brought Nijinsky to the United States.

Our rehearsals were staged in the Maison du Peuple at Lausanne, which we forsook regularly for members of the present Russian government who held their meetings there. Many times, my wife and I have watched Lenin, Trotsky, and their loyal Communist followers entering the hall. Who could understand the meaning of those gatherings then? The Communist movement seemed hopeless, and so, without realizing their greatness or their destinies, we artists, to whom politics were a mystery anyway, chatted with the men destined to transform Russian thought less than five years from that time. They were courteous and kindly with us, willing always to answer whatever questions we had.

Rehearsals were done. We made one stop at Paris, where we gave a charity performance for the benefit of the Red Cross at staggering prices. The next day, January 1, 1916, we boarded the *Lafayette* at Bordeaux bound for the United States. We were thirteen days at sea because of wireless warnings that we were being stalked by a submarine. Diaghilev, faced by the prospect of death, walked the deck interminably, comforted by the thought that he had ordered Vassily to pray constantly for him, forgetful of the antireligious ballet he had worked out! Great as he was, Diaghilev had his little inconsistencies!

One beautiful morning, the inspiring Statue of Liberty rose before us, offering us safe harbor. Something in me responded to the soundless message of the vista opening behind the symbol of freedom, but I set the emotion down to relief from the fears which had beset our crossing. How could I know that that towering Liberty was waiting to claim me—that my Old Russia would be drenched in its own blood, and that I stood greeting the mistress of my new country that morning? We Russians feel deeply. Had I not been so loyal to Russia, I could not have understood how much my oath of fealty meant when I became an American!

XV

NEW YORK CITY

New York seemed a city of fantasy to us, inspiring in its immensity, but depressing. It made us small and insignificant in the midst of synthetic grandeur. When we stood at the bottom of deep chasms yawning up to a ribband of sky, it seemed as though we might be crushed between the monstrous buildings shouldering one another. Traffic, crowding, haste, and speed dinned in our ears. In amazement we learned that those huge piles were constantly being torn down and replaced by greater blocks of masonry, reaching ever higher towards the broad expanse of sky they hid from view. Americans were always seeking to break records, to set new ones!

Our first appearance was at the Century Theater, the best in the city then. Another shock awaited us. In Russia a theater was a theater, but in America it housed a midway lined with shops, cigar stores, florists' nooks, and tiny stores. There was but one big playhouse in New York that was solely a theater, we were told.

Rest was something unworthy of consideration, and so our first night in New York was devoted to a rehearsal! Diaghilev presented us to Otto Kahn, who welcomed us briefly, assuring us that he had no slightest doubt of our success. Three days later our initial appearance was scheduled.

Those were days of furious rehearsing, while a staff of stage hands cleaned and renewed our scenery. The corps of photographers completed our amazement. An army of them had invaded the Century, dogging us wherever we were, whatever we did, whether we were members of the corps de ballet or soloists.

There was an unexpected nudge, a deep-throated, "Pardon me, may I take your picture?" A refusal or affirmative was equally unnecessary, for there would be a "click" and one more question, "What's your name?" before the man with his little black box was off for another victim!

One chorister nearly wrecked the company with her sense of humor. She flirted with a photographer who had pestered the lot of us, assuring him of her position as star ballerina of the company, meanwhile fabricating a most romantic history for his edification.

To her delight and Diaghilev's despair, her name and photograph graced the front page of a popular news sheet, and people began to call the theater frantically to learn when they might see this paragon of Russian beauty. Diaghilev wore a lugubrious air, for the joke nearly cost him his contract before it was forgotten. In Russia such an event would have been impossible, for press persons were required to make themselves familiar with their subject before they approached it. But in America! "Anything may happen," Diaghilev brooded.

Hardly was that over when one day Diaghilev arrived shortly before lunchtime, profoundly assured in his concept of an America similar to Europe where the appearance of a director was sufficient to drive thoughts of anything so material as luncheon far, far into the background. He sat himself in place to begin his day's work, when the chief carpenter walked over to him, addressing Diaghilev, who spoke no English, in that tongue. "Well, well! Diaghilev! You must have overslept! Got here a bit late," the carpenter began, clapping the immaculate Diaghilev on the shoulder familiarly. Like a shot, Diaghilev brushed himself as though he had been touched by a leper, his monocle literally shaking in his eye socket when he burst into a torrent of Russian, demanding of his assistant stage manager how a mere workman dared address a director like an old friend, and put his dirty hands upon him.

None of the workmen, fortunately, had witnessed the incident, and the carpenter had been too busy requesting advice about the scenery to have noticed Diaghilev's repulsion. Furthermore, he couldn't understand Russian, and so he missed the classic oration the stage manager delivered to Diaghilev, the mighty, who was informed for the first time in his life that he must treat

workmen with respect, that there was a union which made stage hands and
workers so loyal to one another that if one was insulted none would work.
Diaghilev's fists clenched and unclenched, his face became a florid sunburst,
with his assimilation of the novel idea that an aristocrat was expected to show
consideration for a man who earned his living with his hands!

He opened his mouth to give orders, but a bell rang, and down went
hammers and awls, while overalls were peeled off hurriedly. Not a soul paid
any attention to the infallible Diaghilev, who stared in blank disbelief. He
had spoken and no one had cared! The stage manager explained that the bell
marked the beginning of a dinner hour, and not one lick of work could be
expected until the men had enjoyed their repast.

"Stop them! They can't have lunch when I am here!" bellowed the infuriated director. "I am Diaghilev. I give orders to that rabble!" But the
stage manager only added to Diaghilev's dismay with his assertion that the
"rabble" was comprised of splendid fellows with a perfect right to enjoy
their lunches, Diaghilev or no Diaghilev. Any outcry against them would
mean a broken contract, he warned. The workmen clustered in the flies
observing the Silver Beaver striding up and down the stage, obviously in a
white-hot temper, obviously angry at them, raving in unintelligible Russian.

One of the group strode over to the stage manager, "Say, tell that boy that
if he don't behave himself he'll get himself in trouble, and we'll give him
plenty!" A snicker ran through the company. When in the memory of any
of us had Diaghilev been called a "boy"?

He had fired directors, stars, conductors, patiently stalking whomever he
disliked, and discharging them with the nonchalance of the king he considered himself to be. It must have been a terrifying shock to unearth a
nation that forced the "king" not only to consider the wishes of others, but
to oblige his workmen, be on time at rehearsals along with his most humble
ensemble girl, and generally conduct himself as a man who might be more
gifted, but who certainly was no better than a scene shifter!

We had all been accustomed to honor and deference in Europe, where an
artist was a superior being. Insulted by the shoves administered by friendly
stage hands who treated us as equals, we resented their attitude until we

glimpsed the philosophy behind it. There was wisdom to be gleaned in this
new country where men were free of class and caste. The more I studied
Americans, the more I found to like in them, eventually becoming a convert
to the American spirit, swearing fealty to my new country with an emotion
too deep for description.

On January 16, 1916, we opened our American tour to the cream of
American audiences, with Lopokova, Idzikovsky, Massine, and Adolph
Bolm dancing the first roles, and achieving success past our fondest dreams,
despite another precursor of a new custom that awaited us. Backstage there
were only reporters, critics, and more photographers. None of America's
great sought us backstage for congratulations! The place was bare of flowers,
crackling with terse questions put by hasty press representatives. We stood
flabbergasted, some of the ensemble girls in tears, questioning childishly:
"How is this? No flowers for us in the richest country in the world!"

For ten weeks we traveled—to Boston, Chicago, Detroit, Cleveland,
Kansas City, Washington—learning the ways of a tremendously intent,
efficient land. Gradually we familiarized ourselves with the enormous posters
and huge advertisements screaming "Russian Ballet" from newspapers, from
signboards, in stores, on trolley cars, everywhere! We ranged the states in
our own Pullmans, well content with an arrangement enabling us to carry
stage hands, carpenters, the orchestra, costumers—and Diaghilev wherever
we went.

Before a fortnight passed, we had made staunch friends of our staff of
workmen, delighted to find them both convivial and intelligent. Of course,
we whiled time away with poker, and inevitably Diaghilev took it upon
himself to stroll through the train. He gazed at me popeyed, motioning me
to follow him.

"Bourman, what is this?" he sputtered. "Do you, a Russian gentleman
and an artist, play poker with carpenters? What is wrong with your sense
of propriety?"

I interrupted. "But, Mr. Diaghilev, those men are fine fellows! They
make more money than we do. They are freer than we! Why shouldn't I
enjoy their companionship?" The poorest-paid stage hand received a hun-

dred dollars a week, and we, if we earned sixty-five dollars per week, were getting good money! The trunks and clothes of the hands looked like millionaires' beside ours.

Pulling into Detroit at midnight, we sought the Statler for rooms, Diaghilev with us. I never shall forget my surprise when I came down in the morning to behold the untouchable aristocrat solemnly breakfasting in the huge dining room, with a carpenter at the next table! I watched the picture rejoicing, for I discerned every symptom of an explosion simmering beneath the impeccable Diaghilev's exterior.

On the train, Diaghilev lay back in his seat glaring at me through a monocle screwed tightly against his eye. "I know well enough that you champion this mad democracy, Bourman," he began. "Be good enough to tell me why—when a man has no deference shown for his position!"

"Because the people are generous, like our own Russians. They aren't stingy and snaky," I replied. "They are upstanding and honest, free with their money, eager to make you at home with them, quick to set you at ease, and not make you aware that you are a foreigner!"

Diaghilev flared. "You know they are common! They belong to a different class than we. They are working men and women. Inside, they feel their European blood. Every one of them knows he is nothing more nor less than a glorified immigrant like you, yourself. I know another class of people. I have several times been the 'honored' guest of those who call themselves leaders of America's society. Everything about them is expensive, but far beneath our standards. It takes me half an hour to discover a European with whom I can converse intelligently. I pick them by their cultured manners, and I never make a mistake. Americans have money inherited from a grandfather, or the result of their own labor. Americans are uncouth, nothing but adventurers under a brittle veneer of polish! They have money, beautiful homes, and clothes. They think they can buy anything with it, but they can't purchase blue blood and good breeding!" He betrayed his deep-seated repugnance with a gesture, continuing: "They're proud of their 'Four Hundred' and their silly *Mayflower*. They imagine the best families of Europe came over here." He swung his monocle superciliously. "How

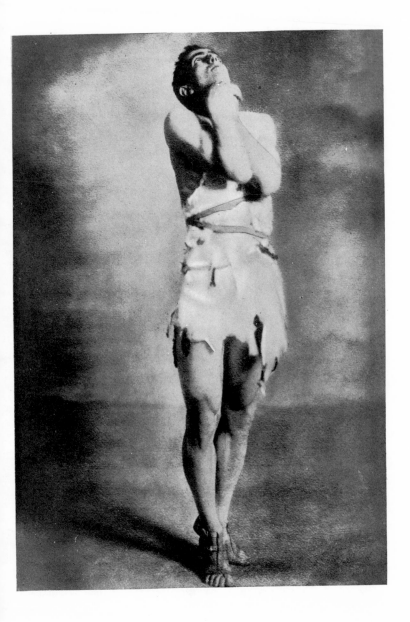

ridiculous they are! Nothing but low-grade failures in Europe would go sail-
ing around the ocean for a couple of months in search of a chance to dig out a
living for themselves! And that, Bourman, is the foundation of this America
you love! America! Bah!"

Perpetually, Diaghilev stormed against the nation that lined his pockets
with gold, against the great personalities who entertained him lavishly. With
them he was the perfectly cultivated gentleman, accepting their hospitality
with ingratiating evidences of enjoyment, yet declaiming against them from
city to city, ridiculing the very ones who sought most sincerely to make his
visit in America happy and worth while. How often I have watched him
stoop over the hand of a woman, justly proud of her name and position, only
to hear the untouchable Diaghilev direct his satire at her and reduce her and
her pride to rags in the retirement of his own car!

"If there is any blue blood here, it isn't advertising itself with diamonds
and gold," Diaghilev would sneer. "It is to be found unpretentiously concerned with cultural pursuits, as would any true aristocrat occupy himself
after being driven from his country by canaille, during the French Revolution, for instance. No true aristocrats can I unmask in this bumptious Four
Hundred! If you choose to prove it, open any society paper on Sunday, and
look at the charming democratic faces peering out at you, graced with a 'II'
or 'III' after their names. A paltry attempt to prove that they have ancestors,
and to prove it publicly! What a show of dignity and breeding! To advertise
one's ancestry in the common press! Most likely her father, or his grandfather, sneaked out of Europe in something not precisely a first-class boat,
nor a first-class cabin. They were lucky, and made money, these people out
of European backwaters, and here we find them—what? America's 'exclusive Four Hundred,' " and Diaghilev would go off into peals of laughter
that carried in its very sound a mortal insult, while he daintily fingered a
beautiful invitation and ordered his acceptance.

"One can always laugh at these Americans," he would observe to his
artists, who mutely wondered whether democracy or aristocracy was the
more admirable, and usually favored the straightforward, honest democracy
that was growing upon all but Diaghilev, to his intense disgust.

"Have you heard that there are kings in the great country?" he would query innocently. "Ah, yes, my good friends, there are *kings* here. Automobile kings, chewing-gum kings, frankfurter kings—but how can they be crowned, these gorgeous American kings? Perhaps with a string of frankfurters to advertise themselves!" With that, Diaghilev would dangle his monocle, muttering, "To be sure, to be sure, some have managed to buy a petty title with a million or so, but what titles! Few are great; many are impostors!" Diaghilev would chuckle with a Machiavellian humor at the expense of his doting hostesses, and their impostor guests.

Again his satirical views would be expressed in a different mood. "It is merely funny when an American heiress decides to marry a policeman, for *all* Americans are eccentric. It is pathetic when they buy meaningless titles for their millions!" After an observation of that sort Diaghilev would terminate his thought with a short laugh. "No wonder I despise this America that fills my pockets with its gold! I shall never return. I am only waiting to see if Nijinsky cannot stir their passion for the dance a little—even though he is not of noble birth. At least he is king of the dance, not king of the sausages! Every city looks the same—a Childs', a United Cigar store, ugly, commercialized! Europe can learn efficiency and comfort, not culture, from this gold-struck nation!"

The company fraternized with our workmen despite Diaghilev's unceasing complaints, extracting every ounce of pleasure from the tour, and hoping for Nijinsky's return. Oddly enough, our arrival at New York coincided with the receipt of a cable from Nijinsky. A few days would find Vaslaw back with us, hampered by Diaghilev's orders to pander to a society both despised.

XVI

NIJINSKY AT THE
METROPOLITAN
OPERA HOUSE

Nijinsky's arrival in New York was an event welcomed unanimously by the company, and especially by me. Two and a half years had elapsed since I had last set eyes on him. With everyone else, I greeted his appearance at rehearsals at the Metropolitan with wild applause, but when I saluted him personally, I realized that a coldness had crept into our friendship during our more than two years of separation. As with all foreign languages, English was also difficult for Vaslaw and he frequently called upon me to assist him when Madame Nijinsky, his wife, was not present. It became painfully apparent to me that Vaslaw's London experiences, his long array of successes, and his entrance into social circles had wrought unflattering changes in the man I had known. He adopted a pompous attitude in his relations with the whole company and appeared to me totally devoid of sincerity or naturalness.

Unwilling to endure his conceit, I suggested that he employ a Russian boy with a command of English to interpret for him. An extra danced attendance on him as a veritable valet, accepting only a few dollars for his services. The career of that boy is interesting. He was Nijinsky's errand boy, and little more, but he was crazy over the Russian Ballet and arranged to

take a few lessons from one of my friends. I was amazed at the gullibility of
the American public when I discovered upon my return to this country five
years later that this lad had become a "ballet master" in New York, advertising himself as a member of the Diaghilev company, and cashing in remarkably well for his ten weeks as an extra who had never danced with the
company! The arrival of Fokine, Bolm, and others of us was sufficient to
enable one of the most discriminating showmen in America to break the
valet's contract and end that phase of his career.

But the story is of Nijinsky. He began severe practice upon his arrival and
within a week our doubts of his supremacy were dissipated. It was an adept
who danced once more. His personality transformation had not affected his
artistry. Publicity about him filled New York's papers until his name was
on every lip, assuring a house jammed with American social lights for his
opening performance. If photographers and reporters had dogged the steps
of extras, they besieged Nijinsky until he literally bumped into them,
stumbling over them wherever he turned.

His first appearance, in *Le Spectre de la Rose,* was barely saved from
disaster. To our dismay, his ballet slipper split up the side with one of his
first leaps. His dance was fraught with danger from that moment forward,
minimized somewhat by a precaution customary with him—he had glued
the heels of his slippers tight to his feet with collodion. He took a position
behind a fauteuil, near the wing where I stood, while Lopokova danced.
Under his breath he muttered in Russian: "What to do! A tragedy! A
tragedy! I cannot dance!"

Instantly I whispered, "Take off your slipper! Kick it free. No one out
front can see! Quick, Vaslaw!" His feet moved like lightning. A soft sigh
was the only sign he gave that the slipper was off without ruining his scarlet
tights and creating a scandal. A moment later he was dancing the final steps
of his great interpretation, hovering an instant motionless in mid-air, and
shooting forward like an eagle. By a hairsbreadth, his first American presentation was a success.

He looked handsomer during his American tour than at any time I had
ever seen him. Offstage, he ran to me. "Anatole!" he gasped, breathless

from his tremendous dance, and hugging me like a bear. "You have saved me once more! That slipper—it nearly ruined me for America!" The moment was gone. Nijinsky's American triumph was secure, for every critic lauded him to the skies.

Messages from America's notables began to pour in the following day, and Vaslaw's fame mounted with every performance. Often backstage the staff of directors of the Metropolitan Opera chattered amiably with Nijinsky and Diaghilev, introducing them to America's great ones. I have watched such informal groups include—besides Otto Kahn, Diaghilev, and Nijinsky —John D. Rockefeller, Jr.; the Vanderbilt family; Vincent Astor; the Gould family; Chalmers, painter and millionaire; Mrs. Harriman, wife of the famous American banker, who invited us to enjoy one of her delightful Bohemian parties; and the Lewisohn sisters, whose patronage has spelled hope to so many artists, besides adding priceless items to the store of treasures American art may boast. Besides these, theatrical celebrities frequently moved in and out of the gatherings. I have often watched the brilliant and beloved David Belasco conversing with motion-picture and stage stars, dancers, and social leaders in his delightful fashion.

Nijinsky was frequently invited to dance at the homes of America's social leaders for astounding fees. One story that he recounted concerned Mrs. Vanderbilt.

"Mrs. Vanderbilt is fine and generous," he remarked, dabbing make-up on before his appearance one night. "You know, Tola, to satisfy a caprice, she gave me ten thousand dollars!"

I sat up. "How? Ten thousand dollars?"

"Of course, ten thousand dollars is not so much in America, Tola."

"But why?"

"It is no mystery and no secret," Nijinsky observed. "Last week Mrs. Vanderbilt announced to a group of friends that she would dance with me the following week at a social affair of hers. Later she asked me, and of course I refused. How could I dance with a nonprofessional? But Mrs. Vanderbilt was delightful. I consented. We did a gavotte together before her guests and she gave me ten thousand dollars! That is all!" and Nijinsky brushed the powder from his tights.

Our season at the Metropolitan was brief. A few weeks, and the Diaghilev company sailed for Europe, but not before Nijinsky had signed a contract with the Metropolitan for the 1917 season, deciding to stay in this country. After his marriage, Nijinsky never contracted with Diaghilev, but dealt directly with the theater. Diaghilev and Nijinsky no longer spoke, nor did Vassily act as Vaslaw's valet. Instead, Massine and Diaghilev walked backstage, both ignoring Nijinsky, who unfailingly returned the compliment.

Meanwhile, Klementowitsch, who had shortened her name to "Klemova" for the benefit of American audiences, and I likewise chose to remain in the United States, and began our dancing before Diaghilev and his Ballet Russe were more than well started for Europe. My wife and I soon found that we were worth four or five times as much to America as we were to Diaghilev. We joined Theodor Kosloff's small but exceptionally fine ballet, and broke the records of the Palace Theater in New York with a five-week run while Nijinsky and his wife lived at the Hotel Claridge, Nijinsky not making any appearances, but enjoying a vacation and recovering his poise after the surveillance and horrors of his Austrian internment.

Occasionally Klemova and I enjoyed informal luncheons and dinners with Nijinsky and his wife. On rare occasions I played for him at the Metropolitan Opera House, where he practiced daily in preparation for his coming season, and there it was that we met when we could.

Up and down Broadway we would walk, entering a bar now and again to chatter away as we had in years past. To my delight, I discovered that Nijinsky still loved informality, although he seldom had an opportunity to indulge that phase of his character. There were many reasons for this, he would explain, apologizing for his relatively few visits with me—and his explanations involved so many persons still living that it is best not to repeat them here. It was the same cry that issued from Nijinsky's lips: "If I could only be free of the responsibilities of fame and position—if I could only forget the crowds!"

Klemova and I were tired, too. Seeking advice, we were informed that

Newport, Rhode Island, was the only place for a retreat, so off we went to Newport! We had a carefree holiday for ten days, when to our disgust, the papers announced that two members of the Diaghilev company were at Newport, and our vacation was ruined with invitations to dance. We made two appearances, one at a dinner in honor of an admiral of the American Navy who was feted at Hilltop Inn, and to our delight our expenses were covered for our entire stay! America was revealed, like Russia, as a nation where people were gay and generous.

I wrote Nijinsky to that effect, telling him of the ease with which one could make money. Apparently Vaslaw decided that if we made money, he most certainly could. Therefore he and his wife followed us to the resort shortly after our departure. They registered at the exclusive Hilltop Inn, but there were no parties to dance at, for Newport had retired behind its clipped hedges and its barred gates to enjoy seclusion, with only occasional parties at Hilltop Inn to break its summer siesta. Nijinsky stayed on for a few weeks without engagements, returning empty-handed to New York, where he met me with more explanations.

"That trip to Newport was bad, Anatole. It was an expensive mistake, but I don't blame myself!"

XVII

SECOND AMERICAN TOUR

During the fall months, Diaghilev's company arrived in New York once more, this time opening in the Manhattan Opera House. The Silver Beaver had given instructions to his stage manager and invitations to rejoin the company were issued to Klemova and me. Nijinsky bolstered up the invitation with a personal call, urging me in these words: "Please, Tola, come back with us. Year after year we have worked together and the company will seem incomplete without you and your wife." It was useless. We had accepted the freedom accorded by American organizations, besides the generosity of American producers.

Nijinsky made the fifty-city tour, however, and with the other members of the Ballet Russe, discovered that, as Pavlowa had said, dancing on tour was "work." Playing a matinee in one city and an evening in another proved no joke, and when letters trickled back to us with their accounts of strenuous shows, Klemova and I both gave thanks for the wisdom guiding our refusal of Diaghilev's invitation.

Meanwhile, Diaghilev and Massine stayed in Europe. The Silver Beaver kept his word never again to set foot on American shores and suffer the agony imposed by American society. Though that decision unquestionably cut wide swaths in his profits from a company touring without his executive genius, he remained obstinate. He had seen America once and sent word that "Once was enough!"

Letters began to reach me from members of the company bearing strange tidings of Vaslaw's doings. He had taken Tolstoy as his prototype, they said, and had adopted an extremely humble mode of life. I knew, of course, of Nijinsky's dislike for crowds and social life, but the notion of his turning completely Tolstoyan was eerie. Two members of the company were reported to be a little moonstruck on the subject of Tolstoy (they disapproved stiff collars and a well-groomed appearance, and forswore good food and the simplest luxuries while they lauded the virtues of self-denial). They must have talked Vaslaw into his ostensible penury, I decided, secretly sympathizing with Madame Nijinsky, who must have suffered public humiliation whenever Vaslaw put in his appearance attired like a muzhik, conducting himself like a peasant. That leap from the heights of luxury into the slough of figurative poverty must have seriously affected Vaslaw's mind, for he was, as a rule, slow to adapt himself to his environment.

In due course, the Russian Ballet arrived in New York and I was at the Grand Central to meet Nijinsky. My first glimpse of him verified all reports. He was garbed in the simplest fashion, staggering under the weight of his heavy luggage, and soberly refusing the services of the porters clustering around him and his wife.

"Vaslaw, are you crazy? Remember for a moment that you are still the great Nijinsky!" I exclaimed, embracing him. "Forget Tolstoy for five minutes and call a porter! Carrying luggage is not for you—besides, you are depriving the porter of his work and tips!"

He drew back half-angrily. "What Tolstoy? What are you talking about? Here, porter!" I exchanged a smile and a greeting with Madame Nijinsky, who, I have no doubt, heaved a sigh of relief with me when Vaslaw relinquished his luggage to face a battery of photographers. Once more, his reputation was saved, and he had escaped the fate overshadowing him even then.

A few days later the company sailed for Europe. Another invitation from Diaghilev waiting for us, coupled with war talk rising, persuaded us. It needed only the company's urging.

"Come with us, Bourman! The smell of gunpowder is already in the air, and America is making ready to play her role with the warriors!" our friends prophesied and the boat crept out of safe harbor with Nijinsky in New York,

Klemova and me on board. Some days later, he and Madame Nijinsky followed us across the seas, and word reached us indirectly that they had taken residence in Switzerland.

No letters passed between us, but the world is small to the traveler who has visited many capitals and entered many harbors. We had friends who brought us firsthand news of Vaslaw. Rumors crowded thick and fast. He was taking part in a few recitals arranged for him in Switzerland. Instead of concentrating on beauty, he was composing weird routines. Nijinsky had declared his mission to be that of introducing "real" modern work, and in a theater jammed to the doors, with a long queue of disappointed patrons stamping restlessly outside, he had introduced an absurdity that had sent laughter rippling through his audience. Wearing ribbons around his neck, around his ears, and around his wrists, he had assumed positions that had rocked the theater with their grotesquerie.

"Is this the great Nijinsky?" people questioned, and for the first time those who knew of my friendship with him asked me: "Is this Nijinsky done with dancing? Is he demented?"

All Europe was bowing its head under the bludgeoning of Mars. The Germans were advancing, and the world waited fearfully for a terrible denouement. Instinctively all thoughts turned towards the United States. *There* were thousands of fresh soldiers ready to die—*there* was hope for victory—*there,* in short, existed the mainstay of the masses of men and women in the allied countries who, without political knowledge, with one accord called on the only source of hope—America!

We traveled with Diaghilev through France and Italy, being stirred out of our berths at all hours of the day and night for passport inspection, standing for interminable hours in way stations or on spur tracks while ambulance trains rumbled past bearing a cargo of wounded men whose suffering surrounded their train like a gruesome shade.

Portugal saw us—and we saw Portugal in the throes of a revolution which nearly cost us our lives, crumbling our hotel with artillery fire. Diaghilev's company proved itself a company of real troupers who went hungry during the days when revolution raged in Lisbon, and still danced the classics of Old Russia.

In Switzerland, Nijinsky waited—for what? We pestered Diaghilev with queries about him. Where was he? Why was he not with us? When would he join us? But Diaghilev screwed his eternal monocle against his eye and kept his own counsel. Nijinsky still would not sign with the Silver Beaver, nor would the Silver Beaver deliberately seek a contract with Nijinsky.

The revolution in Lisbon had effectively blocked our travels for five months when relief came in the form of an engagement to play the Royal Theater in Madrid. The royal family and the Spanish people had previously greeted the Russian Ballet with fiery enthusiasm. King Alfonso and Queen Victoria had made it their business to become acquainted personally with every member of the company.

In Madrid and later in San Sebastian whenever we saw King Alfonso driving we shouted, "Hello!" He knew every one of us by name, and regardless of the crowds he would answer, "Hello, there!"

If he glimpsed us from a window, the same cheery greeting rang out despite his crown and power.

Members of the company were occasionally invited to dance at his palace, a pleasure that was never mine, although Klemova appeared by command.

One of her numbers was a Russian solo, spectacular with its arm work, executed to compelling rhythms, alive with the dash and vigor of spirited stamping and spinning. The King applauded vehemently, searching the company for Klemova when the presentation was over.

"That was an impressive dance," he remarked, "but I'm not sure it was as difficult as it looked. I'll show you my version of it!"

Before Klemova could reply, King Alfonso had posed one hand over his head, the other on his hip, and was capering clumsily, to the intense amusement of his court. Nothing daunted by the laughter about him, he persisted until, with Klemova's instruction, he had managed the position.

"I told you I would do it!" he exulted, leaving her to Queen Victoria, whose admiration for Klemova's costume prompted a conversation interrupted only by Diaghilev's fears that his services as an interpreter were indispensable to the Queen, gaily chatting on about native costumes, and adding to her own knowledge of Russia with the questions she directed to Klemova.

The whole Spanish court and its aristocracy maintained an identical informality, gathering in groups backstage after every ballet to converse with us. There I met Count Romanones, the richest man in Spain and Prime Minister of his country, and Dato, later Prime Minister, who was assassinated within a fortnight after I had seen him. Those were troublous times, threatening danger to us all.

Pastora Imperio, in my opinion the greatest living Spanish dancer, used to sit backstage when we danced. There in the first wing she took up her post, and if anyone jostled her, she spouted a stream of oaths and curses as potent as liquid fire for the unlucky oaf who had disturbed her!

After our engagement at Madrid, a Spanish tour was inevitable, since no other country in a war-riven world could offer us support. Cordova, Barcelona, Seville, Granada—we played them all, with their ancient buildings and their colorful traditions. Weeks might go by without the sight of a foreigner other than ourselves, for in Spain, at least, the Spanish rule and visitors are scarce. More than twenty cities were on our itinerary, and when our train rolled into the stations, whole populations shouted greetings, brilliant in typical Spanish costumes, showering us with the sunny smiles that seem to be natural in Spain. We played to full houses and were rewarded by storms of applause. What if we had no money? Spain loved us and we loved Spain!

At Valencia, Blasco Ibáñez's family invited us to stay in their beautiful palace of white marble on the shores of the Mediterranean. All Bohemia met there. Our visit was one of consecutive delights shared with famous Spanish artists, caricaturists, singers, and dancers, who drank wine with Señora Libertad Ibáñez as a gracious and charming hostess! Not one of us but enjoyed our browsing in a rich library where we might see the writer's original manuscripts.

Our next stop was Barcelona, and there news reached us that Diaghilev had signed for another South American tour. Life was not too difficult, then! South America! The whole company rejoiced.

XVIII

DIAGHILEV'S PLOT
AND ITS TOLL

V AGUE rumors had reached us that Nijinsky had contracted with the Theater Cologne at Buenos Aires, and that he would once more dance with us, but Diaghilev flew off on a tangent with my first question. "What?" he rapped out. "Nijinsky? Why trouble about Nijinsky? We can do well enough without him!" The Silver Beaver silenced curiosity with the same testiness, twiddling his monocle around his forefinger and reiterating, "We can do well enough without Nijinsky!"

We heard that neither Diaghilev nor Massine would journey to South America with the company. That added weight to the supposition that Vaslaw would be there, but an air of secrecy surrounded the Massine-Diaghilev camp, and there was nothing for it but to embark and see what awaited us in Buenos Aires. Nijinsky's roles had been farmed out to dancers without any particular fame, with the exception of *Le Spectre de la Rose* and the premier solos in *Karnival*. Those were assigned to Stanislaw Idzikovsky, whom Nijinsky had long ago lauded as "the greatest living dancer." Fame as great as Nijinsky's might have been Idzikovsky's but for a careless destiny which had deprived him of two inches of height. "Oh! If he were only two inches taller," Pavlowa had sighed. "I could ask for no better partner, for his dancing is superb!"

We sailed from Barcelona, watching the Spanish mainland bury itself in a thin line of mist on the faraway horizon with deep regret mingled with high hope. We were leaving the war and its horrors behind. Ahead of us loomed the possibility of an art no longer submerged by inevitable reminders of war.

Our boat was camouflaged like a futuristic version of a stormy sea and two ominous guns pointed their mouths seaward. An atmosphere of disquiet traveled with us, approximating a panic when some practical joker shouted, "Submarine! Submarine aft!"

Again it was a false signal that sent us flying to our places by the lifeboats, some of us calm, others confused and ridiculous under the strain. I remember one woman who rushed towards the cabins pursued by shouts of "The lifeboats! Don't go down! To the lifeboats!"

Her voice, shrill with terror, came up the stairs: "I'm after my passport! Wait! Wait!"

After eighteen days of tragicomedy, we put in to Rio de Janeiro, where we opened at the Municipal Theater to a packed house after a five-year absence. What a change! There was no more buzz of amazement. Pavlowa had toured the country, dozens of smaller companies had completed the work of education, and an audience almost as sophisticated as any European gathering welcomed us.

We entrained for São Paulo, and miraculously escaped death in a tunnel on our route, a mass of flame and smoke when our train rushed through it at full speed. The company, blinded and choked in heavy rolls of smoke, nearly roasted by the intense heat, must have collapsed in a few moments. As it was, the train roared on, while we gradually recovered both our breath and our eyesight! At Santos we embarked on a tiny steamer bound for Montevideo with only the company on board. Again, a hairsbreadth escape was ours. Less than a full day after we disembarked a German submarine accounted for her, and scuttled the boat with all hands.

At Montevideo we gave a few performances, before going on to Buenos Aires. Though Nijinsky was with us, I was too lost in poker to realize his presence. Everyone who had played his roles in smaller stands resented his forthcoming triumphs, with the exception of Idzikovsky who was sin-

cerely glad to applaud Vaslaw, and whose character has, to this day, remained as inspiring as his art. Gavrilov shared this attitude.

Both Madame Nijinsky and Vaslaw were as happy to see me as I was
to greet them at the moment we met. It was only as I had an opportunity
to talk with Nijinsky that I realized that some terrific change had taken
place in his innermost being. It was as though a strange soul inhabited his
splendid body, for before answering the simplest question, he would pause
for a long moment, searching me with a distrustful look, and finally would
reply haltingly.

I stood his suspicious attitude for a short time in silence, before I objected.
"Vaslaw! Vaslaw! Why do you look at me as though I were a stranger?
Why do you act as though you couldn't trust me?"

"Who knows you?" he countered, cowering away from me. "I have not
seen you for a long time! Perhaps you have grown like everyone else!" His
voice took on a fearful timbre. "Perhaps you are like everyone else and not
my friend! How can I know *what* you have become? Many people are
plotting against me, trying to ruin me, planning to assassinate me. Perhaps
you are one!"

It was a terrifying shock. I grasped his hand impulsively. "Vaslaw!
Think! Think! When have I broken my word to you or betrayed a single
trust?" Some inkling of his trouble glimmered in the back of my mind, but
I thrust it away. My best friend, mad! It was unthinkable.

I urged a more peaceful outlook for his sake and my own. "Vaslaw! That
is foolish. No one wants to kill you. If anything happened to you, the whole
cultural world would mourn! No! No! Nothing must happen to deprive it
of your glorious art! Someone has been filling your ears with foolish tales.
Put them away from you. You are the world's greatest dancer—and I? I am
content to be your friend always!"

Slowly a semblance of the old Nijinsky appeared in the man before me.
I had faced the most awful tragedy I had known in all my years of friendship
with him, and thereafter I was prepared for something that hovered between
us like a black threat.

"Come, I will show you!" he said, leading me to a huge poster, remarking, "There is a chance that you may remain my friend!"

The poster screamed "Diaghilev's Ballet Russe!" and under the caption were listed the names of the artists in alphabetical order, among them that of Vaslaw Nijinsky. No big type, no glory for the man beside me—immediately I proposed a visit to the theatrical director, and together we confronted him.

"You have done an impossible thing!" I blazed. "How dare you refuse to give credit to Nijinsky? Why do the announcements read Diaghilev Ballet Russe instead of 'Nijinsky and Diaghilev's Ballet Russe'? What have you done?"

The director hastened to explain. "It is not my mistake, I swear it is not. The posters came from the Diaghilev company at Rio de Janeiro! They were sent to me!"

Instantly Diaghilev's plot was bared—he, his managers, and his dancers had turned as one against Nijinsky, who stood, dumb-struck, beside me. The solos that had been given to the unknown dancers, Idzikovsky's triumphs, took on new significance. They had been planned to fan jealousy. The posters—everything had been contrived by the Silver Beaver to achieve one purpose—that of leaving Nijinsky distraught and friendless in far-off Buenos Aires. I extracted a promise for the immediate change of the posters, and the next day Nijinsky's name was foremost, the rest of us named as we always had been. Vaslaw's distrust of me lifted a little, but the damage seemed to have been done.

XIX

DELUSIONS AND DANGERS

T HE delusion of persecution showed itself repeatedly during our four weeks at Buenos Aires. It became habitual for Vaslaw to hunt me out, and after glancing about fearfully, half whisper, "Tola, they will kill me here! Watch and you will see that this time, at least, I am speaking the truth. I know I am going to die. They will kill me!"

No particular person or persons seemed to be suspected and the "they" remained a mystery. Meanwhile, from the moment I met him, everything occurred to nurse the specter of madness that was closing in upon him.

There was a beautiful ballet hall in the Theater Cologne where we were playing, but Vaslaw preferred to practice on the stage to familiarize himself thoroughly with it. When I was not engaged in rehearsal, it became my custom to seek Nijinsky, who otherwise would have been alone on the huge dark platform, imagining that secret enemies skulked in every shadow, making himself utterly wretched. Whenever I appeared he rushed to me, crouching with his head turned to discover lurking danger. "Oh! Tola! I am so glad that you are here!" he'd gasp. "Now I am not alone. I am not afraid. Come to me always when you have a moment. Don't leave me alone for them to kill!"

Afraid! It was increasingly apparent that the Vaslaw I knew was dying a strange death. He had never been afraid, and the spectacle of his terror was almost worse than death for me to watch.

I don't want to believe that we had in the company anyone deliberately bent on taking Nijinsky's life, but it wasn't long before I began to be almost as apprehensive as he. Circumstances tended to uphold the fright haunting his mind, allaying my suspicion of his approaching madness. I hardly knew whether to be grateful or more upset, when I witnessed what seemed a deliberate attempt on him.

On friendly terms with the whole company, I made it my business to encourage its discussions of Nijinsky in the hope of discovering who harbored malice against him. I could find no serious cause to suspect any of them. I was faced with a modicum of jealousy overcome by loyalty in every case except on the part of those members of the staff directly under orders from Diaghilev. They contented themselves with disparagements. "What, Nijinsky? Don't bother about him! He's going mad!" they would observe offhandedly.

In vain I tried to find out whether or not Vaslaw had received threatening letters, but no! There was nothing substantial to lay his fears to. He knew someone was going to kill him, and that was all there was to it!

A series of accidents launched his morbid imagination on deeper excursions into that half-world of the demented. During the ballet *Scheherazade,* in which he played the principal role, Nijinsky had to pass backstage where heavy pieces of scenery were stored. As he passed, some instinct, more animal than human, warned him to leap. As he did, huge pieces of wood and scenery, any one of which would have killed him, tumbled harmlessly on the spot he had been startled away from by the eerie inner sense that he swore by and dreaded.

The very next day, before the presentation of the ballet *Petrouchka,* requiring three heavy iron supports upon which the three premier dancers balanced in grotesque positions, Nijinsky apparently experienced another of his uncanny warnings. A minute before the curtain was due to rise, he leaped to the platform upon which the three standards were mounted, supposedly immovably screwed to the flooring. He tried the first and the second. Both were in perfect order, and then he shook the third—his own. It wavered and crashed. Instantly he created a frenzied scene. He turned to the company and wailed: "Look! Boys and girls, they are trying to kill me. This moment the curtain should rise and I should take my position. The standard is not

screwed down. It would crash on me—break my legs, break my skull—kill
me! Who did it? Who did it?" His voice lost itself in a gruesome moan.

Instantly I swept the company with a look. Not one face betrayed anything but anger, concern, indignation. They knew nothing except that
Nijinsky had saved himself by one chance in a million.

At once the stage hands were brought in and a churlish-looking fellow
shuffled up to the stage manager mumbling: "Give me time! Give me time!
I had plenty of time!" Plenty of time, with the curtain due to rise less than
a minute after Nijinsky had leaped like a cat, filled with almost unearthly
cunning, to discover proof of his fears!

A few days later my life and his were both saved by another weird coincidence. Nijinsky, waiting for me to play for him, was seated in the half-
gloom of an empty stage, the only light coming from two wan electric
lights on tall iron stands at opposite ends of the boards. He sat by one of the
lamps, massaging his instep and arch as is customary with Russian dancers.
That spot was his favorite. It was in the light, and he felt less timorous away
from shadows. He had flung his bathrobe over the back of his chair, draping
his towel around his neck. Nijinsky occupied that chair only a moment each
day before he began his workout, for it is against the Russian custom to sit
during practice.

For some reason, I objected. "Don't sit there, Vaslaw. Come on over to
the piano where the light is stronger."

"All right, Tola. As you say!"

He picked up his chair, walking less than three steps at my side before a
frightful sound, like the explosion of a big gun, thundered in our ears. We
stood petrified for a full second before we summoned courage to look behind
us. Great, sharp splinters of glass had sprayed over the floor—by some freak
of fate, away from us. Slowly we both stared awe-struck at the gouge made
by the glass as it fell. It marked the precise spot Nijinsky had occupied!
There was no need for words. His face was bloodless, and my teeth were
chattering.

"Vaslaw! What—who—how did it happen?" I whispered.

Vaslaw clutched his head in his hands, rocking backwards and forwards.

"Anatole! Run from here! Run from here! They will kill me! They will kill me!" he cried, his voice chilled with horror as though his mind had been broken with the glass that glittered in fragments on the empty stage.

By common consent, we fled to the dressing rooms, and there he declared, "It is the end! I will never go on that stage! Run! Run!"

In no time Vaslaw was in street clothes, rushing from the theater, and carrying his woe with him! For him, fate was inexorable. His brain had been obscured by vague premonitions before, but then!—then it fed upon strong food that nourished the canker of fear without respite.

Before long, members of the staff were aghast at news of the accident. Their explanation was as strange as the cause. For no reason at all, a piece of glass fifteen inches in diameter and three inches thick had fallen from a reflector. The electricians were called and questioned, the stage hands were put through a third degree.

"Why should the reflector, after inspection, fall upon a deserted stage at the exact spot where Nijinsky sat?" demanded the director, his face livid with anger at his men.

Shrugs and nothing else answered him. No one could explain how a reflector, in perfect order a short time previous, crashed like magic at the one moment in the day when Nijinsky should have sat beneath it! In utter hopelessness, the director scanned the lights one by one and started in dismay. Not one reflector was without its glass! Not one! However, a shadowy bridge ran through thick darkness over the place Nijinsky had occupied.

XX

SOUTH AMERICAN FINALE

Nᴵᴶɪɴsᴋʏ never practiced on the stage after that, nor did he ever enter the theater alone. Madame Nijinsky was always at his side, and his practice took place in the full light of the ballet hall. There it was that Nijinsky taught his wife daily while he practiced, until he prepared her for an appearance in the ballet *The Blue God*.

She was the only student Nijinsky ever taught outside Russia. I have heard many claim to be his students, but I know how he hated to teach and that his only student was his wife. Some claim to have been his teachers, but only those whose names I have mentioned have any right to assume that honor truthfully. All my life I knew Nijinsky as a brother knows his brother when life arranges their careers together.

For a few days the company buzzed with comment. With the best intentions in the world, they did Nijinsky incalculable harm by adding to his certainty that he was the victim of some dismal plot. "They" menaced him night and day until he was no longer balanced in his attitude towards any of us. Someone constantly attended him. He dared not step foot upon the stage alone, but cowered in his dressing room until it seemed he must miss his cue. Then he tore to the stage and executed glorious dances before a public that applauded and never dreamed that an overpowering delirium was lending fresh nimbleness to his feet.

Only once did I learn that my friendship still meant something to the man who had been my friend. The reason for Nijinsky's sudden refusal to appear on the stage before a full house eludes me. He was in costume and ready, but he just would not appear. The director, the conductor, the soloists, the boys and girls, all did their best, but nothing meant anything to Nijinsky. I sat on the other side of the stage in my own dressing room, unaware of any emergency until one of the boys dashed into the room full of excitement.

"Nijinsky is crazy! He must be crazy! He won't go on the stage! The house is packed! The curtain is late, and I don't know what will happen! Three thousand people in the theater, and the director has shouted that if Nijinsky won't dance, not one of us will get a cent for transportation home! It's no joke! That madman won't go on!"

Terrified at the prospect of being stranded with a twenty-one-day ocean trip between them and home, the boys were speechless with dismay until one turned to me. "Bourman! You know him! Go and talk to him, please!"

Impulsively I consented and ran down to the star's dressing room. The stage manager, the director, the conductor, a dozen well-groomed men and women, and a few members of the company huddled together quietly outside the door. A man's voice was audible: "Ladies and gentlemen, it is impossible to do anything. We must break the whole contract!"

The stage manager had fined me on the previous day and so we weren't speaking, for he had been an old school friend. He stared at me when I passed, and I understood that he would never ask me to talk with Vaslaw, but, if I did, there would be no second fine!

The company clustered around me, whispering: "Go in and talk to him. Perhaps you can help. All else has been useless."

I hesitated. "You don't understand! If he answers me as he has you, 'Get out of my room. I won't see you! Get out!' it will mean more to me than—" The sight of their discouragement was enough. I broke off. "All right, I will try it!" For the first time in many months, I prayed God to let Vaslaw remember our friendship and to grant me influence with him just once, not to increase my prestige, but to help Vaslaw, for the sake of the artists, and to enable me to take care of my wife.

At that moment nervous applause clattered from an audience which had waited half an hour for the curtain. I knocked on the door in absolute silence. "Get out! I won't see anybody! I won't dance! Get away from my door!"

I tried to open the door. It was locked. I rapped again, pleading, "Vaslaw, it's Anatole! Let me talk to you just one moment!"

Madame Nijinsky answered me: "No, Mr. Bourman, it is impossible. He will not see anybody!"

"My dear madame, I am not just 'anybody.' I am his old friend, and a friend who has been dear to him. Please let me come in!" I begged. A short pause, and Madame Nijinsky opened the door.

Vaslaw was completely dressed. He paced backwards and forwards ceaselessly. For a second we confronted each other wordlessly.

Madame Nijinsky spoke, "Surely, Mr. Bourman, you remember everything!" and she offered some explanation which failed to register with me, for I was thinking of the company, and not at all forgetting my own predicament.

"Madame Nijinsky," I countered, "you and Nijinsky may be right, but you have forgotten our point of view. If Vaslaw doesn't dance, I am not worried for myself alone, I am thinking of sixty-five artists waiting out there! If he doesn't appear, not one ticket will be given for our return passage. I know you and Vaslaw are too loyal to the company to leave it stranded, and I am asking you, not for myself, but for the boys and girls! We'll starve in Argentina—which is not the United States, or Europe!"

Vaslaw said nothing. I stood helpless, waiting. My role was done, except for the solitary "Please do something to help us," that was all I could offer.

In a thick silence, Madame Nijinsky opened the door and I left them alone. I faced a company alert with eagerness. "What has been done? What?" they clamored.

I flung my hands out, "I don't know," and a tremendous burst of applause broke from the theater. We stood through an awful moment. Nijinsky's door opened with a crash, and Nijinsky, his head down, rushed onto the stage, looking neither to the right nor the left.

Madame Nijinsky's voice cut a sound of little rustling, the only sign the company gave of its relief. "You may go on," she said.

Perhaps I was responsible for saving the situation, and perhaps I was not. I do know that for the balance of our season, all was peaceful. Thereafter I spoke with Vaslaw occasionally, but his answers were eccentric. He was planning a series of original interpretations, but they were dances that I, who knew dancing, recognized as physical impossibilities. He told, too, of a peculiar system he had invented to describe the dance, and I listened saddened.

I had had my prayer answered. He had remembered our friendship that once, but henceforth he would yield to no influence of mine whenever his fantasies gripped him in their frenzied power.

Vaslaw, my friend, seemed mad.

XXI

THE LAST TRAGEDY

A LITTLE more than a year after I saw Nijinsky for the last time, harrowing news flew around the world. Brief, terse, and cruel, the headlines stared from a London paper—"Nijinsky Is Insane"—and Diaghilev read them as he made his way unsteadily to the Empire Theater. He came onto the stage with his eyes full of tears. His voice broke when he called us together and announced, "Boys and girls, Nijinsky. is mad. He is insane. This is not publicity. It is, alas, the truth!" The Silver Beaver walked away, his shoulders sagged, his superiority completely crushed by the news.

I cannot explain my feeling. I had known, yet I had not known. I didn't weep; I couldn't. Something in me was killed, and only memory was left. Before my mind's eyes the whole pageant of our lives passed in an instant, from the moment of Nijinsky's entrance into the Imperial Russian Ballet School until I shook hands with him for the last time in South America—his school tragedy, his first appearance on the stage, his Parisian triumphs, his fame, his longing for forgetfulness, his South American trials.

I turned and faced Diaghilev. My brain was staggered by the knowledge that never again could I talk with Vaslaw, never play for him, never watch the supreme art that was his—and I remembered in a flash Diaghilev's remark: "Nijinsky? We can do well enough without him!" I stared at the Silver Beaver, whose eyes fell before mine as the wild accusation stirred in my mind: "Perhaps you helped him on towards this, you and your plots—and now you weep!"

Such thoughts are futile, for they are born of shock and sorrow, not of reason. To this day I know exactly why Diaghilev dropped his eyes from mine and wept when the one man in the world who knew a hundred secrets arraigned him in silence. His conscience was his own, and I have told as many of his secrets as concern the world that loved Vaslaw Nijinsky.

Nobody knew his soul, and dreams, and hopes, and fears as I knew them, for I shared his sorrows and his joys alike from the day I swore my friendship after the custom of Old Russia until I begged him to dance for the company.

Now that my memories of that generous friend and mighty artist are almost done, two pictures leap into the present from the past. One is of that old beggar-woman in the golden sunlight of Old Russia hobbling forward and squinting up at Nijinsky, tall and straight and happy. Once more I hear her words auguring ill: "Poor boy! Poor boy! Always at the moment of your greatest triumphs, tragedy will spoil everything for you!"

Again, there is the vision of Gillert, whose days of triumph were over, and who gave his talisman to Vaslaw on his graduation day: "As long as you wear my ring no sorrow or misfortune can touch you, but I warn you, the ring must stay on your hand!"—and Vaslaw threw that great gift aside for diamonds! It was one of the few petty acts of his life, that tossing aside of Gillert's gift—yet, from that time forth, the beggar-woman's prophecy began its sad fulfillment.

I look into the present and the future. Then alone can I appreciate what the world has lost of art and culture with Nijinsky's mind. I am forgetting, for a moment, what his tragedy has meant to us who loved him, his mother, his sister, his wife, his family, his friends—myself! Instead, I am realizing what the world has lost—the greatest dancer who ever lived, perhaps the greatest who ever will live, for it will be a titanic soul who comes again with Vaslaw's art, Vaslaw's mastery, Vaslaw's loyal heart, and the equal of his splendid body.

Yet he is not dead—it is only the shining soul of him that has fled, leaving a tragic shell to mock its glory and its woes.

Two years ago in London, I met many of my old friends, among them Karsavina and Kyasht, and we spoke once more of that great living dead man, Vaslaw Nijinsky. Especially did Karsavina sorrow over him, for she shared his acclaim so many times. Business was calling me to New York, but I was only a few hours from Paris—a postwar Paris that had offered a haven for Mother Nijinsky, Bronia, and Kshessinskaya.

Kshessinskaya met me with her customary warm greeting. Forgetful of her lost millions, she was thrilling to the joy of teaching young girls to carry on the art of Old Russia. Again, it was memories of the life that has gone that we discussed. Vaslaw's name was mentioned, and Kshessinskaya choked with emotion. "It is the greatest tragedy I know of, Bourman, I who have watched life and death in many lands!"

Then I told her how she, and she alone, had made him renowned as he deserved, fo. in all Russia, Kshessinskaya alone could have assured Imperial favor in the days that are done. She chose Nijinsky for her partner, and saved him an arduous climb up the ladder of fame. That is what I told her, while she shook her head and cried afresh. "I? Not I, Bourman! His genius and his talent would have won him laurels had I never lived!"

There remained one other visit, and I left Kshessinskaya in tears to seek out Vaslaw's mother. During my life, I have had to watch hideous tragedies played out before my eyes. I have had to watch men killed, and I have had to walk through rows of dead, searching for the face of a friend, but never, never have I had to face more sorrow and more tragedy than when I saw Madame Nijinsky, Vaslaw's mother, for the first time in fifteen years.

The door was opened to me by a boy about fourteen years old who stood beside a girl of about seventeen, Bronia's children. They stared at me unbelieving, as though they had known me. I gave no name, but asked instead, "Is Madame Nijinsky, Mother, at home?" At that moment, I saw an old lady standing in the doorway inside, a crutch clutched under one arm. She saw me!

"Tola!" she screamed, throwing her arms out towards me, forgetful of her crutches, of everything, it seemed, but me—and Vaslaw. My throat was dry. How could I speak? I ran to her and knelt before her, kissing her hands, so wrinkled, so old—as I would kiss my mother's hands. There were no words to say. Mother Nijinsky held me close, repeating simply two names with a voice that was hardly more than a sob. "Tola! Vaslaw! Vaslaw! Tola! Tola!"

She stroked my hair as she had done when I was a boy, the while her body shook with sobs, and then she gave me her greatest compliment. "Tola," she whispered "you are my Vaslaw's dearest friend. My son! My son!"

In that moment I realized that Nijinsky's tragedy was not his—but hers —and mine.

IMPORTANT DATES IN THE LIFE OF VASLAW NIJINSKY

1890—*Born in Kiev, Russia.*

August 20, 1900—*Entered Imperial Russian Ballet School at St. Petersburg.*

1900–1902—*Trained under Nicolai Legat's direction.*

1902–1908—*Trained under Michail Obouchov's direction.*

1904—*Severe injury to head and chest suffered at school.*

1905–1912—*Studied ballet composition and interpretation with Michail Fokine from the time of Fokine's first production of ballet in Russia, and throughout the period of their work together in Diaghilev's company. Thus Fokine is credited as one of his teachers.*

May 20, 1908—*Graduated from Imperial Russian Ballet School.*

Autumn, 1908—*Met Sergei Diaghilev for first time.*

1908–1911—*Soloist, officially ranked as a member of the Imperial Russian Ballet at the Marinsky Theater, St. Petersburg.*

Summer, 1909—*Appeared in Paris with Diaghilev's summer company, including Pavlowa, Bolm, Kosloff, and Karsavina.*

Winter Season, 1911—*Expelled from Imperial Russian Theaters by Director Teliakovsky.*

Spring, 1911—*Opened European career with Diaghilev's company as permanent soloist.*

1913—*Married Romola de Pulszki, left Diaghilev's company, and produced with his own company in London, England.*

1914–1916—*Prisoner of war in Austria-Hungary.*

1916—*Exchanged as prisoner of war and permitted to go to the United States.*

1917—*Toured United States and South America.*

1917—*Obvious indications of mental derangement began to interfere with career in South America.*

1917–1919—*Returned to Europe where he remained seeking treatment for mental disorder.*

May, 1926 or 1927—*Attempt made by Diaghilev to shock Nijinsky's mind into remembrance.*

Nijinsky has remained in a sanatorium under treatment since 1919. In 1930, Bronia Nijinsky reported his ailment to be non-violent and described her brother as spending his days quietly sitting in a chair, staring blankly ahead, apparently unconscious of anything about him.

AFTERWORD

To Vaslaw, who is still my best friend:

                              Forgive me for describing all
of your life in this book. That is the cry that rises from my heart. I have
done it because of the untruths that have been published about you in the
press throughout the world, and because no other living person can clear
the life I know so well of the unjust criticisms I have read. This book has
forced me to relive thirty years—twenty years of which we lived together.
It has been fraught with sorrow and with joy, this journey through my
memory with you.

I have remembered the many tricks I played upon you at school, and now
that I have reached adult stature, I wonder why I hated you at first—perhaps because you were a Pole and great. If I have forgotten any who should
have found a place within my pages, or if I have made mistakes in dates,
forgive that, too, for I have had so much to recall—so much to tell. I have
tried to remember the greatness of your life and your career.

I will be the happiest man living if one day you can recover and read
what I have disclosed of your life, for you, and you alone, will know that
not one word of fantasy has been indulged in to mar the truth of you. Your
suffering is done, they tell me, and that my hope for you is vain. You, then,
are happy. It is we who knew you and remember—your relatives, your wife,
your friends—whose prayers rise constantly invoking health for you—we
suffer still—remembering.

The privilege that has been given to me as your intimate comrade to immortalize your name and art, if not perfectly, at least sincerely, makes me happy—for some other man, perhaps more gifted than I, may use it as the foundation for a monument of literary art raised in your honor.

Perhaps it is a blessing that has mantled you at the peak of your great triumphs, for tragic indeed is the destiny of one who has known fame and triumph, and must live the anticlimax of existence—with a host of gloried memories.

ANATOLE BOURMAN

October 6, 1932
Springfield, Massachusetts

INDEX